MW00700394

The Best Boring Book Ever™ of
Tableau *for* Healthcare
third edition

by

Daniel Benevento
Katherine Rowell
Janet Steeger
Ann Cutrell
Marnie Morales

The Best Boring Book Ever™ of
Tableau *for* Healthcare
third edition

Copyright @ 2017 by HealthDataViz

ISBN 978-0692938508

Designed by:

Breviloquent
Lexington, Massachusetts | Charlottesville, Virginia
www.breviloquent.com

More information:

www.healthdataviz.com

LIMITATION OF LIABILITY
HealthDataViz, LLC and its affiliates (hereinafter "Publisher") make no representation regarding the completeness, correctness or accuracy of the contents of this work. The Publisher shall not be liable for any loss, damages, injury, claim, liability or damages of any kind resulting in or arising from this work. This work is provided by the Publisher on the basis that the Publisher is not engaged in rendering medical, legal or other professional advice. The work and its strategies may not be suitable for all audiences and situations.

DISCLAIMER OF WARRANTY
HealthDataViz, LLC and its affiliates (hereinafter "Publisher") provides this work without warranties of any kind either expressed or implied, statutory or otherwise including but not limited to warranties of merchantability, or warranty of fitness for a particular purpose and non-infringement.

TRADEMARK/SERVICE MARK NOTICE
An "®" following a trademark indicates that the trademark has been registered in the United States Patent and Trademark Office. A "™" following a trademark indicates that the mark is currently an unregistered trademark. All Trademarks/Service Marks are the property of their respective owners. Tableau and Tableau Software are trademarks of Tableau Software, Inc. All other company and product names may be trademarks of the respective companies with which they are associated.

Contents

Preface

A couple of us at HealthDataViz (HDV) remember the first time we encountered Tableau. It was in a beta version—not quite ready for primetime, but intriguing all the same. As we watched it develop, becoming easier to use and more powerful with each release, our imaginations were captured by the promise of being able to explore our data faster and easier than ever before and of creating beautiful, enlightening visualizations. We were nothing short of ecstatic about an emerging application that would empower us to display the stories buried in the mountains of health and healthcare data we worked with every day—revelatory data that (we were certain) had the power, once it had been clearly presented, to improve health and healthcare across the board and across the globe.

Using our substantial experience with and broad knowledge of health and healthcare data, and advanced skills in data visualization and the use of Tableau, we designed both Beginner|Intermediate and Advanced Tableau training courses for health and healthcare professionals. A book to reach an even wider healthcare audience was the next logical—albeit at times a seemingly quixotic—step. The Best Boring Book Ever™ of Tableau for Healthcare (now in its 3rd Edition) is the result. Each learning unit walks a reader through one of many particular types of visualizations or tasks from start to finish, with particular emphasis on clarity, logic, simplicity, and the smooth flow of ideas. Reading these chapters in order allows a user to build on what has already been accomplished, but doing so is not mandatory: each unit stands alone to teach one type of lesson fully.

As with the first (and second) Best Boring Book Ever, this third edition would have never seen the light of day without the skill, dedication, hard work, support, and advice of a number of our colleagues. It is our deepest pleasure to express our gratitude to them now.

First, we could never have written this book without our Tableau guru, Dan Benevento. His gift for explaining how Tableau works built the solid foundation for this book's clear structure and effective instruction.

Our gratitude to Janet Steeger and Ann Cutrell is hard to express in mere words. It is through their tireless efforts and determination to not only update this text but to vastly improve it as well that our 3rd Edition has seen the light of day. Never satisfied with "good enough," they used their extensive experience and the feedback they and the entire HDV Team received as they trained hundreds of clients in using Tableau to search out new datasets, update examples, and improve the flow of the entire book. Their dedicated and creative efforts have produced this edition, and clearly reflect their exceptional intellect and professionalism.

We also wish to thank the newest member of our team, Marnie Morales, Ph.D., for her contribution, especially to some of the new chapters. It is terrific to have her on our team.

Yet again, we are eternally grateful to our editor, Anne W. Jackson, Ph.D. (Grammar Lady—or GL, as we call her), for keeping us on the grammatical straight and narrow, and our design partners at Breviloquent, Jim Leightheiser and Peter Massarelli, for the beautiful design and layout of this book.

This list of gratitudes would not be complete without a final thanks to Sandy Lawson, who kept things running day to day at HealthDataViz so that we could write this book. If you look up "Den Mother" in the dictionary, you will see a portrait of Sandy.

Thanks to you all: for this "baby," as with the other kind, it really did take a village.

Katherine S. Rowell
on behalf of the HDV team

Introduction to Tableau

1

Introduction

A Book Designed for Health and Healthcare Professionals

Designed specifically for health and healthcare professionals by the health, healthcare, data-visualization, and report-design experts at HealthDataViz, this updated volume introduces and describes in detail Tableau 10's features for analyzing health and healthcare data and creating dashboards and reports.

As we did in the first edition of Tableau for Healthcare (Tableau 8), we have used health and healthcare data (real, but rendered neutral and anonymous) from a wide range of sources (public health, hospital, clinical) to demonstrate Tableau's functionality in concrete, practical ways immediately useful for real-world application by health and healthcare professionals.

What's new in Tableau 10?

DATA PREPARATION AND MANIPULATION

- Cross-Database Joins and Union updates
- Filtering across data sources
- Data Interpreter enhancements
- New data source connections including PDFs

ANALYTICS

- Level-of-Detail Expression improvements
- Data Pane enhancements
- New Table Calculation experience

DESIGN AND USER INTERFACE

- New design for user-interface and workbook-formatting capabilities
- New Device Designer for creating device-specific dashboard layouts
- Story Point improvements
- New Map Options
- Auto-save

What's new in the latest edition of Tableau for Healthcare?

In addition to covering the latest enhancements and features available through **Tableau 10.4**, we have also updated the third edition of this book with:

- Six new and five updated data sources
- Twelve improved step-by-step walk-throughs
- In-depth tips and tricks, a new formatting chapter, and more call-outs throughout the book

Before presenting and explaining all of this book's useful and innovative features, we'd like to briefly consider several significant visualizations that have informed recent trends in making modern healthcare systems and research stronger and more effective, thus improving care globally.

Visualizing Health and Healthcare

Even before modern-day visualization research validated the direct and powerful relationship between the way information is presented and the way we see and understand it, pioneering healthcare statisticians and caregivers like John Snow (1813-1858) and Florence Nightingale (1820-1910) understood that visual display could be a highly effective method for grasping and communicating the messages buried in data.

No one who has ever taken an epidemiology course can forget Dr. John Snow's classic work "On the Mode of Communication of Cholera." By mapping the London street addresses of residents who had become sick (and in many cases died) and their distance from City water pumps, Snow could visually and effectively communicate the relationship between a single pathogen-tainted water source and the homes of people who contracted the disease. Most people who had fallen ill, it turned out, lived near the Broad Street pump. Snow persuaded the town council to remove the pump's handle, and the outbreak abated.

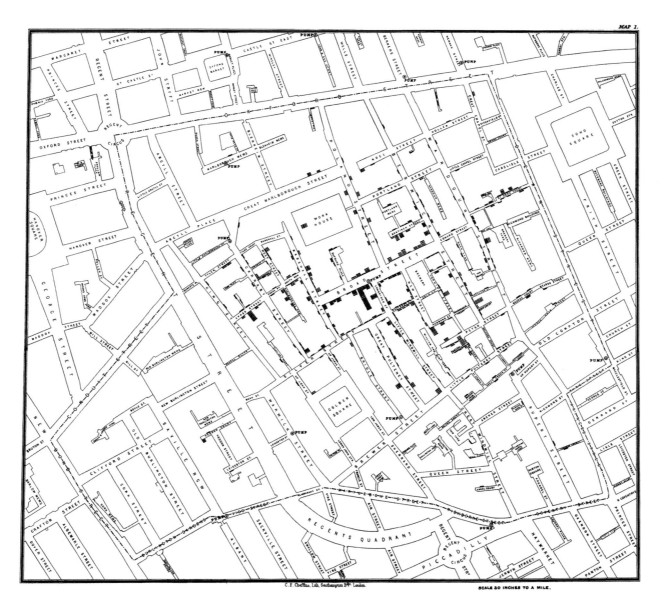

(Image in the public domain.)

In 1868, British nurse Florence Nightingale—distressed by the alarmingly high mortality rates in the Crimean War—began to compile statistics on causes of death. Her analysis revealed that of the 900,000 soldiers who died during the war—more than half of 1,650,000 combatants from all countries involved—most had succumbed to preventable diseases arising from unsanitary conditions in the hospitals where they were treated, and not as a direct result of battlefield wounds. Nightingale recognized the buried message: better hygiene could have saved—and could still save—thousands of lives.

As impressive as her statistics were, Nightingale worried that the tables she presented to Queen Victoria would seem tedious, even incomprehensible, and feared that members of the British Parliament were unlikely to be swayed by numbers lying flat on a page. So Nightingale devised clever ways of presenting the information in charts.

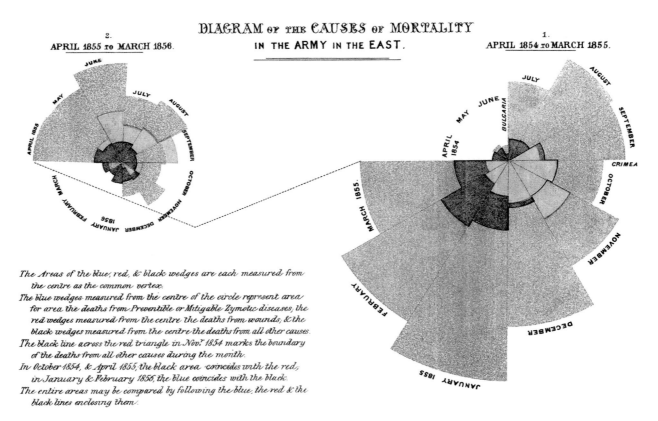

(Image in the public domain.)

In the now-famous "Diagram of the Causes of Mortality in the Army in the East," each month is represented as a twelfth of a circle; months with more deaths are shown with longer wedges, so that the area of each wedge represents the total number of deaths. Preventable deaths are blue, deaths due to wounds are red, and deaths from all other causes are black. Over the months after March 1855, when members of the Sanitary Commission began repairing, cleaning, and otherwise improving field hospital conditions, the blue wedges shrank dramatically. Showing wonderful insight into the power of displaying the data in this way, Nightingale said her graph was designed "to affect thro' the Eyes what we fail to convey to the public through their word-proof ears."

More recent efforts by healthcare researchers like those led by Dr. Jack Wennberg at the Dartmouth Atlas Project have documented glaring—and, for the most part, inexplicable—variations in how medical resources are apportioned and delivered in the United States. The project builds on Medicare data to provide comprehensive information and analysis about national, regional, and local markets, as well as individual hospitals and their affiliated physicians.

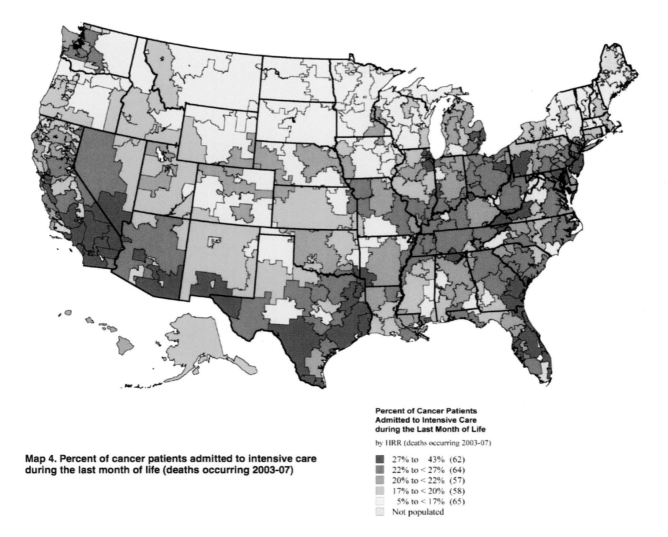

Map 4. Percent of cancer patients admitted to intensive care during the last month of life (deaths occurring 2003-07)

Percent of Cancer Patients
Admitted to Intensive Care
during the Last Month of Life

by HRR (deaths occurring 2003-07)

■	27% to 43% (62)
■	22% to < 27% (64)
■	20% to < 22% (57)
■	17% to < 20% (58)
□	5% to < 17% (65)
□	Not populated

Source: *The Dartmouth Institute: The Dartmouth Atlas of Healthcare*

Consider the map reproduced above from the Dartmouth Atlas Report: "Quality of End-of-Life Cancer Care for Medicare Beneficiaries." It displays the percent of cancer patients admitted to intensive care during the last month of life compared by hospital referral regions. About 24% of cancer patients nationwide were admitted to intensive care at least once during that last month. However, the percent thus admitted varied more than sevenfold across those regions (dark red versus light yellow areas on the map), leading the viewer to ask "Why are these rates so dramatically different across the country?"; and perhaps to add an even more significant question: "What should the rate be?"

Geospatial displays of data like this one make the variation in end-of-life care jump off the page in a way that it never would if the data were buried in a table or report narrative. Such geospatial maps and accompanying reports, along with the research upon which they are based, have helped policymakers, the media, healthcare analysts, and others improve their understanding of the efficiency and effectiveness of our health care system. As with the map created by John Snow, the visualizations built for the Dartmouth project make the story easy to see and understand, and have formed the foundation for many of the nation's ongoing efforts to improve U.S. American health and health systems.

Using Vision to Think – The Power of Tableau ™

The power of these and similar visual displays (and by extension the power of Tableau™) is that they help us use what we see to improve the way we think—how we comprehend, reason, deduce, and respond. Tableau empowers users to quickly grasp the stories and potential opportunities buried in the bottomless oceans of data that surround us.

As with all truly great technology and design, the apparent simplicity of Tableau™ belies the complex concepts and mechanisms used to create it. Building on a new technology that combines Structured Query Language (SQL™) for databases with a descriptive language (Visual Query Language|VizQL™), Tableau translates a user's actions into a database query, then expresses the response graphically. Tableau's drag-and-drop and "Show Me" functionality, as well as its high-quality graphics, are the products of complex engineering built on a solid foundation of substantial research into visual intelligence and information visualization, and their connections to vision, perception, and visual cognition.

No Tool is the Total Solution: Knowledge of the Subject and Visual Intelligence Required!

Clearly we are Tableau fans, but we also know that no tool is a total solution. Designing and building transparent, revelatory dashboards and reports requires subject-matter expertise in health, healthcare, and statistics; knowledge of best practices; and awareness of current research in visual intelligence.

None of these abilities is intuitive; data-visualization skills in particular, often assumed to be instinctual, must in fact be honed over time. Further, while it is unnecessary for every team member to become an expert in visual intelligence, each should be aware of it to avoid working at cross-purposes with those members who specialize in data visualization best practices. (That is, everyone should know better than to ask for 3D red, yellow, and green pie charts.) Building a team with these multiple and complementary knowledge areas has enabled us to become even better at creating effective visualizations, and will help you *"See how you're doing©."*

How to Use this Book: Tips & Tricks

Each chapter begins with a brief discussion of a chart or other display type and its appropriate use, illustrated by a graphic of the finished chart to be built in the chapter, coupled with a brief description of the health and healthcare data's source and significance.

The main body of the chapter contains meticulous, logical, step-by-step instructions on how to build the chart, with frequent screenshots and other images to help orient the reader and clarify each action.

» Directions formatted like this (with a yellow arrow bullet) indicate an action to be performed by the reader.

Key information is highlighted in call-outs containing images or side-text in the following categories:

Tableau Call-outs ▶

Call-outs formatted like this (black header; orange italic body type) indicate Tableau-specific information and functionality.

Best Practice

Blue boxes display data visualization best practices.

Refreshers ▶

Call-outs formatted like this (orange header; blue italic body type) contain reminders of information discussed in previous chapters.

9

Those knowledgeable and confident about building a particular chart type can skip the detailed instructions in favor of using our concise and handy, innovative ***HDVizoom*™**—all the necessary steps distilled into a compact list at the end of each chapter.

We have also included introductory overviews of how Tableau connects to data, and of Tableau Server—emphasis here on "introductory." More in-depth explanations, tutorials, forums, and online Tableau communities are found at http://tableausoftware.com/support.

Downloading and Using the Datasets

Although you can successfully and effectively use this book without working with the datasets we have created for its teaching|training exercises, we believe that completing a visualization using the same data is a terrific, hands-on way to see how Tableau works. To that end, we have stripped the datasets included of all formatting or other distractions, freeing you to fully immerse yourself in learning, step-by-step, how to create visualizations using Tableau.

To download the datasets you'll need, please visit HealthDataViz at:

`http://www.healthdataviz.com/Tableau-for-Healthcare`

and follow the instructions we have posted there.

To learn more about the different types of health and healthcare classification systems and databases, we encourage you to take a look at our award-winning companion work, *The Best Boring Book Ever™ of Select Healthcare Classification Systems and Databases* (available from Amazon). And we invite you to join the ongoing conversation about health and healthcare data and data visualization by subscribing to our free newsletter, *Unleash Your Inner Healthcare Data*, at http://www.healthdataviz.com.

Thank You

Thank you for your interest in this book—for supporting our mission, and sharing our vision of creating clear and compelling dashboards and reports that create opportunities to improve our health and healthcare systems, and move people to action.

Sincerely,

The HealthDataViz Team

CHAPTER 2

Tableau Desktop Interface and Navigation

This chapter lays the foundation for working with Tableau Desktop, beginning with an overview of its interface and operational workflow, followed by a discussion of the core concepts that govern how visualizations are displayed. The rest of this chapter—layout, workflow, and field attributes—will help you become familiar with Tableau, so you can use its rich and powerful features with confidence.

Tableau Desktop Layout

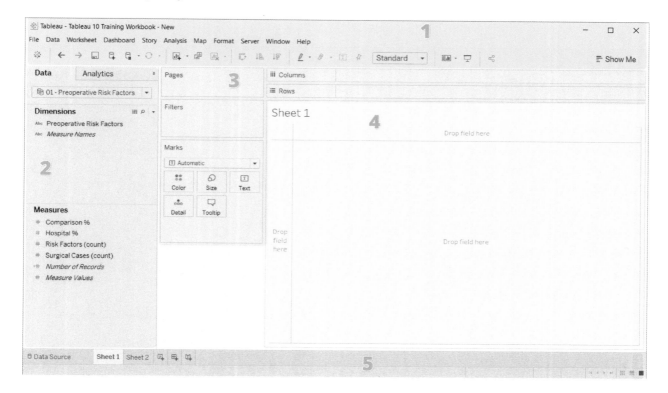

1 - Workbook Title, Menu Bar, and Toolbar

In the image above, a workbook title is displayed at the top of the space. Below it, a Menu Bar and Toolbar (with icons for most commonly used features) extend across the top of the workspace.

2 - The Side Bar

This multi-purpose pane on the left side of the screen contains different features and controls, depending on the task being performed. The Data pane (shown above) is the default display; it shows the list of connected data sources with corresponding fields organized as Dimensions and Measures (discussed later in this chapter). The images below show a selection of other possible content of this pane, depending on what function the user chooses.

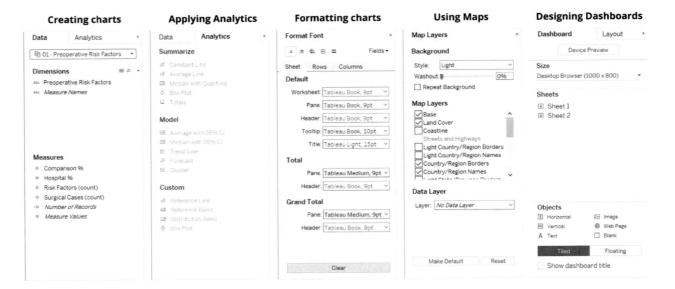

▲ Collapse, Show, or Close the Side Bar

Each Side Bar has either a double caret ⌃ *or an 'x'* ✕ *in its upper right corner. Click the double caret to collapse the Side Bar to the bottom left of the screen. Click it again to re-display the pane. Click the 'x' in Format and Map panes to return to the default view.*

3 - Shelves and the Marks Card

Shelves (Columns, Rows, Pages, and Filters) and the Marks card (Color, Size, Label, Details, and Tooltips) are landing areas for dragging and dropping data fields to build and format visualizations. Data fields placed on any shelf or Marks card are called "pills."

4 - The View

The View is the work area where the visualization is displayed. Data fields can be added directly to the View as well as to the shelves and to the Marks card.

5 - Data Source tab, Sheet tabs, New Worksheet/Dashboard/Story tabs, Navigation Tools

The Data Source tab contains the data sources and their corresponding connections to Tableau. Data connections are covered in Chapter 3.

Each workbook contains three sheet types:

1) **Worksheet** allows the creation of individual charts.

2) **Dashboard** displays one or more worksheets in a single view.

3) **Story** organizes worksheets and/or dashboards into a narrative presentation.

Sheet tabs are a quick path to individual worksheets, dashboards, or stories created in a Tableau workbook. Every newly created sheet has a corresponding sheet tab. Dashboard tabs display a small "window" icon, Story tabs an "open book" icon.

Three small icons at the bottom right of the workbook enable toggling the sheet tab view between a sheet sorter, a sheet filmstrip, and the default sheet tabs.

Data Sources and Fields in Tableau

The top of the Data pane lists all available data sources and their designated connection types. The fields from a selected data source appear below it and are grouped into sections: Dimensions, Measures, and, if applicable, Sets or Parameters. These are the building blocks of any Tableau visualization.

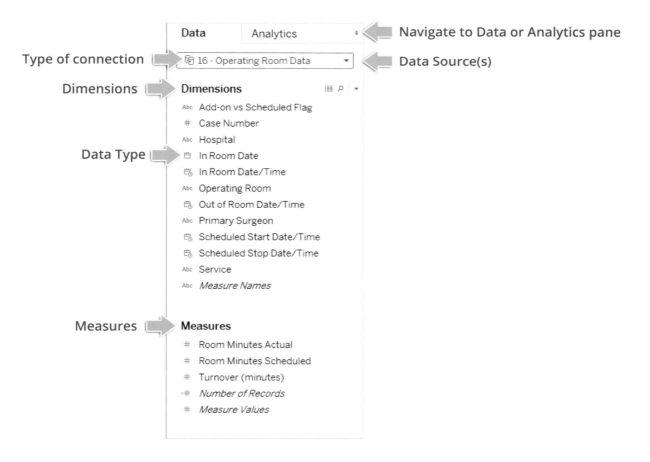

Each data field displays an icon to its left representing its data type, and is colored according to whether it is discrete or continuous (discussed later in this chapter). The three italicized field names shown—Measure Names, Number of Records, and Measure Values—are auto-generated by Tableau and serve valuable functions, discussed throughout this book.

Data Sources

Datasets imported into Tableau appear in the Data pane. The icon to the left of each data source indicates the type of data connection.

Live connection to a relational data source.

Connection to an extract of the data source.

Connection to a multidimensional or cube data source.

A **blue** checkmark superimposed on the data-source icon means that the source is the *primary* one for the worksheet; an **orange** checkmark indicates a *secondary* source used in data blending.

Data Types

Each field is automatically assigned a Data Type reflecting the kind of information stored in that field. Types might be integers (932), dates (1/23/2017), or strings ("General Hospital"). The Data Type is identified by a unique icon placed to the left of each field in the Data pane.

Icon	Value Description
Abc	Text
#	Numerical
📅	Date
📅🕐	Date and Time
T|F	Boolean
⊕	Geographic

◀ **Data Type Icons**

An = sign preceding any icon denotes a user-defined calculated value field or a copy of another field—for example =# or =Abc.

Sometimes Tableau matches a field with an incorrect data type—for example, a field that contains dates may be identified as Numerical rather than as Date. To correct this, right-click the field in the Data pane, select Change Data Type, and choose the appropriate Type.

Mechanics of Data Field Placement in the Workspace

The layout of any chart created in Tableau is controlled by the placement of data fields from the Data pane in specific locations on the worksheet. Possible targets for data fields include the Columns or Rows shelf, the Filters or Pages shelf, or the Marks card. Tableau offers several ways to place data fields on the shelves and Marks card:

- **Drag and Drop.** Drag a field from the Data pane and drop it directly onto the View, or onto any shelf or Marks card. A field present in the View can also be dragged from one location to another. Alternatively, drag a field with the right mouse button to generate a Drop Field menu with shortcuts to additional field options.

- **Double-Click.** Double-clicking a data field prompts Tableau to add the field to the shelf it deems most appropriate based on the field's data properties. Once a field is moved onto a worksheet, it becomes a pill and can be dragged and dropped onto any location.

- **Type-In.** Double-click any blank space in Rows, Columns, or on the Marks card, to type in a field name. Tableau auto-completes field names.

- **Show Me.** The Show Me window suggests visualization type(s) for data selected in the Data pane or data fields already present in the View. Tableau evaluates the chosen fields and determines what chart options are appropriate based on the data's attributes.

Hovering the cursor over each thumbnail in the Show Me dialog box displays, at the bottom of the box, a chart name and the number of Dimensions and Measures required to generate the chart. Click the thumbnail to create the desired chart. It is possible to build an enormous variety of charts in Tableau; Show Me is a one-click option, not a comprehensive list of all possible choices.

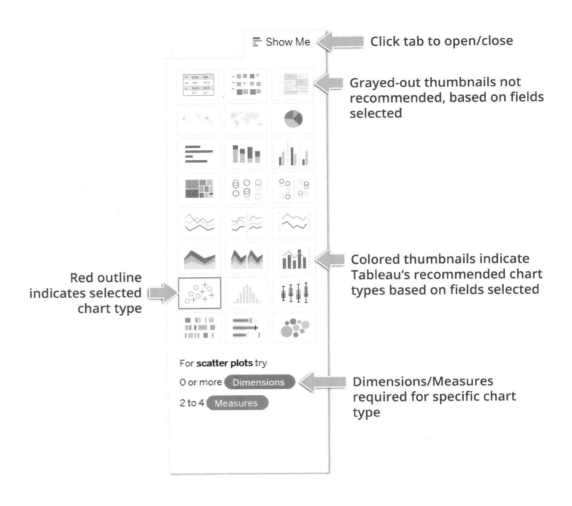

Click tab to open/close

Grayed-out thumbnails not recommended, based on fields selected

Colored thumbnails indicate Tableau's recommended chart types based on fields selected

Red outline indicates selected chart type

Dimensions/Measures required for specific chart type

Marks Card

The Marks card controls the type of chart rendered and its display properties. The drop-down menu displays the default or "Automatic" chart type as determined through Tableau logic or the Show Me selection, but can be manually edited if needed.

Marks Card ▶

The Marks card offers these display-customization options:

Color *and* ***Size****: can be manually set or dynamically calculated by a field dropped onto either of these buttons.*

Label *and* ***Tooltip*** *add written information to the View. Label displays information directly on the marks; Tooltip does so in a pop-up box when the cursor is hovered over marks in the View.*

Detail *affects the level of granularity for the chart. Dimensions added to the Detail shelf are part of the chart's level of aggregation and Measures added to the Detail shelf can be used in chart elements like reference lines.*

The ***blue box outline*** *is an area that changes depending on the chart type selected. For example, if a Line or Polygon chart type is chosen, a Path button appears; if Shape is selected, a Shape card does.*

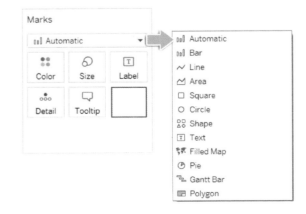

Dimensions vs. Measures

When connecting to a dataset, Tableau evaluates each field, then places categorical data in the Dimensions window and quantitative data in the Measures window.

DIMENSIONS	MEASURES
Categorical Data, Independent Variable	Quantitative (numerical) Data, Dependent Variable
Organize data into groups	Are used in calculations, (Sum, Average, Count)
Answer: • Who? • What? • Where? • When?	Answer: • How much? • How many? • How long?
Dimensions group or slice Measures. The combination of values of all Dimensions in the view defines the lowest *Level of Detail* for that view by default.	Measures aggregate in real-time and recalculate with every Dimension incorporated into the visualization.
Dimensions are not typically aggregated.	Measures are most often aggregations.
Each Dimensions pill displays as its field name.	Measures pills display the aggregation along with the field name.
iii Columns Hospital	☰ Rows SUM(Room Minutes..)

▲ Aggregation and Reassigning Dimensions and Measures

Aggregation is the task of collecting multiple values (individual numbers) into a single result by, for example, summing values (SUM), counting the number of values (CNT), averaging values (AVG), or displaying the smallest individual value for a group of rows (MIN). In a worksheet, performing an aggregation on a Dimensions field requires it to be changed or treated as a Measure.

Aggregate a Dimension in one of three ways: 1) right-click the field pill on the worksheet and change its default selection to Measure and choose the desired aggregation; 2) drag the field from the Dimensions window to the Measures window; or 3) right-click the field in the Dimensions window and select Convert to Measure. The last two approaches can be used conversely to convert a field from a Measure to a Dimension.

If Tableau is connected to a cube data source, Dimensions and Measures are predefined in the database and cannot be reassigned.

Discrete (Blue) vs. Continuous (Green)

Besides the Dimensions and Measures distinction, fields are also either Continuous or Discrete, a contrast signaled by **blue** for a discrete field and **green** for a continuous one.

17

"Discrete" and "Continuous" are mathematical terms. "Discrete" means individual, separate, countable, finite. Such fields can be reordered and still make sense. "Continuous" means a range (containing an infinite number of values). Reordering these numbers renders them meaningless.

Field data type icons are either blue or green, discrete or continuous. When a field is moved to the worksheet, it becomes an oval "pill" of the same color as the icon.

In many cases, Dimensions are discrete (**blue**) fields that create category headings, and Measures are continuous (**green**) fields that create axes along a continuous scale. If required, Dimensions (only date or numeric fields, or those aggregated to produce counts) can be changed to continuous; all Measures can be changed to discrete, producing a list of all the distinct values of the field.

▲ **Blue and Green Pills**

Date and numeric Dimensions can be either discrete or continuous, as can all Measures. A pill's background color indicates whether it is discrete (blue) or continuous (green).

Right-click a pill to change discrete to continuous or vice versa. This change can also be made from the Data pane: right-click a field and select the "Convert to" option.

When a field is placed on a worksheet, Tableau creates headers for Discrete fields and axes for Continuous fields.

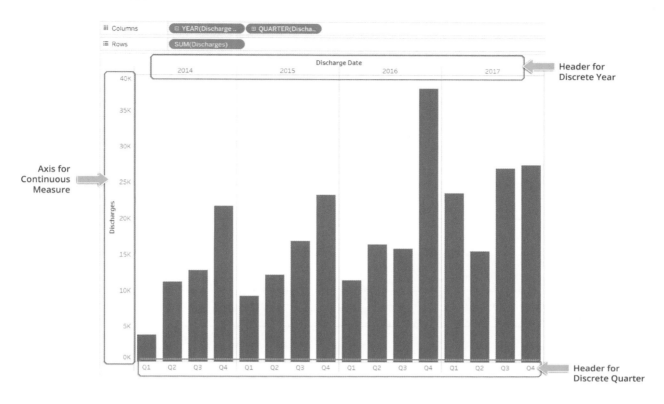

There are other functional differences between leveraging discrete and continuous fields in a worksheet; these will be discussed in future exercises.

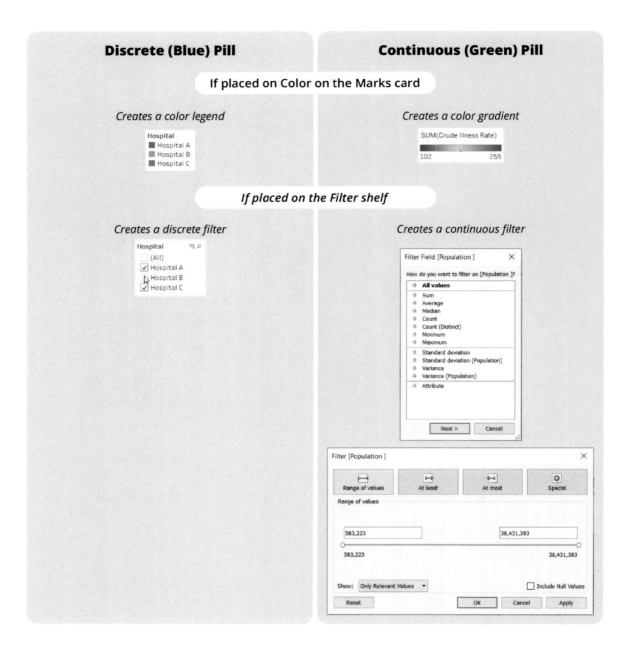

Tableau-Generated Data Fields (*Italicized Font*)

Italicized field names—*Measure Names*, *Measure Values*, and *Number of Records*—are Tableau-generated fields and not part of the underlying data source. Tableau creates them when the data source is created.

Measure Names and Measure Values

These Tableau tools allow two or more Measures to be compared side by side along the same axis. Tableau automatically adds these two fields to every dataset, placing the Measure

Names field at the bottom of the Dimensions list, and the Measure Values field at the bottom of the Measures list. "Measure Names" contains multiple Measures' names in a single, discrete (blue) pill. "Measure Values" contains multiple Measures' values in a single, continuous (green) pill. These unique fields make it possible to build data views involving multiple Measures.

▲ Measure Names and Measure Values

The Measure Values pill represents all user-selected Measures; however, since they are not visible in the pill itself, a shelf appears below the Marks card listing all field names that the pill contains.

If user chooses to display only certain Measures, a Measure Names pill appears on the Filters shelf. Right-clicking this pill and selecting Edit Filter shows a list of both excluded and displayed Measures.

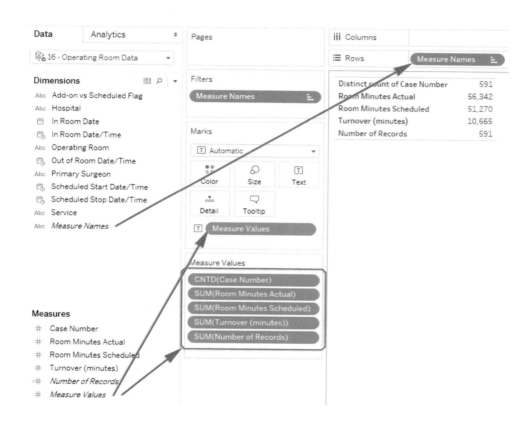

▲ Data Exploration Tip

Measure Names and Measure Values allow easy exploration of a dataset by creating a text table. Moving "Measure Names" from the Dimensions window to the Rows shelf, and Measure Values from the Measures window to Text on the Marks card gives effortless access to the data.

Latitude and Longitude

In fields that have a Geographic role (these can be used to create maps), Tableau automatically geocodes the data and includes Latitude (generated) and Longitude (generated) fields. These fields can be used to overlay data on live maps.

Number of Records

This field represents the number of rows in the data source. It is a Tableau-generated calculated field with a value of 1 whose SUM is the number of records (rows of data) in the dataset. When working with a new dataset, use Number of Records to determine the size of the data source and to understand what one row of data in the dataset represents.

File Types and Saving

Work can be saved as several different Tableau-specific file types described below.

Tableau Workbook (.twb)

This file format is Tableau's default way of saving work. Tableau workbooks contain one or more worksheets, dashboards, or stories, as well as all the information required to draw visualizations, such as fields used in each view; measure-aggregation methods; and style and formatting applied. Workbooks also include data-source connection information and any metadata created for that connection (see .tds file type below); however, they do not include the data itself.

To create a .twb file:

> » On the Tableau Menu Bar, select "File."
>
> » Select "Save."

Tableau Packaged Workbook (.twbx)

A Packaged Workbook bundles the information in a workbook with any associated files including local data (any data not on a server). This file type is for sharing work with those who do not have access to the data source. (Note: .twbx files are the only format viewable in Tableau Reader .

To create a .twbx file:

> » On the Tableau Menu Bar, select "File."
>
> » Select "Save As."
>
> » Choose the ".twbx" option from the dropdown menu at the bottom of the Save As dialog box.

Recovered Tableau Workbook (.twbr)

New in Tableau Desktop version 10.2, the Autosave feature runs every few minutes. If Tableau crashes, a recovered Tableau workbook (.twbr) file is saved in the same location as the original file or in the My Tableau Repository/Workbooks folder. When Tableau is reopened, a recovery dialog box appears containing a list of the recovered files to resume or delete. Autosave is turned on by default, but can be disabled from the Help menu.

Tableau Data Source (.tds)

This file type contains only the information needed to connect to data sources, such as data source type, location, and metadata. If local file data sources (Excel, Access, Text, extracts)are used, the file path is stored in the data source file.

 ### Tableau Packaged Data Source (.tdsx)

A Packaged Data Source (.tdsx) contains all the information in the Data Source (.tds) file as well as any local file data sources. This file type is a single zipped file and is good for sharing a data source with people who do not have access to the original data source.

> » On the Data menu, select a data source, then choose Add to Saved Data Sources from the context menu.

> » Complete the Add to Saved Data Sources dialog box by specifying a file name and type of data source file. The new .tds or tdsx file is then listed in the Saved Data Sources section of the Connect pane.

Tableau Data Extract (.tde)

Data Extracts are a local copy of an entire data source or a subset of that source. They are highly compressed and can be used to share data, work offline, or speed up database performance. Connecting to data using Tableau can be either "Live" or "Extract"[ed] into a .tde file. The disadvantage of using an Extract is that the Tableau visualization no longer points to the Live data source; however, the ability to refresh an Extract is only a few clicks away, and can be scheduled using Tableau Server.

To create a .tde file:

In an initial connection,

> » Select the "Extract" radio button.

If the live connection has already been established,

> » Right-click the data source connection.

> » Select "Extract Data."

Connecting to Data

CHAPTER 3

Connecting to Data

3.1 Common Data Source Connections

The first step toward creating a visualization in Tableau is to connect to the desired data source. Most organizations have data stored across multiple systems, often including live databases and static files. Tableau connects to these in a variety of ways, enabling fast development of dashboards and reports. These visualizations can then be distributed to other users through multiple channels (described in the chapter "Report and Dashboard Distribution").

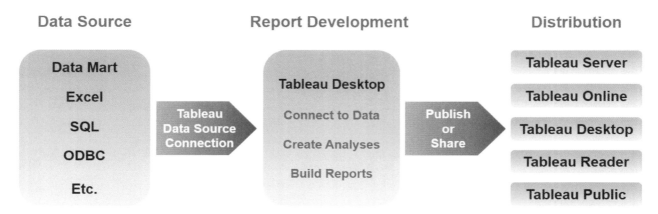

There is no limit to the number of data source connections Tableau can have in one workbook, making it possible to analyze data from multiple sources in the same report. A given data environment may have several tables of related information needed for a report. Tableau can join these tables into a single data connection, or work with them separately. Once a connection is created to the desired data table(s), it can be kept as a live connection to the data source, or a subset or "snapshot" of the data can be extracted from the data source and saved as a Tableau Data Extract (.tde) file.

Connections to data sources are created and modified on the following two pages:

- The **Tableau Start Page** allows the user to select the appropriate connector for the specified data source.

- The **Data Source Page** displays additional details to validate and modify the data connection.

Each page is explained below, along with instructional examples of how to connect to two common data sources: CSV files and MS SQL Server.

The Tableau Start Page

The Start Page contains three sections, shown in the screenshot below. From this central location, the user can (1) **Connect** to data, (2) **Open** most-recently used Tableau workbooks, and (3) **Discover** resources such as training materials, Viz of the Week, and other content produced by the Tableau community.

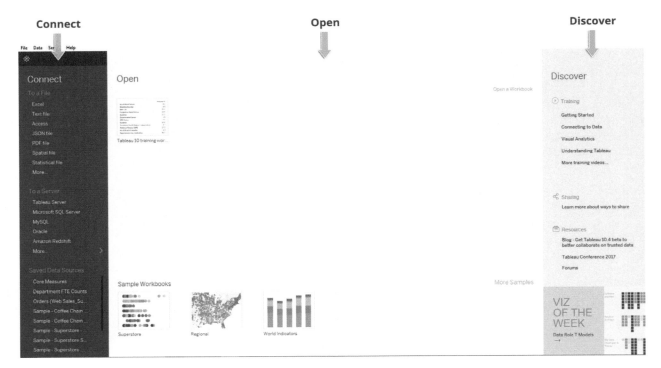

⚠ Tableau Editions

In the Tableau Personal Edition, the menu title To a Server is not visible on the screen. Only Tableau Professional Edition allows the user to connect to data on a server.

Connect

◄ **Connect**

The small Tableau logo icon at the top left of the Connect pane is a handy button to toggle between the Tableau Start Page and any active Worksheet.

The left pane lists connections to an ever-expanding library of file- and server-based data source types. It also displays a list of shortcuts to saved data sources for quick access.

1) **To a file:** Connect to data stored in Excel, text files, PDFs, statistical files, etc.

2) **To a server:** More than 50 server-based data source connections are available here. Each connector has been optimized for performance when working with the capabilities of the particular data source. If the desired data source is not listed, it may still be possible to connect to it using an Open Database Connectivity (ODBC) standard connector.

3) **Saved data sources:** Access frequently used data sources quickly and easily through shortcut links created by saving Tableau Data Source (.tds) files. Saved data sources

allow the user to set up data source customizations once for reuse across multiple reports and analyses.

Open

Open

Open a Workbook

Tableau 10 training wor... Tableau 10 Training wo...

The Open pane facilitates quick access to workbooks:

1) **Recently viewed workbooks** – these can be pinned (kept on the recent workbook list), unpinned (removed from that list), or opened from this pane.

2) **Open a workbook** –This link opens a navigation window to select other workbooks than those displayed.

3) **Sample workbooks** –Tableau displays these at the bottom of the Open pane for demonstration and learning purposes.

Discover

This pane contains training materials from Tableau, the Viz of the Week from the Tableau community, and Resources, such as Blog posts, Tableau Conference information, and Forum links.

HOW TO CONNECT TO A NEW TABLEAU DATA SOURCE

All Tableau data source connections occur via these five steps:

Step 1 - Choose a Connector. Under "Connect" on the Start page, click a type of file or database and, if required, enter authentication information to open the Data Source page.

Step 2 - Locate the Data. Select the file, database, or schema, then choose the data table(s) within it to be used for analysis.

Step 3 - Validate. Preview and edit metadata if needed.

Step 4 - Customize. Select connection options.

Step 5 - Begin. Go to worksheet to start analysis.

The Data Source Page

After the initial connection to the data is established, Tableau automatically navigates to the Data Source Page. This Page can also be accessed from any location in a Tableau workbook by clicking the Data Source tab at the bottom left of the workbook screen. The Data Source Page can look different according to the type of data connection; however, it will contain the same sections in all cases.

In this image, the four sections of the Data Source Page have been numbered to show work-flow sequence and direction.

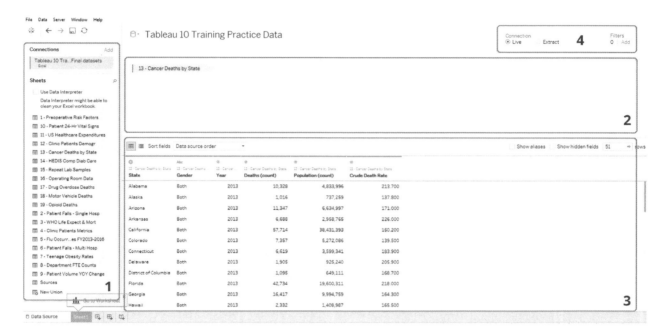

Section 1 - Data Source Information. Displays the default title of the data connection as inherited from its file or database name, as well as details of the connected data. This section's display may differ slightly depending on the capabilities of the connected data source. If prompted, choose the desired database to see its data tables displayed in a list below. Connect to desired tables by double-clicking or dragging and dropping them to Section 2, the Canvas or Join Area. To retitle the data connection, highlight the title and type in a new one.

Section 2 - Canvas or Join Area. Choosing a data table from the list in section 1 and placing it here connects to its data. Multiple tables with related data can be placed here to specify Joins and Unions. More information on Joins and Unions is in section 3.2, below. Once selected, the data will populate the data grid area for preview and validation.

Section 3 - Data Grid. Here the dataset can be previewed, modified, and validated. The Data Grid is a preview of rows of data values. It can be changed to a Metadata Grid—which is a simplified list of the columns in the data source and their properties—by clicking the icons in the upper left corner of the section.

Either the Data or the Metadata Grid can be used to modify column/field properties. To hide or rename a field, hover over the field header and click the caret that appears. Select the appropriate option from the drop-down menu. To change the data type, click the icon by the field name, then select the correct type from the menu.

For data sources including Excel, Text files, and Google sheets, columns of data can be pivoted and split into new fields. These tools are explained in section 3.3 "Reshaping Data Files: Using Data Interpreter, Pivot, and Column-Splitting."

Section 4 - Customize Connection & Filters.

- **Connections** are either Live or Extract. "Live" connects directly to the data source; "Extract" imports data into Tableau's fast data engine.

- **Filters** can be used to define a subset of the data, reducing the number of records in the data source. Filters can be applied to both Live and Extract connections. Data Source Filters limit the number of records queried; Extract Filters limit the amount of data extracted into the .tde file.

▲ Data Connection: Live vs. Extract

The decision to create a live connection to the data or to extract data from the data source into Tableau's data engine depends on user requirements and available network resources.

Live: Tableau connects directly to the data source and queries this source in real time as the report is rendered. This is the best choice when data is constantly updated and time-sensitive analysis is required. With Llive connections, the queries' speed will depend on the performance capabilities of the source system.

Extract: Tableau takes a snapshot of the data and puts it into a Tableau Data Extract file, a proprietary, columnar data format optimized for querying by Tableau. Once an Extract is made, queries are directed to the .tde rather than the originating data source. The Extract can then be refreshed manually or via Tableau Server on an automated schedule as frequently as every 15 minutes and/or as fast as the database is able to refresh the query for the extracted data.

Best Practice

There are many reasons to consider extracting data when developing and distributing Tableau reports.

1) If a Live connection is slow, a Tableau Data Extract may enhance performance.

2) End users may not have access to the underlying (possibly remote) data source. A Tableau Data Extract file (.tde) can be combined with a .twb workbook file to create a Tableau Packaged Workbook file (.twbx) that can be distributed and used for offline analysis.

3) Data Extracts can aggregate data for visible Dimensions and hide unused fields to improve performance and enhance security.

If real-time analysis is needed or the data is too large to extract, a Live data connection can be used.

Go to Worksheet. Once a data connection is set up appropriately, click "Go to Worksheet" or "Sheet 1" to start the analysis.

Data Connection Examples

The following examples are intended to be conceptual walk-throughs, illustrating the steps required to connect to common data sources.

EXAMPLE 1: CSV FILE CONNECTION

This example illustrates connecting Tableau to a text data file to set up a single table data source.

Choose a Connector

» On the Tableau Start page, in the Connect section, click "Text File."

Locate the Data

» Click the desired data source title, then click "Open."

» On the Data Source page, drag and drop the selected table from the left pane onto the Join Area. (If there is only one table in the left column, Tableau automatically places it in the Join Area.)

Validate

» Preview the data.

Customize

» Rename column headers, hide columns, and/or edit data types as needed.

» Under "Connection," click the radio button for "Extract."

» Replace the pre-assigned title with a descriptive one of your choice by highlighting the title field (upper left corner of the workspace) and typing in the chosen name.

Begin

» Click "Go to Worksheet" to start the analysis.

Note: Dragging and dropping more than one sheet to the white canvas activates Table Joins and Unions. These processes are explained in section 3.2 "Table Joins." This example assumes that only one sheet is needed.

EXAMPLE 2: MICROSOFT SQL SERVER

Connecting to server-based data sources, like Microsoft SQL Server, requires additional steps for user authentication and locating the desired data tables.

Choose a Connector

» On the Tableau Start page under "Connect," go to the "To a Server" section, and click "Microsoft SQL Server."

Locate the Data

» Enter the name of the server.

» Provide login credentials for the server by specifying whether to use Windows Authentication or a specific Username and Password.

» Check the "Require SSL" box if connecting to an SSL server.

» Specify whether to "Read uncommitted data."

» Click "OK."

» On the Data Source page, choose a database from the "Select Database" drop-down menu.

» Drag and drop the desired table onto the Join Area.

Validate

» To minimize queries to the database, the data grid may not update immediately—in which case an "Update Now" button will display. Select it to preview the data.

Customize

» Under "Connection," leave the selection on "Live," or click the radio button for "Extract" to generate a Tableau Data Extract.

» Replace the pre-assigned title with a descriptive one, if desired, by highlighting the title field (upper left corner of the workspace) and typing in an appropriate name.

Begin

» Click "Go to Worksheet" to start analysis.

3.2   Table Joins

Table Joining combines records from two or more tables into a *single Tableau data source* using fields common to all the tables.

Tableau can join tables within a single data connector or across multiple data environments. The example below demonstrates the basics of these variations via a simple Table Join between two tables in a single Excel file. The section following it explains the process for joining tables across data environments, called a Cross-Database Table Join.

Joining Tables in Tableau: Within a Single Data Connector

This walk-through explains how to join two tables from a single Excel workbook. Follow these steps using the "Tableau 10 Training Workbook - New" .twbx file in the download files for this book.

The process is similar to that for joining multiple tables from a single database such as MS SQL Server.

» Double-click the downloaded "Tableau 10 Training Workbook - New" file to open it in Tableau Desktop.

» In the Data pane, select the "12 - Clinic Patients Demographics" dataset.

» Click "Data" on the Menu bar.

» Click "12 - Clinic Patients Demographics to display its submenu.

» Select "Duplicate" to make a copy of the dataset.

» At the very bottom of the Side Bar, click the "Data Source" tab.

The "12 - Clinic Patients Demographics (copy)" table has been placed on the Join Area. The data from Clinic Patient Demographics is displayed in the data grid, allowing the user to view the contents of that data source.

Next, join "12 - Clinic Patient Demographics (copy)" with the "06 - Patient Readmission Days" table:

» Double-click the "06 - Patient Readmission Days" sheet.

This sheet is added to the Join Area, and Tableau automatically performs a Table Join. The joined dataset preview is visible in the lower half of the screen.

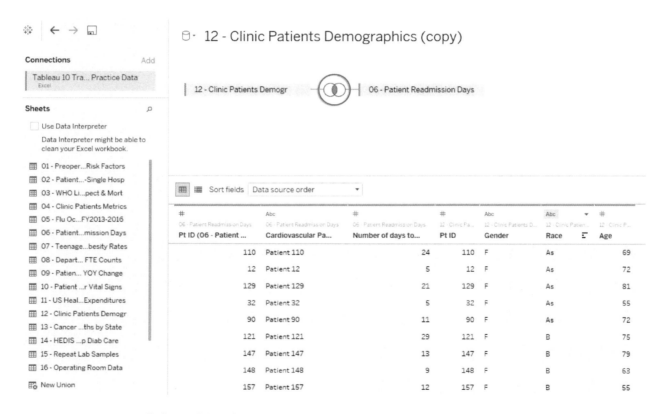

▲ Defining Table Joins

When a second table is added to the Join Area, Tableau makes a guess as to how the tables should be joined by identifying fields with the same name. If Tableau chooses incorrectly, or no shared field names exist, the join clause can be manually defined. Tableau also updates the preview in the data grid below to reflect the new data source being created by the Table Join.

»

» Click the Join icon to view the options.

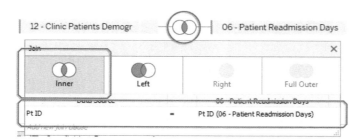

Tableau recognized that both tables have a common data field—Pt ID—and has joined the tables via an Inner Join. If this choice is incorrect, select other Join options.

▲ Table Joins

The type of Table Join used will determine how two tables are combined to form a new table with fields from both.

An in-depth analysis of Table Joins is beyond the scope of this book, but below is a quick overview of the four Joins that Tableau allows:

Inner Join: A row is returned only when the value is matched in both tables.

Left Join: All rows are returned from the left table; matching records only are returned from the right table. If no matching records exist, the fields from the right table return NULL.

Right Join: All rows are returned from the right table; matching records only are returned from the left table. If no matching records exist, the fields from the left table return NULL.

Full Outer Join: A row is returned when a value is present in either table. If no matching records exist, the fields from the other table will return NULL.

Tableau correctly selected the fields to join (Pt ID) in this example. However, it is possible to change the field on which the Join is performed. To view available fields for a possible join:

» Hover the cursor over either field name in the Join box to display a caret.

» Click the caret to view the drop-down menu of available fields to join. In this example, Age, Gender, and Race are additional data fields available for a join.

» For this example, leave the join on "Pt ID."

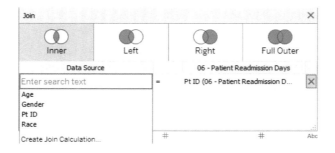

◀ Join Calculations

In version 10.2 and later, it is possible to make calculations part of Join criteria. Select "Create Join Calculation" to achieve more complex joins or to resolve field mismatches between tables.

»

» Click the title bar to highlight the title.

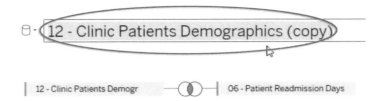

» Change the title to: "20 - Clinic Patients - Demographics and Readmission Data."

» Click the worksheet tab to go to the worksheet.

The tables are now joined.

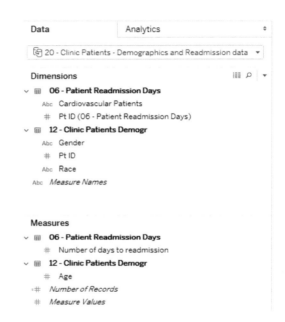

Data-Pane Organization ▶

When multiple tables are joined in a single data source, Tableau automatically groups the fields by table name (as displayed here, at right) to keep them organized. To use Folders as an organizing device instead, right-click the white space of the Data pane, select Group by, then Folder. Right-click again to choose Create Folder. Drag and drop selected fields into this new Folder.

Unions vs. Table Joins

Table Joins in their simplest form place one table next to another, lining them up row by row based on the data values of key field(s) to create a wider final dataset. Table Joins can also increase or decrease the number of rows in the resulting data source based on the type of join and whether any matches are found for the key field. Unions align two tables column by column, essentially appending the rows of data to make a longer final dataset. Another way to think of this difference: joining tables is a way to append new columns to a dataset; creating a Union is a way to append rows to existing columns in the dataset.

38

Join   **Union**

Column 1	Column 2	Column 3
John		
Jean		
Jane		

+

Column 1	Column 4	Column 5
John		
Jean		
Jane		

Column 1	Column 2	Column 3
John		
Jean		
Jane		

+

Column 1	Column 2	Column 3
Kenny		
Kathy		
Kaitlin		

↓

Column 1	Column 2	Column 3	Column 1	Column 4	Column 5
John			John		
Jean			Jean		
Jane			Jane		

↓

Column 1	Column 2	Column 3
John		
Jean		
Jane		
Kenny		
Kathy		
Kaitlin		

Unions

Unions are useful in any situation in which data tables are generated at regular intervals with identical columns, but with new data values, and where a compilation of data across those intervals is needed for analysis. For example, monthly financial reports are sometimes stored as individual tabs in an Excel workbook. Unions are a fast way to merge these tabs for analysis in Tableau. Unions can occur only between tables in the same data source. Not all data sources support Unions; when they *are* supported, the bottom of the left pane of the Data Source Page displays a "New Union" option.

Here are the conceptual steps to create a manual Union:

>> Double-click the "New Union" option to open the Union dialog box.

>> Drag and drop the desired tables from the left pane into the dialog box.

>> Select "Apply."

Where possible, tables should have the same structure, column headers, and data types. If this is not possible, mismatched columns can nevertheless be merged.

>> Select the columns to merge.

>> Click the drop-down arrow; select "Merge mismatched fields."

Additional notes on Unions:

• Unmatched columns (one exists in the first table, but not in the second) are retained; missing data are treated as NULL.

• Tableau generates meta-data fields about the Union and adds them to the data, including Sheet and Table names.

- A wildcard search from the Union dialog box can find all matching tables, so they can automatically be included in the Union.

Joining Tables in Tableau: across Data Sources ("Cross-Database Join")

New to Tableau is the ability to join tables across different databases and data environments. The conceptual walk-through below uses screen shots to show how to join an Access and an Excel table; many different cross-database combinations are possible. Much of what has been said so far about Table Joins in a single data source applies to Cross-Database Joins as well; note however, the important difference highlighted below.

To create a Cross-Database Join, start in the Data Connection page view.

»   Select the first table for the join by dragging it to the Join Area.

»   Next, Click the "Add" button to the right of the Connections header.

»   Select the desired File or Server connection from the Connection List menu that appears. The list displays only the databases for which Cross-Database Joins are supported. Once the multi-connection data source is established, joins can be created as usual.

»   Drag and drop the desired table/sheet onto the Join area, then set the Join criteria using the steps described for Table Joins, above.

Once you have a multi-connection data source, Tableau color-codes each table and its corresponding columns as an added visual cue.

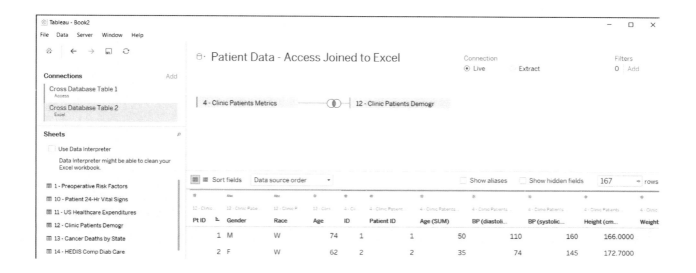

Cross-Database Join Notes:

Any grayed-out connection types are not supported for Cross-Database Joins.

When using an Extract as part of a multi-connection data source, designate it the primary connection to retain any metadata customizations (default property settings, calculated fields, groups, and aliases). Should a multi-connection data source require multiple Extracts, only the customizations in the primary connection Extract will remain.

To troubleshoot multi-connection data sources, verify that the data types of the key fields match. It is often possible to create a calculated field to fix column mismatches as long as calculations are supported by all active connections.

3.3 Reshaping Data Files: Using Data Interpreter, Pivot, and Column-Splitting

EXAMPLE: MICROSOFT EXCEL FORMATTED AS A REPORT

Excel data files are often formatted as reports that include titles, row spacing, merged cells, and other features, making them hard to work with in Tableau. Tableau's data-connection process provides tools to mitigate this difficulty: Data Interpreter, Pivoting, and Column-Splitting.

For Tableau to correctly use imported data, data table(s) must be in a "raw" format, with variables in columns and values in rows. The table must be free of all processing; even common, easily read formatting seen in spreadsheets or pivot tables, such as totals and line breaks, must be omitted. (The first row in the file can contain field headers or column names.) Everything else, including empty columns and/or rows, should be deleted.

Comparing the tables below further illustrates this point.

Incorrect Data-Table Formatting

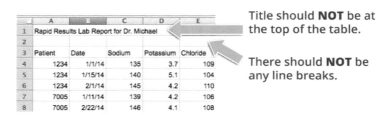

Title should **NOT** be at the top of the table.

There should **NOT** be any line breaks.

Correct Data-Table Formatting

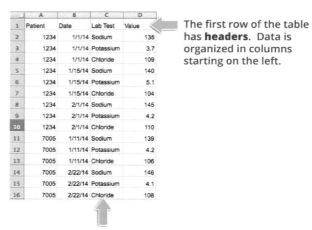

The first row of the table has **headers**. Data is organized in columns starting on the left.

Data has been "**pivoted**," or reshaped. Lab tests appear as a single column; test results appear in a second column named Value. This arrangement changes lab results from three Measures into a Dimension (Lab Test) and a Measure (Value).

The pair of images above shows "before" and "after" versions of an Excel file whose data has been modified to work more smoothly in Tableau. (The original Excel file is not affected.) Tableau data-preparation tools can be launched from the Data Connection Page:

- **Tableau Data Interpreter** detects the data, including sub-tables, and removes extra formatting such as titles and blank space from Excel data sources.

- **Pivot** converts Excel or text table data to a narrower table structure. Multiple, adjacent columns are transformed into a column with the field names and a separate column containing the field values.

- **Split** and **Custom Split** generate new fields according to user-defined requirements.

EXERCISE: USING TABLEAU'S DATA-PREPARATION TOOLS

This exercise lists the steps to connect to the Excel worksheet displayed below. Follow them using the "Data Interpreter Example – WHO Death Projections.xls" file in the download dataset for this book.

This spreadsheet has been created in a typical report format: title on the first row, followed by several empty rows, then column headers (separate from the first row of data and spread across multiple rows), and data values divided across several columns.

Projection of deaths per 100,000 Population

| | 2030 | | | | | | | | | | | | 2015 | | | | | | | | | | | |
| | Male | | | | | | Female | | | | | | Male | | | | | | Female | | | | | |
	0-4 years	5-14 years	15-29 years	30-49 years	50-69 years	70+ years	0-4 years	5-14 years	15-29 years	30-49 years	50-69 years	70+ years	0-4 years	5-14 years	15-29 years	30-49 years	50-69 years	70+ years	0-4 years	5-14 years	15-29 years	30-49 years	50-69 years	70+ years
All Causes	201	50	165	284	1010	5483	164	23	53	137	652	4676	304	56	184	308	1141	6192	244	27	60	157	728	5461
Communicable & other Group I	58	5	9	27	61	447	69	5	6	20	41	420	178	6	11	57	79	490	139	5	11	23	48	459
Infectious and parasitic diseases	13	2	6	20	33	134	11	2	1	14	21	123	33	4	6	29	47	145	28	5	5	15	26	132
Tuberculosis	0	0	0	0	2	5	0	0	0	0	1	2	0	0	1	2	6	13	0	0	0	1	2	5
STDs excluding HIV	0	0	0	0	0	0	0	0	0	0	0	0	0	0	0	0	0	0	0	0	0	0	0	0
Syphilis	0	0	0	0	0	0	0	0	0	0	0	0	0	0	0	0	0	0	0	0	0	0	0	0
Chlamydia	0	0	0	0	0	0	0	0	0	0	0	0	0	0	0	0	0	0	0	0	0	0	0	0
Gonorrhoea	0	0	0	0	0	0	0	0	0	0	0	0	0	0	0	0	0	0	0	0	0	0	0	0

» On the Tableau Start page, under the Connect header, click "Excel."

» Select the "Data Interpreter Example - WHO Death Projection" file, then click "Open."

Sheets in Excel are treated just like tables in a database. Since there is only one file displayed in the Data Source section, the data automatically appears in the Join Area.

» Preview the data. Since this is an Excel data source, Tableau recognizes that the data is eligible for Data Interpreter.

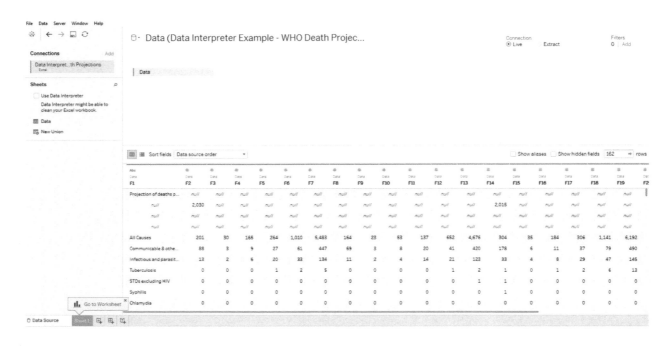

Data Interpreter scans all data to find Excel sheet areas convertible to well-structured tables, automatically discarding header/footer text and flattening multi-level table headers. If the sheet is already structured properly, these actions do not occur.

»   Click the "Use Data Interpreter" box.

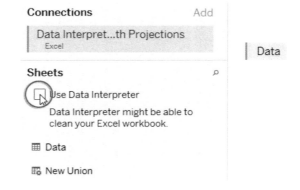

Data Interpreter looks for patterns of well-structured tables in the Excel data source. It restructures only the Tableau data source, never modifying the underlying data file.

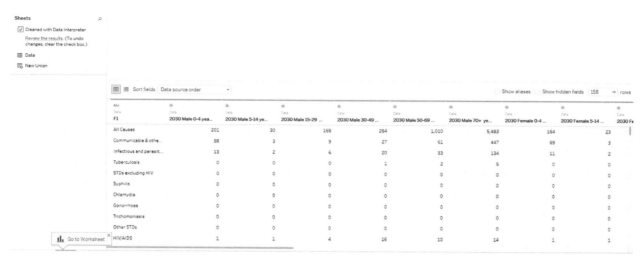

▲ Data Interpreter

When Data Interpreter is turned on, Tableau does its best to clean up titles, blank rows, multiple header rows, and other formatting anomalies. It will not, however, pivot or split fields automatically.

Data Interpreter works only on Excel workbooks.

To ensure quality control, look over Data Interpreter's modifications.

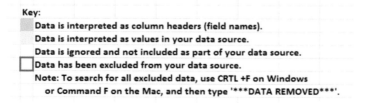

» Click "Review the results"; this opens a separate Tableau-generated Excel file.

The first spreadsheet tab is a color key that assists in clarifying Data Interpreter's results.

Key:
Data is interpreted as column headers (field names).
Data is interpreted as values in your data source.
Data is ignored and not included as part of your data source.
Data has been excluded from your data source.
Note: To search for all excluded data, use CRTL +F on Windows
    or Command F on the Mac, and then type '***DATA REMOVED***'.

The next tab displays the underlying details of the changes Data Interpreter has made to the mirror file it created.

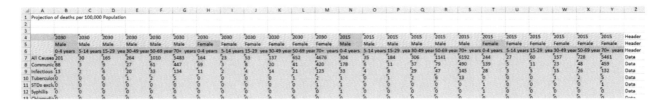

» Unless the viewer wishes to dismiss the changes, "Review the results" can be closed.

Pivot Tool

Data Interpreter correctly identifies data values and flattens multi-line column headers. This does not guarantee, however, that data is optimally structured. The table layout is in a cross-tab format—useful for report consumption, but not for data analysis. Year, Gender, and Age Range variables are spread across multiple columns, making it necessary to reduce columns to one per field. This can be done using the Pivot Tool. The number of rows then increases, providing a narrower data structure better suited for report creation in Tableau.

» Select the columns to be pivoted. Click the first column header "2030 Male 0-4 years."

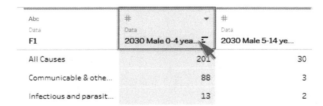

» Scroll all the way to the right and, while holding down the Shift key, click the last column header. This will highlight all columns from the first through the last selected one.

» Hover the cursor over the last selected column header to make its caret visible.

» Click the caret to display a dropdown menu, then select "Pivot."

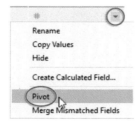

Pivoting displays multiple column headers in one column labeled "Pivot Field Names" and numeric values in a second column labeled "Pivot Field Values."

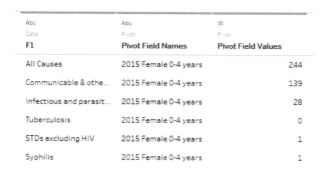

Abc	Abc	#
Data	Pivot	Pivot
F1	**Pivot Field Names**	**Pivot Field Values**
All Causes	2015 Female 0-4 years	244
Communicable & othe...	2015 Female 0-4 years	139
Infectious and parasit...	2015 Female 0-4 years	28
Tuberculosis	2015 Female 0-4 years	0
STDs excluding HIV	2015 Female 0-4 years	1
Syphilis	2015 Female 0-4 years	1

Column-Splitting

"Pivot Field Names" contains multiple categorizations in one column. The column can be split into three columns: Year, Gender, and Age Range. Tableau's Split and Custom Split text field functions identify patterns that use separator-characters such as hyphens, symbols, spaces, or a repeated pattern of values present in each row of the field. Splitting uses the separator to organize the values into individual columns. Our example will demonstrate a Custom Split, relying on a blank space as a separator.

» Right-click the "Pivot Field Names" header; select "Custom Split."

» Place the cursor in the "Use the separator" text box and enter one space by pressing the space bar. This action removes all greyed-out separators and replaces them with a single blank space to use as a separator.

» For "Split off," select "First" and "3" columns, then click "OK."

» Right-click the "F1" column header, then select "Rename" from the menu.

» Rename it "Cause of Death."

» Right-click the "Pivot Field Names" column header, then select "Hide."

» Name the resulting three new columns "Year," "Gender," and "Age Range (years)."

» Rename "Pivot Field Values" "Projected Deaths per 100,000."

» Connect via "Extract"; do not select any filters.

» Click the data connection title, then rename it "WHO Deaths Projection per 100,000."

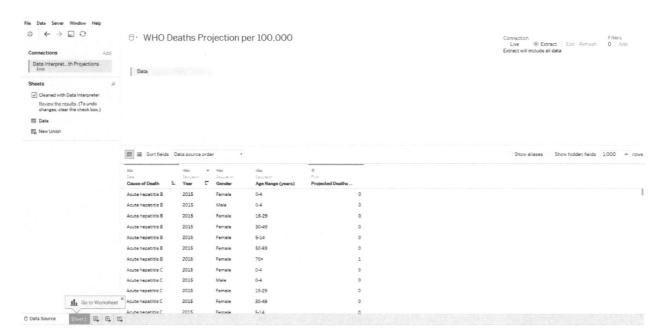

» Click "Go to Worksheet" (or New Worksheet icon to its right) to begin analysis.

▐▙ *HDVizoom*™ ...to Connecting to Data

Basic Data Connection

Choose a Connector

» On Tableau Start page, in Connect section, click desired Connector

Locate the Data

» Click desired data source file, then click "Open"

» On Data Source page, drag and drop selected table from left pane onto Join Area (If there is only one table in left column, Tableau automatically places it in Join Area)

Validate

» Preview data

Customize

» Rename column headers, hide columns, and/or edit data types as needed

» Under "Connection," click radio button for desired Connection type

» Replace pre-assigned title with descriptive one by highlighting title field (upper left corner of workspace) and typing in chosen name

Begin

» Click "Go to Worksheet" to start analysis

Joining Tables in Tableau: within Single Data Connector

» Double-click downloaded "Tableau 10 Training Workbook - New" file to open in Tableau Desktop

» In Data pane, select "12 - Clinic Patients Demographics" dataset

» Click "Data" on Menu bar

» Click "12 - Clinic Patients Demographics to display its submenu

» Select "Duplicate" to make copy of dataset

» At very bottom of Side Bar, click "Data Source" tab

» Double-click "06 - Patient Readmission Days" sheet

» Click Join icon to view options

» Hover cursor over either field name in Join box to display a caret

» Click caret to view drop-down menu of available fields to join

» For this example, leave join on "Pt ID"

» Click title bar to highlight title

» Change title to "20 - Clinic Patients - Demographics and Readmission Data"

» Click worksheet tab to go to worksheet

Unions

» Double-click "New Union" option to open Union dialog box

» Drag and drop desired tables from left pane into dialog box

» Select "Apply"

» Select columns to merge

» Click drop-down arrow; select "Merge mismatched fields"

Joining Tables in Tableau: Across Data Sources ("Cross-Database Join")

» Select first table for join by dragging it to Join Area

» Click "Add" button to right of Connections header

» Select desired File or Server connection from Connection List menu that appears

» Drag and drop desired table/sheet onto Join area, then set Join criteria using steps described for Table Joins, above

Reshaping Data Files: Using Data Interpreter, Pivot, and Column-Splitting

» On Tableau Start page, under Connect header, click "Excel"

» Select "Data Interpreter Example - WHO Death Projection" file, then click "Open"

» Click "Use Data Interpreter" box

» Click "Review the results"; this opens separate Tableau-generated Excel file

» Unless viewer wishes to dismiss changes, "Review the results" can be closed

» Click first column header "2030 Male 0-4 years"

» Scroll all way to right and, while holding down Shift key, click last column header

» Hover cursor over last selected column header to make its caret visible

» Click caret to display dropdown menu, then select "Pivot"

» Right-click "Pivot Field Names" header; select "Custom Split"

» Place cursor in "Use the separator" text box and enter one space by pressing space bar

» For "Split off," select "First" and "3" columns, then click "OK"

» Right-click "F1" column header, then select "Rename" from menu

» Rename it "Cause of Death"

» Right-click "Pivot Field Names" column header, then select "Hide"

» Name resulting three new columns "Year," "Gender," and "Age Range (years)"

» Rename "Pivot Field Values" "Projected Deaths per 100,000"

» Connect via "Extract"; do not select any filters

» Click data connection title, then rename it "WHO Deaths Projection per 100,000"

» Click "Go to Worksheet" to begin analysis

Basic Charts and Skills

CHAPTER 4

Text Table

A Text Table encodes words and numbers and arranges them in columns and rows. Also called "crosstabs" or "pivot tables," Text Tables are used to display simple relationships between quantitative values and corresponding categorical subdivisions. This structure makes tables ideal for looking up and comparing individual values. When deciding between building a Text Table and a chart, always think about how the information will be used. Choose a Text Table when your audience will need either to look up individual values or compare those values.

How To: Build a Text Table to look up specific preoperative risk factors to compare a hospital's results to benchmark data.

Preoperative Risk-Factor Rates: Hospital vs. Comparison

Preoperative Risk Factors	Hospital %	Comparison %
Acute Renal Failure	4.0	3.0
Bleeding Disorder	3.3	2.0
BMI > 30	33.3	40.0
Congestive Heart Failure	10.0	15.0
Diabetes	25.3	35.0
Disseminated Cancer	1.6	1.2
DNR Status	0.5	0.3
Dyspnea	12.0	15.0
Functional Health Status < Independent	8.7	10.0
History of Severe COPD	17.3	15.0
Hx of MI w/in 6 months	5.3	4.5
Hypertension req. medication	56.7	61.0
Sepsis within 48 hours	6.4	4.5
Smoking	20.0	17.0
Stroke	4.7	4.0
Transfusions	3.3	5.0
Ventilator Dependent	6.7	4.2

Data Source: *Mock preoperative risk-factors for patients having surgery*

About the Data: *Preoperative risk factors are important for the fair comparison of surgical outcomes. We created this mock data based on similar information captured by different surgical outcome programs such as the National Surgical Quality Improvement Program (NSQIP), the Society for Thoracic Surgeons General Thoracic Surgery Database (STS GTSD), and the Bariatric Longitudinal Outcomes Database (BOLD), which capture, report, and benchmark, clinical, risk-adjusted surgical outcomes for the improvement of surgical care in hospitals.*

1 Connect to the data

» Open the file "Tableau 10 Training workbook - new.twbx" downloaded from the HealthDataViz website.

» In the Data pane, click the caret to open the drop-down menu. Click on "01 - Preoperative Risk Factors" to select the dataset.

Creating Drop-down Menu Options ▷

When multiple datasets are present in a workbook, this drop-down menu option can be created by dragging up the border between the Data window and the Dimensions window until the view compresses.

2 Create the chart

» Double-click the following three fields:

- "Preoperative Risk Factors" in the Dimensions window.
- "Hospital %" in the Measures window.
- "Comparison %" in the Measures window.

Populating Fields Via Double-click ▷

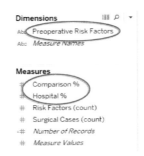

There are several ways to populate a worksheet with data: double-clicking fields; dragging and dropping; typing directly onto a shelf; or using the Show Me button. When a field from the Dimensions or Measures window is double-clicked, Tableau makes its best guess as to where that field should go based on what is already populated in the active worksheet. The order of double-clicking will affect the data display, but fields can always be rearranged once they are on the worksheet.

The table initially looks like this:

Refresher ▷

Measure Names and Measure Values pills are Tableau's way of letting more than one measure appear in the same place. Tableau automatically adds the above two fields to the data set, placing the Measure Names field at the bottom of the Dimensions window, and the Measure Values field at the bottom of the Measures window. For certain chart types, when multiple measures are used in the same location, Tableau automatically adds the Measure Names and Measure Values pills to the worksheet, and a Measures Values shelf appears showing the Measures fields.

Preoperative Risk Factors	Comparison %	Hospital %
Acute Renal Failure	3.00	4.00
Bleeding Disorder	2.00	3.33
BMI > 30	40.00	33.33
Congestive Heart Failure	15.00	10.00
Diabetes	35.00	25.33
Disseminated Cancer	1.20	1.60
DNR Status	0.30	0.53
Dyspnea	15.00	12.00
Functional Health Status ..	10.00	8.67
History of Severe COPD	15.00	17.33
Hx of MI w/in 6 months	4.50	5.33
Hypertension req. medica..	61.00	56.67
Sepsis within 48 hours	4.50	6.40
Smoking	17.00	20.00
Stroke	4.00	4.67
Transfusions	5.00	3.33
Ventilator Dependent	4.20	6.67

3 Format the data

The next step is to format the data; all numbers should be displayed with one decimal place.

» Right-click the "SUM(Comparison %)" pill on the Measure Values shelf.

» Select "Format..."

◄ Measure Formatting

By default, Tableau will typically display Measures in the same data format as the underlying data source. Adjusting formatting not only permits great precision (i.e., how many decimal places to include), but also allows correct formatting of elements such as percentages, monetary amounts, and numerical prefixes/suffixes.

Format Measures in one of two ways:

1. Default format change: *Change the default formatting from the Measures window, so all future uses of the Measure will display the new format. Selected formatting will then persist when the field appears in other worksheets.*

2. Single-use format change: *Change only the formatting of a Measure field already in the worksheet.*

To change the default format: *Right-click the field in the Measures window. Select Default Properties, then choose a new formatting option.*

To make a single-use format change: *Right-click the field pill already in the worksheet. Select Format; select Number drop-down; change to an appropriate format.*

Selecting "Format" opens the Format pane, replacing the Data pane at the left of the screen.

» Ensure the "Pane" tab is selected.

» Click the caret to the right of the "Numbers" field to open the drop-down menu.

» Select "Number (Custom)."

» Change "Decimal places" to "1."

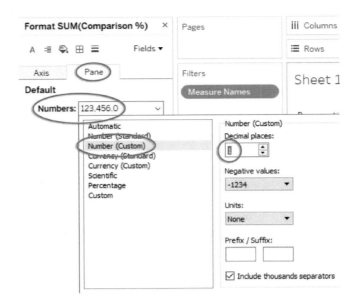

» Follow the same steps for the "SUM(Hospital %)" pill on the Measure Values shelf.

To return to the Data / Dimensions / Measures window:

» Click the "X" in the upper right corner of the Format pane.

4 Format the columns

The data columns need to be switched so that the "Hospital %" data is displayed to the left of the "Comparison %" data.

To transpose the columns:

» Drag and drop the "SUM(Comparison %)" pill below the "SUM(Hospital %)" pill on the Measure Values shelf.

To ensure clear, readable column and row width formatting, adjust the width as follows:

» Hover the cursor between the first two columns until it changes to a horizontal bi-directional arrow.

» Click and drag the width to completely display all text.

Preoperative Risk Factors	Hospital %	Comparison %
Acute Renal Failure	4.0	3.0
Bleeding Disorder	3.3	2.0
BMI > 30	33.3	40.0
Congestive Heart Failure	10.0	15.0
Diabetes	25.3	35.0
Disseminated Cancer	1.6	1.2
DNR Status	0.5	0.3
Dyspnea	12.0	15.0
Functional Health Status ..	8.7	10.0
History of Severe COPD	17.3	15.0
Hx of MI w/in 6 months	5.3	4.5
Hypertension req. medica..	56.7	61.0
Sepsis within 48 hours	6.4	4.5
Smoking	20.0	17.0
Stroke	4.7	4.0
Transfusions	3.3	5.0
Ventilator Dependent	6.7	4.2

◀ **Column Sizing**

Column widths containing text can be customized as described above. Columns containing figures will remain proportional.

◀ **Row Sizing**

Rows must remain proportional and evenly spaced in a text table. Adjusting the height of one row by hovering and dragging will change all rows to maintain proportions.

Best Practice

Tableau automatically right-justifies values in a Text Table to ensure that values are correctly aligned (i.e., ones, tens, and hundreds) for ease of comparison.

» Hover the cursor on the right edge of the "Comparison %" column until it changes to a horizontal bi-directional arrow.

» Click and drag the width to completely display the column headers.

5 Add a title

To add a title to the Text Table:

» Double-click the title row "Sheet 1" at the top left of the Work Area. A dialog box will appear.

◀ **Hide/Show Title Row**

The Title Row defaults to display on the worksheet. It can be hidden, if desired, by navigating to the Menu Bar, selecting the Worksheet option, and clicking Show Title to uncheck it. To redisplay the Title Row, click Show Title again.

»

» The Title text defaults to the generic Tableau worksheet number. Highlight and delete the current title.

» Enter the new title, "Preoperative Risk-Factor Rates: Hospital vs. Comparison."

» Highlight the Title text and click the "B" icon to bold the title font.

» Click "OK."

Title Formatting ▶

Titles provide a powerful tool for conveying metadata about a worksheet. In addition to including and formatting normal text, the Insert option at the top right of the Title menu screen can be used to add fields, data-connection information, and/or captions.

The final table looks like this:

Preoperative Risk-Factor Rates: Hospital vs. Comparison

Preoperative Risk Factors	Hospital %	Comparison %
Acute Renal Failure	4.0	3.0
Bleeding Disorder	3.3	2.0
BMI > 30	33.3	40.0
Congestive Heart Failure	10.0	15.0
Diabetes	25.3	35.0
Disseminated Cancer	1.6	1.2
DNR Status	0.5	0.3
Dyspnea	12.0	15.0
Functional Health Status < Independent	8.7	10.0
History of Severe COPD	17.3	15.0
Hx of MI w/in 6 months	5.3	4.5
Hypertension req. medication	56.7	61.0
Sepsis within 48 hours	6.4	4.5
Smoking	20.0	17.0
Stroke	4.7	4.0
Transfusions	3.3	5.0
Ventilator Dependent	6.7	4.2

Insight: Presenting Hospital Preoperative Risk Factors in a text table allows the audience to see exact numbers in a clearly presented format. In this example, it is easy to tell that the Risk Factor Rate for Diabetes is 25.3% for the primary hospital vs. 35.0% for the comparison hospital.

6 Rename the worksheet tab and save the worksheet

» Right-click the "Sheet 1" tab at the bottom of the screen.

» Click "Rename Sheet."

» Enter a new title ("Text: Preop Risk Factors"), then press Enter.

» Click the Save icon on the Toolbar.

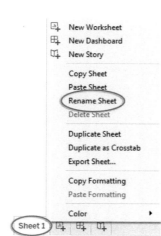

Best Practice

Always use intuitive names for worksheets to keep them organized and easier to find.

Best Practice

Save, save, and then save again! Saving during and after each chart is constructed is a sensible habit.

61

▐▌ *HDVizoom*™...to the Text Table

1 **Connect to data**

» Open file "Tableau 10 Training workbook - new.twbx" downloaded from HealthDataViz website

» Click "01 - Preoperative Risk Factors" to select dataset

2 **Create chart**

» Double-click following three fields:

- "Preoperative Risk Factors" in Dimensions window

- "Hospital %" in Measures window

- "Comparison %" in Measures window

3 **Format data**

» Right-click "SUM(Comparison %)" pill on Measures Values shelf

» Select "Format..."

» Ensure "Pane" tab is selected

» Click caret to right of "Numbers" field to open drop-down menu

» Select "Number (Custom)"

» Change "Decimal places" to "1"

» Perform same steps for SUM(Hospital %) pill on Measure Values shelf

» Click "X" in upper right corner of Format window to close

4 **Format columns**

» Drag and drop "SUM(Comparison %)" pill below SUM(Hospital %) pill on Measure Values shelf

» Hover cursor between first two columns until it changes to horizontal bi-directional arrow

» Click and drag width to completely display all text

» Hover cursor on right edge of "Comparison %" column until it changes to horizontal bi-directional arrow

» Click and drag width to completely display column headers

5 **Add title**

» Double-click "Sheet 1" at top left of Work Area

» Highlight and delete current title

» Enter new title, "Preoperative Risk-Factor Rates: Hospital vs. Comparison"

» Highlight title text and click "B" icon to bold title font

» Click "OK"

6 **Rename worksheet tab and save worksheet**

» Right-click "Sheet 1" tab at bottom of screen

» Click "Rename Sheet"

» Enter new title ("Text: Preop Risk Factors"), press Enter

» Click Save icon on Toolbar

CHAPTER 5

Bar Charts

Bar Charts are the most effective way to compare values across Dimensions or Measures, where the value of the Measure is represented by the length of the bar, revealing high and low values at a glance. One axis of the chart shows the specific categories being compared; the other represents the value. Sorting (ranking) data in descending order highlights high values; ascending order highlights low values. Because Bar Charts encode data values according to the length of the bar, they should begin at the value zero. (Tableau's default value for Bar Charts is therefore zero.)

5.1 Horizontal and Vertical Bar Charts

How To: **Build a Bar Chart to compare rates of patient falls per 1,000 patient days across types of care for a single hospital.**

Rate of Patient Falls (per 1,000 Patient Days) by Type of Care for FY2017

Data Source: Mock patient-fall data

About the Data: *The American Nurses Association (ANA) National Database of Nursing Quality Indicators (NDNQI®) is a repository for nursing-sensitive indicators, reported at the nursing-unit level, designed to provide comparative information to hospitals for use in quality improvement activities. For this exercise, we created mock patient-fall data, similar to that captured by the NDNQI and other groups such as the Centers for Medicare & Medicaid (CMS), to compare patient-fall rates per 1,000 patient days across types of care for a single hospital.*

1 **Create a New Worksheet and Connect to the Data**

» A new worksheet can be created in one of three ways:

Option 1: Select "Worksheet" on the Menu Bar and then select "New Worksheet."

Option 2: Click the "New Worksheet" tab at the very bottom of the workbook.

Option 3: Click the "New Worksheet" icon on the toolbar.

» To select the dataset, click the caret in the dataset menu of the Data pane then click "02 - Patient Falls - Single Hospital."

2 Create the Chart

» Drag and drop "Type of Care" from the Dimensions window onto the Rows shelf.

Primary Data Source ▶

Notice that once a field is added to the sheet, the data source for that field is marked with a blue check mark icon. This indicates the primary data source for this worksheet. Data from other sources can be combined with this primary data source only by using a technique called "Data Blending," which will be covered in Data Blending chapter.

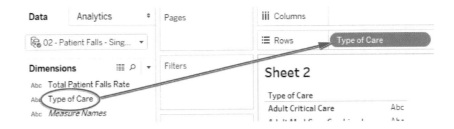

The next step has two parts: move, then edit "Total Patient Falls Rate." Begin by dragging it from the Dimensions window to the Measures window.

» Drag and drop "Total Patient Falls Rate" from the Dimensions window to the Measures window.

Dimensions and Measures ▶

The difference between a Dimension and a Measure was discussed in Chapter 2. To set a field as a Dimension or a Measure, drag and drop the field to the appropriate window. This will not affect the fields already present in your worksheet.

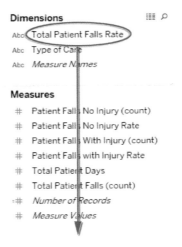

Notice the **Abc** icon to the left of "Total Patient Falls Rate," indicating that the data type is a String. Change the type to Number, as follows:

» Click the data type icon.

» Select "Number (decimal)."

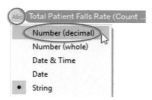

▲ **Data Types**

When Tableau connects to a new data source, it makes its best guess about the type of data being displayed (number, string, date, etc.). The data type will determine the types of calculations that can be performed on a particular field. For example, a SUM calculation can be performed only on a Number value; a date function, like DATEADD, can be performed only on a Date or Date & Time field. Data Types are easy to change by right-clicking the data-type icon, or right-clicking the field and selecting Change Data Type.

» Drag and drop "Total Patient Falls Rate" onto the Columns shelf.

3 Validate the Data

Notice that the "Total Patient Falls Rate" pill on the Columns shelf is labeled "CNTD (Total Patient Falls Rate)." CNTD stands for Count Distinct; this aggregation counts the number of unique values in the Measure, not the number of falls. In order to return an accurate rate, the aggregation needs to be changed. Because there is only one value (one row) per Type of Care, the Total Patient Falls Rate always returns accurately whether the aggregation is set to AVG, MIN, MAX, or SUM. This exercise will use the MAX aggregation:

» Right-click "CNTD(Total Patient Falls Rate)" on the Columns shelf.

» Select "Measure(Count (Distinct))."

» Select "Maximum."

Aggregation ▷

Note: *In this example, each Type of Care represents one row in the dataset. Therefore, Sum, Average, Median, Minimum, and Maximum of Total Patient Falls will return the same result. Count and Count (Distinct), however, will not.*

It is important to notice how a measure is being aggregated in a report. A Maximum will provide a very different result from that of a Count (Distinct).

Change the aggregation in one of two ways:

Aggregation of the Pill: *this is a one-time change to the aggregation of a field already present in the worksheet. Right-click the pill, click Measure, then select the desired aggregation.*

Aggregation of the Measure: *this will change the default aggregation so the change will persist when the field is used in other worksheets. Right-click the field in the Measures window, click Default Properties, then select the desired aggregation.*

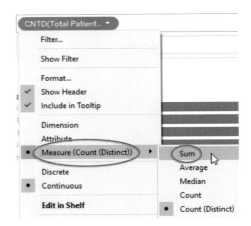

The chart now looks like this:

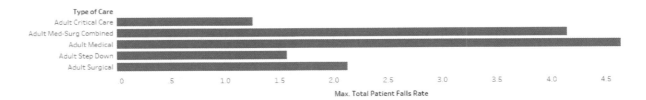

4 Sort and Format the Chart

The default Sort order (the one displayed above) is alphabetical by the single Dimension on the Row shelf—here, "Type of Care." The desired order, however, is from highest to lowest, according to the Measure "MAX (Total Patient Falls Rate)." To make the necessary change, access the quick Sort icon in one of the following two ways:

Option 1: Click the Sort icon on the Toolbar for ascending or descending order.

Option 2: Hover over the top of the chart to display the Sort icon, then click to select the desired ranking order—once to sort ascending, twice to sort descending, and a third time to return to the original order.

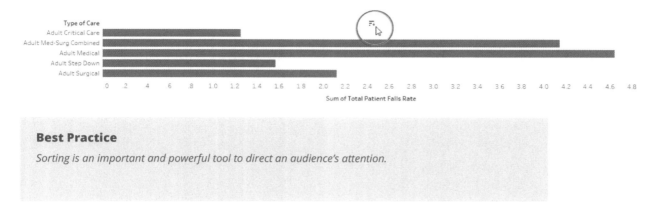

Best Practice

Sorting is an important and powerful tool to direct an audience's attention.

The Dimension, Type of Care, is now sorted by the Measure, Total Patient Falls Rate, from the highest rate to the lowest.

To label each bar with the actual rate of "Patient Falls per 1,000 Days":

» In the Toolbar, click the framed "T" icon. The label will appear automatically.

◀ **Labeling**

Alternatively, click Label on the Marks card, then click the box "Show mark labels." There are additional formatting options under Label.

The chart now looks like this:

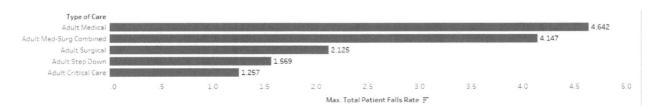

In the above image, the bar labels are carried out to the third decimal. This is unnecessary and creates clutter. To limit the label to one decimal place:

» Right-click "MAX(Total Patient Falls Rate)" on the Columns shelf.

» Select "Format..."

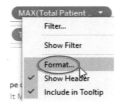

» Select the "Pane" tab.

» Under "Default," click the "Numbers" caret to open the drop-down menu.

» Select "Number (Custom)."

» Change "Decimal places" to 1.

» Click the X at the top right of the Format pane to close it and return to the Data/Dimensions/Measures window.

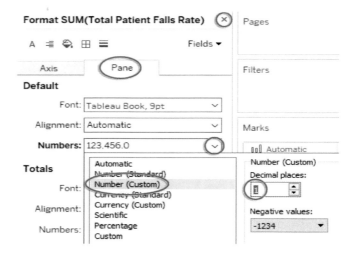

To hide the X axis:

» Right-click the X axis.

» Select "Show Header" to remove the checkmark and hide the X axis.

Best Practice

Since the labels in this example report are visible on each bar, the X axis can be hidden to reduce visual clutter. The decision to do this depends on the level of precision needed.

To hide the Column grid lines:

» Click "Format on the Menu Bar.

» Select the "Lines…" option.

» Select the "Columns" tab.

» Click the caret to the right of "Grid Lines."

» Select "None."

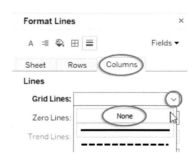

69

To remove the header on the Y axis:

» Right-click the Y axis header label ("Type of Care").

» Click "Hide Field Labels for Rows."

Best Practice

Field headers are sometimes needed to clarify the dimensions being viewed. If, however, field values are well-defined (as with the "Type of Care" categories in this example), remove the headers to reduce clutter.

5 Add a title

» Double-click the Title Row at the top of the Work Area. A dialog box will appear.

» Highlight and delete the current title "<Sheet Name>."

» Enter the new title, "Rate of Patient Falls (per 1,000 Patient Days) by Type of Care for FY2017," and click "OK."

6 Rename the worksheet tab and save the worksheet

» Right-click the "Sheet 2" tab at the bottom of the screen.

» Click "Rename Sheet."

» Enter the new title, "Bar: Patient Falls."

» Select "Enter," then "Save."

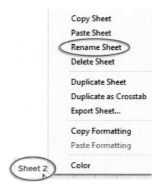

The final bar chart looks like this:

Rate of Patient Falls (per 1,000 Patient Days) by Type of Care for FY2017

Insight: The chart now makes it clear that in this example hospital for FY2017, Adult Medical has the highest rate of patient falls per 1,000 patient days (4.6), while Adult Critical Care has the lowest rate (1.3).

▗▖ *HDVizoom*™ ...to Bar Charts

1 **Create new worksheet and connect to data**

» Choose one of three options:

Option 1:

- Select "Worksheet" on Menu bar, then select "New Worksheet"

Option 2:

- Click "New Worksheet" tab at very bottom of workbook

Option 3:

- Click "New Worksheet" icon on Toolbar

» In Data pane, click caret to open drop-down menu

» Select "02 - Patient Falls - Single Hospital"

2 **Create chart**

» Drag and drop "Type of Care" from Dimensions window onto Rows shelf

» Drag and drop "Total Patient Falls Rate" from Dimensions windows to Measures window

» Click its data type icon

» Select "Number (decimal)"

» Drag and drop "Total Patient Falls Rate" onto Columns shelf

3 **Validate data**

» Right-click "CNTD(Total Patient Falls Rate)" on Columns shelf

» Select "Measure"

» Select "Maximum"

4 **Sort and format chart**

» Choose one of two options:

Option 1:

- Click Sort icon on Toolbar to arrange in ascending or descending order

Option 2:

- Hover over top of chart to display Sort icon, then click to select desired ranking order – once to rank ascending, twice to rank descending, and a third time to return to original order

» On Toolbar, click framed "T" icon

» Right-click on "MAX(Total Patient Falls Rate)" on Columns shelf

» Select "Format..."

» Select "Pane" tab

» Under "Default," click "Numbers" caret to open drop-down menu

» Select "Number (Custom)"

» Change "Decimal places" to 1

» Click "X" at top right of Format pane to close

» Right-click X axis

» Select "Show Header" to remove checkmark and hide X axis

» Click "Format" on Menu Bar

» Select "Lines"

» Select "Columns" tab

» Click caret to right of "Grid Lines"

» Select "None"

» Right-click Y axis header label ("Type of Care")

» Click "Hide Field Labels for Rows"

5   **Add a title**

» Double-click Title Row at top of Work Area

» Highlight and delete current title "<Sheet Title>"

» Enter new title, "Rate of Patient Falls (per 1,000 Patient Days) by Type of Care for FY2017"; and click "OK"

6   **Rename worksheet tab and save worksheet**

» Right-click "Sheet 2" tab at bottom of screen

» Click "Rename Sheet"

» Enter new title, "Bar: Patient Falls"

» Select "Enter," then "Save"

5.2 Bar Chart Variants: Side-by-Side Chart and Stacked Bar Chart

Side-by-Side and Stacked Bar Charts are variations of simple bar charts. Placing bars side by side to compare several variables enables use of both color and placement for enhanced data interpretation.

Stacked Bar Charts can be useful for the display of some part-to-whole data, but it is important to note that in the presence of numerous variables, a viewer's ability to quantify them is severely compromised. It is better to limit use of Stacked Bar Charts to the display of only two to three different variables. Use other types of charts, such as Small Multiples, to enhance display and interpretation of this type of data.

How To: Build a Side-by-Side Bar Chart and a Stacked Bar Chart as options to compare patient-falls rates per 1,000 patient days with and without injury across a range of types of care.

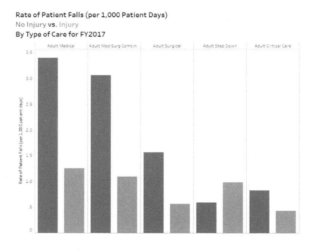 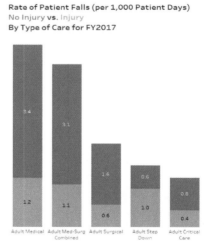

Data Source: Mock patient-fall data for a single hospital for FY2017

About the Data: The American Nurses Association (ANA) National Database of Nursing Quality Indicators (NDNQI®) is a repository for nursing-sensitive indicators, reported at the nursing-unit level, designed to provide comparative information to hospitals for use in quality-improvement activities. For this exercise, we created mock patient-fall data, similar to that captured by the NDNQI and other groups, such as the Centers for Medicare & Medicaid (CMS), to compare patient-fall and falls-with-injury rates per 1,000 patient days across types of care for a single hospital.

1 **Create a new worksheet and connect to the data**

» At the bottom of the Tableau workspace, click the icon for a new worksheet.

» In the Data pane, select the "02 - Patient Falls - Single Hospital."

2 Create the chart

» Holding down the Control key, click:

   • "Type of Care" in the Dimensions window.

   • "Patient Falls No Injury Rate" and "Patient Falls With Injury Rate" in the Measures window.

» Click the "Show Me" tab.

» Select the "side-by-side bars" image.

Show Me ▶

When several fields are either selected in the Data window or present in the active worksheet, the Show Me menu highlights the most likely visualizations to fit the specific combination of Dimensions and Measures present. Choosing one of these options rearranges the fields onto the appropriate cards and shelves to create the chosen chart type. (Note: Tableau can only make its best guess; adjustments are often necessary.)

◀ Show Me Recommendations

At the bottom of the Show Me menu, Tableau lists the number of Dimensions, Measures, and dates necessary to create a particular visualization. Hovering over a grayed-out chart type reveals how many and what types of fields are needed to create that chart.

» Click the "Show Me" tab again to close the tab.

Tableau's Show Me feature has automatically added a field called "Measure Names" to Color on the Marks card. A different color is assigned to each field on the Measure Values shelf.

The chart now looks like this:

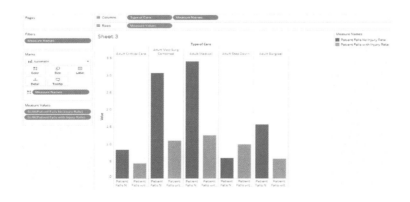

3 Format the chart

When two or more Measures display, Tableau labels the Y axis "Value" by default. To edit the title:

» Right-click the Y axis.

» Select "Edit Axis..."

» Change the title to: "Rate of Patient Falls (per 1,000 patient days)," then click "OK."

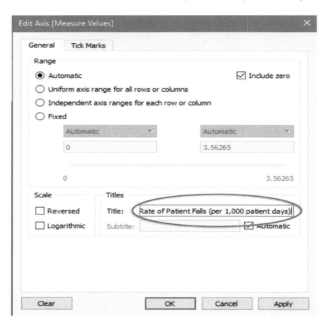

Widen the columns so that labels are fully visible:

» Hover the cursor over the far right column divider until it changes to a horizontal bi-directional arrow.

» Drag the column indicator to the appropriate width.

Remove the unneeded header "Type of Care":

» Right-click the column header "Type of Care."

» Select "Hide Field Labels for Columns."

Hide unneeded row grid lines:

» Click "Format on the Menu Bar.

» Select the "Lines..." option.

» Select the "Rows" tab.

» Click the caret for the "Grid Lines" drop-down menu.

» Select "None."

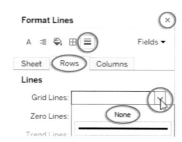

» Click the "X" at the top right of the Format pane to close.

Sort the bars from highest to lowest. Note that with two Dimension pills on the Column shelf, clicking the quick Sort icon will default the sort to the most nested Dimension (that is, the pill farthest to the right on the shelf—in this case, the Measure Names pill). If applying the Sort to the other Dimension is desired, the corresponding pill must be highlighted before the quick sort is selected.

» Click the "Type of Care" pill on the Columns shelf to highlight.

» Click the Descending Sort icon on the Toolbar.

The chart now looks like this:

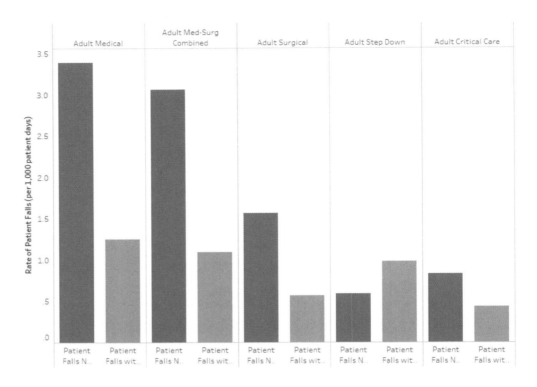

▲ **Sorting Measure Values**

When more than one Measure is present in the Sort (as in this Side-by-Side chart), Tableau will, by default, sort on the aggregation of the Measures.

4 Add a title

» Double-click on the Title Row at the top of the workspace to open the Edit Title dialog box.

» Highlight and delete the default title, "<Sheet Name>."

» Enter the title:

Rate of Patient Falls (per 1,000 Patient Days)
No Injury vs. Injury
By Type of Care for FY2017

» Highlight the title and bold the font.

» The bars and their labels in the title should be color-coordinated for clarity. Highlight "No Injury" and click the Color icon. Change the color to blue.

» Perform the same steps for "Injury," changing the color to orange.

With the bar categories identified by color in the title, the Measure Names headers may now be hidden.

» Right-click any header below the bars.

» Click "Show Header" to remove the checkmark.

The final Side-by-Side Bar Chart looks like this:

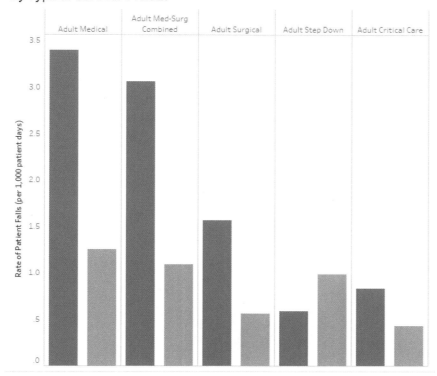

5 Rename the worksheet tab and duplicate the worksheet

» Right-click the Sheet Tab at the bottom of the workspace, then select "Rename."

» Enter a new name, "Side-by-Side Bar: Patient Falls."

» Right-click the Sheet Tab again, then select "Duplicate Sheet."

▲ **Duplicate Worksheets**

Duplicating an existing worksheet to create a new report is a common time-saver in Tableau. Duplicated sheets retain all filters, titles, and formatting customizations of the original sheet. Duplicating sheets is also a great way to test different chart variations without altering the original view.

6 Stack the bars

To change each pair of side-by-side bars to a stacked bar:

》 Drag the "Measure Names" pill off the Columns shelf and drop it onto any gray non-workspace area to delete it.

Removing Pills ▷

As the pill is being dragged to the gray area, a small red X should appear just under the cursor. This X indicates that once the mouse is released, the pill will disappear. If the red X is not visible, the pill will not be removed.

▲ **Why Not Select "Stacked Bar" in Show Me?**

The stacked bar option in Show Me plots a single Measure on the worksheet as a bar and breaks out the color of this bar based on the categories from a single, selected Dimension. However, the visualization in this chapter requires two chart Measures to be stacked one atop the other. This display is best accomplished by selecting the Side-by-Side option, then dragging the Measure Names pill off the shelf and into the gray non-workspace area.

The Measures are now stacked for each Type of Care. The Sort previously performed on the aggregation of the two Measures is easy to see in this chart.

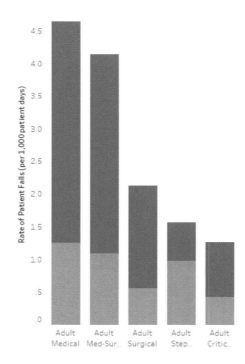

7 Format the chart

Sorting With the Sort Dialog Box

In the Side-by-Side Bar chart exercise, the Sort was performed on the selected Dimension using the "quick" Sort icon. Because there were two Measures represented by the Measure Values pill on the Rows shelf, Tableau sorted on the aggregation of the two Measures. To sort on a single Measure (for example, Falls with Injury Rate), use the Sort dialog box.

>> Right-click the "Type of Care" pill.

>> Select the "Sort..." option.

>> Click "Field" in the "Sort by" section.

>> From the corresponding drop-down menu, click the caret and select the field "Falls with Injury Rate."

>> Click "Descending" in the "Sort order" section.

>> Click "OK."

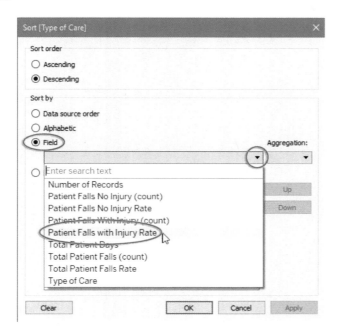

◄ Sort by Field

The Sort menu provides additional flexibility and precision for ordering data. This feature permits sorting based on data-source order, alphabetical order, or any valid aggregation of a Dimension or Measure within the selected dataset. (The field being sorted does not need to be on a shelf in the worksheet.) It is important to specify ascending (from smallest to largest) or descending (from largest to smallest) sort order.

81

The orange bars, representing Patient Falls with Injury Rate, are now sorted from highest to lowest:

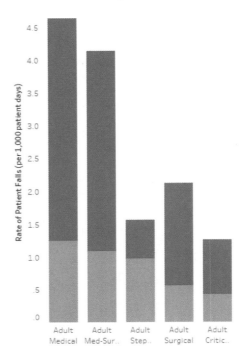

For clarity, add labels to the newly created stacked bars.

» Click the "T" icon on the Toolbar.

Reduce the label values to one decimal place:

» Right-click the "Measure Values" pill on the Rows shelf.

» Select "Format..."

» Select the "Pane" tab.

» Under "Default," click the "Numbers" caret to open the drop-down menu.

» Select "Number (Custom)."

» Change "Decimal places" to 1.

» Click anywhere outside of "Numbers (Custom)" to close.

To view the full headers:

» Hover the cursor over the right border of the chart until it changes to a bi-directional arrow.

» Click and drag the width to the right until the headers are fully displayed.

8 Edit the title

The sort order of "Patient Falls with Injury" from highest to lowest should be clarified in the title.

» Double-click the title.

» Change the third line to "Type of Care, sorted by Injury, for FY2017."

» Click "OK."

9 Rename the worksheet tab and save the worksheet

» Right-click the worksheet tab at the bottom of the workspace, then select "Rename."

» Enter a descriptive title.

» Click the "Save" icon on the Toolbar.

The final Stacked Bar Chart looks like this:

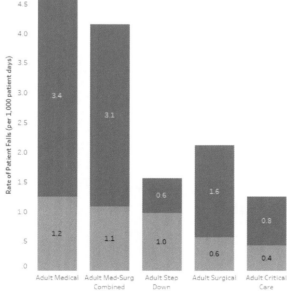

Insight: Adult Medical has both the highest rate of falls (4.6) and the highest rate of falls with injury (1.2) per 1,000 patient days.

▉▉ *HDVizoom*™ ...to Side-by-Side Bar then Stacked Bar Charts

1 Create new worksheet and connect to data

» Open new worksheet

» Select "02 - Patient Falls - Single Hospital" dataset in the Data pane

2 Create chart

» Holding down Control key, click on:

- "Type of Care" in Dimensions window

- "Patient Falls No Injury Rate" and "Patient Falls With Injury Rate" in Measures window

» Click "Show Me" tab

» Select "side-by-side bar" image

» Click "Show Me" tab again to close tab

3 Format chart

» Right-click Y axis

» Select "Edit Axis..."

» Change title to: "Rate of Patient Falls (per 1,000 patient days)"

» Hover cursor over far right column divider until it changes to horizontal bi-directional arrow

» Drag column indicator to appropriate width

» Right-click column header "Type of Care"

» Select "Hide Field Labels for Columns"

» Click "Format" on Menu Bar

» Select "Lines..." option

» Select "Rows" tab

» Click caret for Grid Lines drop-down menu

» Select "None"

» >> Click "X" at top right of Format pane to close

» Click "Type of Care" pill on Columns shelf to highlight

» Click Descending Sort icon on Toolbar

4 Add title

» Double-click Title Row at top of Work Area to open Edit Title dialog box

» Highlight and delete default title <Sheet Name>

» Enter title, "Rate of Patient Falls (per 1,000 Patient Days) – No Injury vs. Injury by Type of Care for 2017"

» Highlight title and bold font

» Highlight "No Injury" and click Color icon

» Change color to blue

» Perform same steps for "Injury" changing color to orange

» Right-click any header below bars

» Click "Show Header" to remove checkmark

5 Rename worksheet tab and duplicate worksheet

» Right-click Sheet Tab at bottom of workspace, then select "Rename"

» Enter new name, "Side-by-Side Bar: Patient Falls"

» Right-click Sheet Tab again, then select "Duplicate Sheet"

6 Stack Bars

» Drag "Measure Names" pill off Columns shelf and drop onto gray non-workspace area to delete

7 **Format chart**

» Right-click "Type of Care" pill

» Select "Sort..." option

» Click "Field" in "Sort by" section

» Click caret for Field and select "Falls with Injury Rate"

» Click "Descending" in "Sort order" section

» Click "OK"

» Click "T" icon on Toolbar

» Right-click "Measure Values" pill on Rows shelf

» Select "Format..."

» Select "Pane" tab

» Under "Default," click "Numbers" caret to open drop-down menu

» Select "Number (Custom)"

» Change "Decimal places" to "1"

» Click anywhere outside of "Numbers (Custom)" to close

» Hover cursor over right border of chart and drag width to right to display full headers

8 **Edit title**

» Double-click title

» Edit third line to "Type of Care, sorted by Injury, for FY2017"

» Click "OK"

9 **Rename worksheet tab and save worksheet**

» Right-click worksheet tab at bottom of workspace, then select "Rename"

» Enter descriptive title

» Click "Save" icon on Toolbar

CHAPTER 6

Formatting

F ormatting requires skill, patience, and meticulous attention to detail. Some people find it tedious; but good formatting reveals the story in your healthcare data with clarity and simplicity. If on the other hand, you burden your text with inconsistent fonts (mis-matched in type, size, or color), odd alignments, or distracting lines, your audience must wade through the visual "noise" to find that story. Drawing on the best practices of data visu-alization to effectively format your charts will help move your reports and dashboards (and all your hard work) from good to great.

Tableau incorporates many visualization best practices into the default designs of its tables and graphs; however, additional formatting may be required, depending on the data in the view, the available space, and the message to be conveyed by the chart. Tableau's formatting options (specifically, Fonts, Alignment, Shading, Borders, and Lines) allow the report-creator to customize the visualization's appearance and to focus the message.

Consider the following best practices for these formatting options:

Shading/Borders/Lines

- Keep in mind a fundamental principal: maximize the "data-ink to non-data ink ratio" (Tufte, 93). The "data ink" should be showcased on the page, while the "non-data ink" should play a supporting role to the chart, helping to convey, and not distract from, the message of the data.

- Ask this question about each component of a chart: "Would the data suffer any loss of meaning or impact if this element were not present?" If the answer is "no," then remove it. (Few, 142). Any non-data ink that makes the cut should be muted so that it doesn't compete with the data ink.

In the "Don't do this" example below, the non-data ink—gridlines, row shading, font bolding, unnecessary labels ("Race" and "Gender/Date"), decimals out to two places, redundancy in Y axis and line labeling—is overwhelming the data ink.

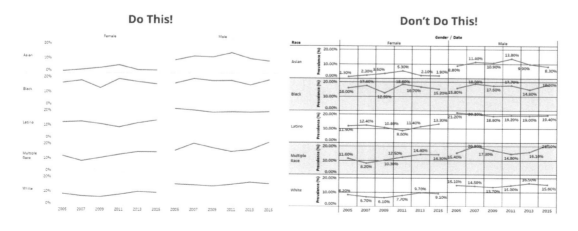

Remember, non-data ink needs to play a supporting role to strengthen the message in the data, not distract from it.

Fonts

- Should be as legible as possible

- Should be consistent throughout reports

- Should have a number set that lines up properly and is clear and easy to read

Fortunately, Tableau has default font selections suited for data visualization, but font style still requires consideration.

Choose Sans-Serif Fonts for Visualizations

A serif font has embellishments that look like little feet attached at a 45- or 90-degree angle to the upright lines of the font, linking the letters one to the next so they appear connected and flow across the page. For example: this text is printed in a serif font. Fonts with serifs are intended for a long sequence of words that exceeds one line. Though research is inconclusive, such fonts are considered by many to be easier to read for printed text, but can make reading on screens difficult, depending on resolution.

Conversely, sans-serif fonts (*sans* = "without") do not have the little feet. They are simpler and easier to take in at a glance—a good choice for labels and titles on graphs and charts, or for data displayed in a table. As this discussion makes clear, sans-serif fonts are the best choice for visualizations.

Alignment

- Quantitative values should be right-justified so that the numbers line up: the ones, tens, hundreds, and so on fall correctly into columns.

- Text usually works best when it's left-justified, because readers in Western cultures read left to right (the opposite would apply for audiences who read right to left).

The example below compares two text tables: one containing left-justified text and right-justified numbers; the other with centered text and numbers. The centered text is difficult to read because our focus must adjust to the place where the text begins and that point shifts on each line. Further, centered numbers are difficult to read, understand, and compare because their digits do not line up evenly.

Left-Justified Text and Right-Justified Numbers

Preoperative Risk Factors	Hospital %	Comparison %
Acute Renal Failure	4.0	3.0
Bleeding Disorder	3.3	2.0
BMI > 30	33.3	40.0
Congestive Heart Failure	10.0	15.0
Diabetes	25.3	35.0
Disseminated Cancer	1.6	1.2
DNR Status	0.5	0.3
Dyspnea	12.0	15.0
Functional Health Status < Independent	8.7	10.0
History of Severe COPD	17.3	15.0

Centered Text and Numbers

Preoperative Risk Factors	Hospital %	Comparison %
Acute Renal Failure	4.0	3.0
Bleeding Disorder	3.3	2.0
BMI > 30	33.3	40.0
Congestive Heart Failure	10.0	15.0
Diabetes	25.3	35.0
Disseminated Cancer	1.6	1.2
DNR Status	0.5	0.3
Dyspnea	12.0	15.0
Functional Health Status < Independent	8.7	10.0
History of Severe COPD	17.3	15.0

Formatting Hierarchy in Tableau

Formatting can be performed at different levels, from the overall Workbook level, to individual Worksheets, and down to individual parts of a view. Understanding the levels will help guide formatting- option selection.

1) **Workbook** - Formatting at the Workbook level affects all Worksheets, Dashboards, and Stories in any single workbook. Workbook Themes, Fonts, and Lines are formatting options at this level.

2) **Worksheet** - Formatting at the Worksheet level affects either the entire active Sheet or its Rows or Columns only. Worksheet-level formatting choices are Font, Alignment, Shading, Borders, and Lines.

3) **Individual Components** - The individual components of a chart include Headers, Axes, Panes, Labels, Lines, and Title. The available formatting options are component-specific.

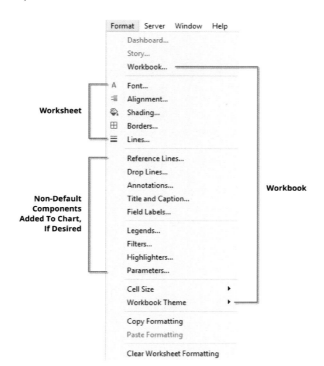

◄ **Format Menu**

Selecting "Format" from the Menu bar accesses formatting options at Workbook and Worksheet levels.

Default (intrinsic) chart components can most efficiently be modified by right-clicking them directly in the chart. (That is, features built into charts are best managed by right-clicking.) Optional features can be formatted from the menu shown at left. If you cannot find a feature you wish to modify on the menu, try right-clicking that feature in the chart.

Formatting at the Workbook Level

Two main components can be formatted at the Workbook level: Workbook Theme and Workbook Fonts & Lines.

Workbook Theme

Each of the four available Workbook Themes corresponds to a version of Tableau Desktop.

1) **Default:** Version 10.0 and higher

2) **Previous:** Versions 8 and 9

3) **Modern:** Versions 3.5 to 7

4) **Classic:** Versions 1 to 3.2

To view these themes:

» Click "Format" on the Menu Bar.

» Select the "Workbook Themes" option.

Workbooks retain the themes originally selected for them even when Tableau versions change.

In our training workbooks, the Workbook Theme is set to "Default."

Workbook - Fonts & Lines

Fonts in Tableau 10 can now be set at the Workbook level to ensure consistency across Worksheets, Dashboards, and Stories. To do this:

» Click on "Format" on the Menu Bar.

» Select "Workbook..."

The Format pane on the left of the screen displays editing options for Fonts and Lines. Fonts for several high-level components of the workbook can be controlled here. Choose "All" (all fonts across all Worksheets, Dashboards, and Stories), or specific components (Worksheets, Tooltips, and Titles for Worksheet, Dashboard, and/or Story).

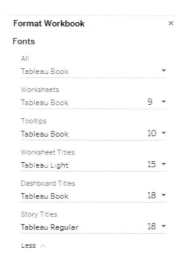

The default font is "Tableau," a custom face created to meet best practice criteria. It is available in six styles:

Tableau Light
Tableau Book
Tableau Regular
Tableau Medium
Tableau Semibold
Tableau Bold

The Worksheet Titles in this training workbook have been changed from Tableau Light to Tableau Medium. This change both demonstrates how to change a font and highlights titles more effectively.

◀ **Edited Settings**

When a default setting is changed, a dot appears to the left of the selected option. This visual cue is a helpful guide in future editing. Clicking the "Reset to Defaults" button at the bottom of the pane clears all edits.

Formatting Lines—Grid, Zero, Trend, Reference, and Drop, as well as Axis Rulers and Ticks—ensures a consistent look across the Workbook. Beginning in version 10.2, editing options include Line type, weight, color, and opacity, as well as an option to turn them all "Off." Gridlines can serve to orient the viewer; however, since they are non-data ink, removing them often results in a cleaner look.

Formatting changes can be made at any point, and will apply globally to both existing and new Worksheets, Dashboards, and Stories.

Formatting at the Worksheet Level

Worksheets can be individually formatted; use the Format menu on the Menu bar of the currently active worksheet. Font, Alignment, Shading, Borders, and Lines display editing options for the Sheet, Rows, or Columns.

Selecting any format option from the menu opens a Format pane on the left of the screen, replacing the Data pane. In the screenshot below, the Font option icon has been selected. Its header indicates the selection; a corresponding icon is outlined with a square. Icons in the Format pane enable easy navigation among Worksheet formatting options. (The Fields option will be discussed in the next section.)

Three tabs—Sheet, Rows, and Columns—offer access to formatting options at the Worksheet level.

- **Sheet** means the currently active worksheet. Any editing under the Sheet tab affects the entire Worksheet (exclusive of Title and Tooltip).

- **Rows** run horizontally across the active Worksheet and are represented by discrete or continuous pills. If a discrete pill is on the Rows shelf, the rows are easy to distinguish; a continuous pill, however, with its axis, looks like one big row. Editing under the Rows tab affects all rows in the chart.

- **Columns** run vertically through the active Worksheet and can also be represented by discrete or continuous pills. If a discrete pill is on the Columns shelf, the columns are easy to distinguish; a continuous pill, however, with its axis, looks like one big column. Editing under the Columns tab affects all columns in the chart.

Other Worksheet Formatting

Formatting options on the Format menu bar can be applied specifically to features that have been added to the chart: Reference Lines, Drop Lines, Field Labels, and Annotations in the chart; Title, Caption, Legends, Filters, Highlighters, and Parameters positioned at the periphery of the chart.

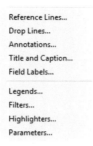

Two commonly used Worksheet format options are Row/Column Dividers and Row/Column Shading. Both help the viewer to keep track of figure alignment while reading the chart.

Steps to Format the Row/Column Dividers

If the Format pane is open, click the "Borders" icon in the top row of icons; otherwise, click "Format" in the Menu Bar, then select "Borders."

The Sheet tab displays options for both the Row and Column Dividers. Each Divider section displays Pane, Header, and Level formatting options.

- **Pane** displays data marks.

- **Header** shows Dimension members labeling the view

- **Level** controls where formatting occurs, depending on the number of pills on the Row/Column shelf.

In the example below, an already-created Text Table will be formatted with Row dividers. (Row shading was a default feature when the Table was created.) Column dividers are formatted in the same way.

The Row Divider Pane and Header each displays the selection of a thin, light-gray line. The Level slider, however, is at the far left, essentially showing "no level" of divider; the resulting chart has no Row Divider lines.

Row Divider

Pane: [⌄]

Header: [⌄]

Level: ▊

Preoperative Risk Factors	Hospital %	Comparison %
Acute Renal Failure	4.0	3.0
Bleeding Disorder	3.3	2.0
BMI > 30	33.3	40.0
Congestive Heart Failure	10.0	15.0
Diabetes	25.3	35.0
Disseminated Cancer	1.6	1.2
DNR Status	0.5	0.3
Dyspnea	12.0	15.0

Slide the Row Divider Level to the right; Row Divider lines appear. The number of Dimensions on the corresponding Row shelf (in this case, one Dimension, Preoperative Risk Factors) determines the number of available levels.

Steps to Format the Row/Column Shading

Shading can be applied to Rows or Columns in bands of color to make data easier to differentiate. Click the paint-bucket icon to access Shading options.

Row and Column Banding options here (under the Sheet tab) are the same as for Dividers described above. In each Banding section, Pane, Header, and Banding Size options are available. If more than one Dimension shares a Row or Column shelf, the Level option also appears. The Banding Size slider permits banding every other row/column or every two, three, four, or more rows/columns.

With reference to the same Text Table, the examples below display the options for the Row Band Size slider. (The banding color has been darkened for better visibility here.)

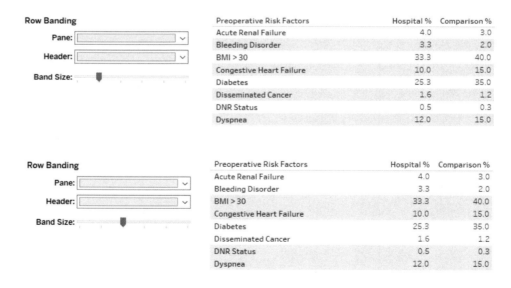

Formatting Individual Chart Components

The same formatting options—Font, Alignment, Shading, Borders, and Lines—available for Sheets, Rows, and Columns can be applied specifically to individual components of a chart. Such components include Headers, created by discrete (blue) pills; Axes, continuous (green) pills; Panes (where data marks are displayed); Axis Titles; Field Labels; Mark Labels; and Totals (if displayed). The available formatting options are determined by the selected component.

Access these components in one of two ways, with Option 1 recommended:

> **Option 1:** Right-click a pill or component on the chart
> - Right-click the pill or chart component.
> - Select "Format" from the submenu.

▲ Pane Formatting

Right-clicking in the Pane seems like a natural approach to formatting mark labels, but it does not open the necessary formatting controls; instead, the global Format Font controls for the worksheet appear. For a precise and targeted path to formatting in the pane, right-click on the Header, the Axis, or the pill itself. Additional formatting options for labels in the Pane are located under Label on the Marks card.

> **Option 2:** Select Format on the Menu bar
> - Click "Format" on the Menu bar.
> - Select the desired Formatting option: Font, Alignment, Shading, Borders, or Lines.
> - Click the "Fields" caret.
> - Select the field corresponding to the component to be formatted.

The Format pane will remain open until manually closed (click the "X" in the top right corner).

Header, Axis, Pane Formatting

The most commonly formatted sections of a chart are the Header, Axis, and/or Pane. It is important to identify which pill on the Rows or Columns shelf generates the particular component to be formatted. Discrete (blue) pills create Header labels; continuous (green) pills create Axes. The Pane displays the Measure figures as "marks" (in the example below, the marks are bars).

The Bar chart created in a previous chapter (with the axis re-displayed), shows the components for this particular chart. The Header represents the Dimension "Type of Care" pill on the Rows shelf; the Axis represents the Measure "MAX(Total Patient Falls Rate)" pill on the Columns shelf; the Pane displays the marks for the Measure "MAX(Total Patient Falls Rate)."

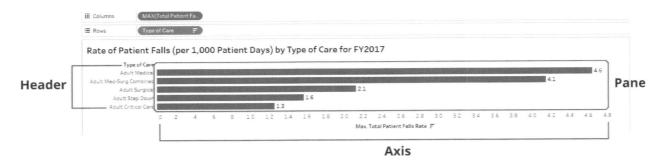

Availability of formatting options is determined by individual chart components:

- **Header:** any Font (type, size, style), Alignment, Shading, and Totals label used can be formatted.

- **Axis:** any Font, Shading, Scale layout along the axis, and Title font can be formatted.

- **Pane:** any Font, Alignment, Numbers, and Totals used can be formatted.

  Because numbers need to be presented in a variety of ways, it is helpful to have multiple formatting options. Fortunately, Tableau offers several; Number (Custom) and Percentage (with Decimal place adjustment) are most commonly used in this manual.

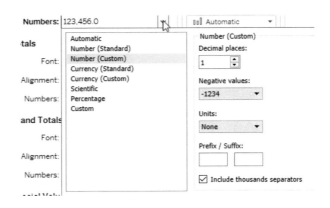

Dates

Right-clicking a Date field presents an additional Default Date formatting option. Available options are determined by the pill type (Discrete or Continuous).

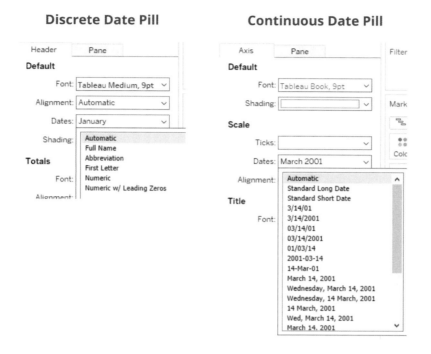

Titles

Worksheet title formatting can be a bit confusing because formatting tools are in two locations. The Edit Title dialog box (which appears when the Title Row is double-clicked) allows the creation and alignment of a title and font formatting (type, color, size, style). The Format Title control that appears in the Format pane affects only background shading and borders. Right-click the title to access this option.

Mark Labels

Default fonts, text color, and number or date formatting can be controlled from the Pane tab of the Format pane as described above. However, it is easier to format these labels by using the Label button on the Marks card (recommended). This button offers many additional display and formatting options. A user can control font type, size, color selection, color matching, and opacity; choose which marks to label; and label display parameters within the constraints of the view. The Labels button on the Marks card provides more options to control how labels are displayed.

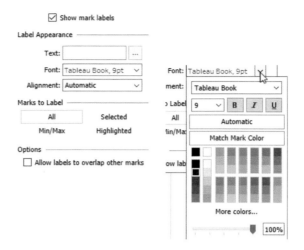

Reference Lines and Trend Lines

Right-click any Line and select "Format" from the menu to edit that Line's type, weight, color, and opacity. Shading can be added above or below it. Any labels identifying line values can be formatted here (font, alignment, numbers, shading).

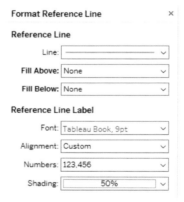

Troubleshooting Tip

If an edit made in the Format pane does not display where expected, check the following:

- Does the header on the Format pane address the correct location of the desired formatting?

- Has the correct tab been selected?

- Has the correct section been selected?

Header ———— Format Type of Care   ×

Tab ———— Header | Pane

Section

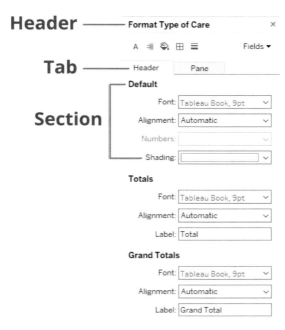

CHAPTER 7

Tooltips

T ooltips reveal useful details for a worksheet or dashboard feature when a data point is hovered over. Tooltips are helpful for presenting data that would be too granular, potentially distracting, or space-consuming if displayed in the primary visualization.

A Tooltip is made up of the "Body," which contains the details of the selected mark(s), and two optional components, the Command Buttons and Action Filter Links. The Command Buttons can be displayed to allow the user to filter, create groups or sets, and/or view underlying data. Action Filter Links display only when an action is configured to run on "Menu" (Actions are discussed in the Dashboards Basic Interactivity chapter).

Tooltip Formatting

Tableau creates default Tooltips for every chart. Each Tooltip is organized to display many of the Dimensions and Measures present on a worksheet when the cursor is hovered over a particular mark on a chart. Below is an example of a Tooltip on the "Rate of Patient Falls" bar chart. The two fields displayed in the Tooltip, "Type of Care" and "Max. Total Patient Falls Rate," are the two fields used to create this chart.

For better readability, Tooltips can be formatted with both static and dynamic text using tools in the Edit Tooltip dialog box. Supporting information can be added; unnecessary fields can be removed. Below is a reformatted example.

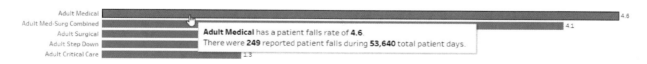

To create this Tooltip:

> » Select the "Bar: Patient Falls" tab at the bottom of the workbook to open the bar chart.

Two Measures, "Total Patient Falls (count)" and "Total Patient Days," are not in the view, and need to be added to the Tooltip.

» Drag and drop "Total Patient Falls (count)" from the Measures window to Tooltip on the Marks card.

Tooltip on the Marks card ▶

For a field to appear in the Tooltip, it must be present on the worksheet. An easy way to add a field to the work- sheet is to drag it to Tooltip on the Marks card.

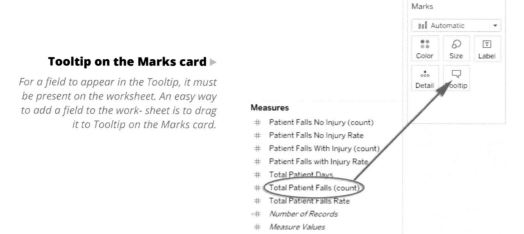

102

» Drag and drop "Total Patient Days" from the Measures window to Tooltip on the Marks card.

» Click "Tooltip" on the Marks card to open the Edit Tooltip dialog box.

Tooltip Details ▶

The Tooltip defaults the list of fields to alphabetical order, first by Dimensions, then by Measures. The text contained within < > is dynamic: it changes according to user selection in the chart. The Insert option displays fields available to add to the Tooltip.

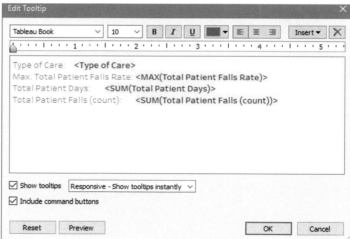

» Edit the Tooltip to read as follows:

<Type of Care> has a patient falls rate of <MAX(Total Patient Falls Rate)>. There were <SUM(Total Patient Falls (count))> reported patient falls during <SUM(Total Patient Days)> total patient days.

To insert the new fields:

» Click the cursor in the body of the text to place it where the new field is to be inserted.

» Click the "Insert" caret and select the desired field from the drop-down menu.

» Highlight the text and change the font color to dark gray.

» Highlight "<Type of Care>" and change the font to "Tableau Semibold."

» Highlight each of the remaining dynamic fields and change the font to "Tableau Semibold."

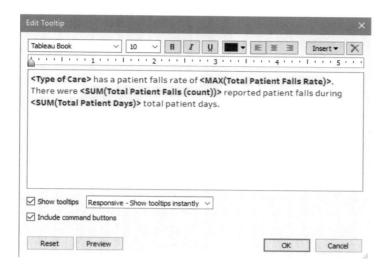

Best Practice

Use color, spacing, font, and plain language to encode information quickly and effectively. Supporting information can be added for clarity.

◄ **Previews**

Use the "Preview" button to preview the Tooltip during editing.

There are three Tooltip display options:

1) **Responsive** – Show tooltips as soon as the cursor passes over the data point. This is Tableau's default.

2) **On Hover** – Show tooltips when the cursor lingers over the data point.

3) **Hide tooltips** – Uncheck the "Show tooltips" checkbox to prevent them from displaying.

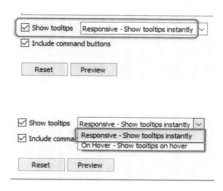

◄ **Tooltip Display Options and Command Buttons**

*When a Tooltip is set to "Responsive," moving the cursor over a mark displays the Tooltip instantly, **without** Command Buttons. Click a mark or marks to display Command Buttons (unless that option has been manually turned off).*

*When a Tooltip is set to show "On Hover," the Tooltip will not appear until the cursor lingers over a mark. Doing so makes the entire Tooltip appear, **including** the Command Buttons (unless that option has been manually turned off).*

Include Command Buttons ▶

Tooltips can embed interactive functions such as those allowing the user to filter, create groups or sets, or view underlying data. These functions can be seen at the top of the Tooltip. If these interactive functions are not desired, uncheck the "Include command buttons" box to disable them

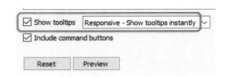

Action Filter Links

Tooltips are the place where Action Filter Links appear if an action is configured to run on "Menu" instead of Select or Hover (see the Dashboards Basic Interactivity chapter on formatting Action Filters).

If "Menu" is selected, the Tooltip will include an embedded link for the desired action.

■.■ *HDVizoom*™ ...to the Tooltip

To create this Tooltip:

» Select "Bar: Patient Falls" tab at bottom of workbook to open bar chart

» Drag and drop "Total Patient Falls (count)" from Measures window to Tooltip on Marks card

» Drag and drop "Total Patient Days" from Measures window to Tooltip on Marks card

» Click Tooltip on Marks card to open Edit Tooltip dialog box

» Edit Tooltip to read:

<Type of Care> has a patient falls rate of <MAX(Total Patient Falls Rate)>.

There were <SUM(Total Patient Falls (count))> reported patient falls during <SUM(Total Patient Days)> total patient days.

To insert new fields:

» Click cursor in body of text to place it where new field is to be inserted

» Click "Insert" caret and select desired field from drop-down menu

» Highlight text and change font color to dark gray

» Highlight "<Type of Care>" and change font to "Tableau Semibold"

» Highlight each of remaining dynamic fields and change font to "Tableau Semibold"

CHAPTER 8

Table Lens

A Table Lens is a type of data visualization that provides the viewer with a quick way to see any potential correlations and/or outliers in a multivariate dataset.

A Table Lens contains a series of side-by-side horizontal bar charts that share the same categorical variable, but with each chart showing different quantitative variables. These variables in the same chart are ranked (from high to low, or low to high) keeping the associated variables in alignment with them. As a result, any potentially interesting correlations or outliers in the data are easy to identify. If warranted, more rigorous statistical analysis may be performed.

How To: Build a Table Lens to compare life expectancy at birth, neonatal mortality rate, under-five mortality rate, and per capita health expenditure by different countries.

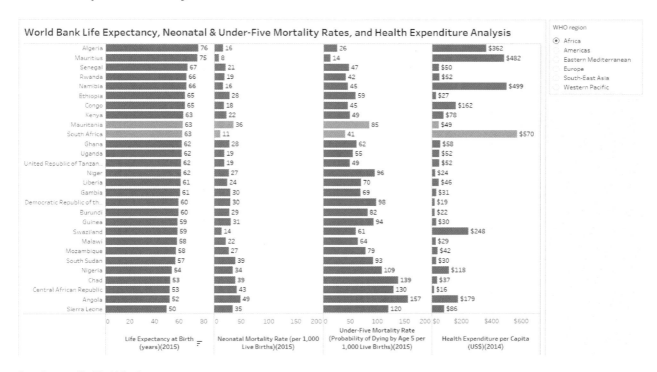

Data Source: The World Bank

About the Data: *The data for this exercise are taken from publicly available information captured by the World Bank Group in alignment with the two goals it hopes to achieve by 2030: 1) the ending of extreme poverty; 2) the promotion of shared prosperity.*

The potential correlations to be examined (by country) in this exercise are:

- Life Expectancy at Birth

- Neonatal Mortality Rate (per 1,000 Live Births)

- Under-Five Mortality Rate (Probability of Dying by Age 5 per 1,000 Live Births)

- Health Expenditure per Capita

1 **Create a new worksheet and connect to the data**

» At the bottom of the Tableau workspace, click the icon for a new worksheet.

» In the Data Pane, select the "03 – WHO Life Expectancy, Mortality, & Health Expenditure" dataset.

2 **Create the chart**

» Drag and drop the following Measures (in the order below) onto the Columns shelf:
  - Life Expectancy at Birth (Years) (2015)
  - Neonatal Mortality Rate (per 1,000 Live Births) (2015)
  - Under-Five Mortality Rate (Probability of Dying by Age 5 per 1,000 Live Births) (2015)
  - Health Expenditure per Capita (US$) (2014)

» Drag and drop "Country" from the Dimensions data window onto the Rows shelf.

» Click the "T" icon on the Toolbar to add labels to the bars.

The chart now looks like this:

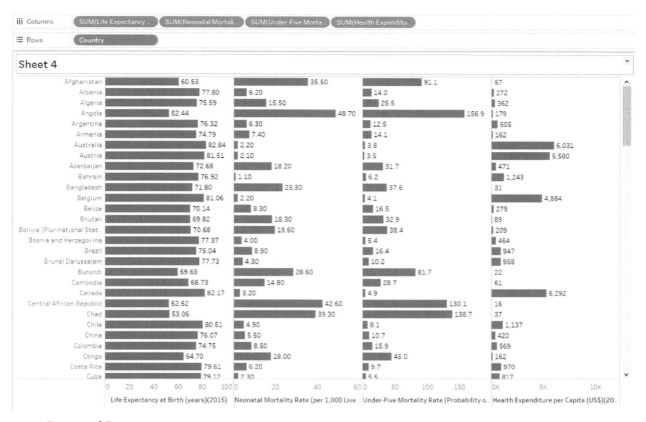

▲ **Drag and Drop**

Tableau's Drag and Drop interface makes it easy to explore data and test different visualizations quickly. Tableau also permits dragging a field already in the worksheet (represented as a blue or a green pill) to another place on the worksheet to change the visualization.

3 Sort the data

The data is currently sorted alphabetically by country. For this exercise, the default sort order should be by country based on "Life Expectancy at Birth," from lowest to highest.

» Click the "Sort" icon once to sort descending.

◀ **End-User Sorting**

The Sort icon in the Measure header and the Measure axis are visible to the end-user as well as to the report-builder. Hovering over the Measure header or axis makes the icon appear, allowing viewers to sort the Table Lens with one click.

4 Edit the axes

Notice that Neonatal Mortality Rate and Under-five Mortality Rate are the same "per 1,000 Live Births." To make an accurate comparison, both measures' axis range must be set to the same value.

First, determine the top range value for both axes. The "Under-Five Mortality Rate" axis in the view has a higher value in the upper range (200) than the Neonatal Mortality Rate (60). To determine the exact upper range value and to fix the axis:

» Right-click the "Under-Five Mortality Rate" axis.

» Click "Edit Axis…"

» Under the General tab, in the dialog box Range, click the Fixed radio button.

» Round the value in the Fixed end box up to a desired whole number, then click "OK."

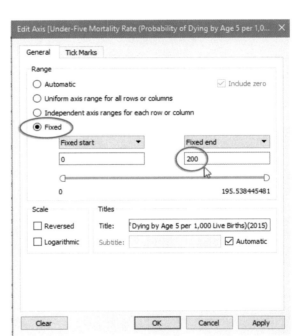

Best Practice

Each Measure in a Table Lens has its own X axis. If two or more Measures are based on the same unit type, the range of the scales must be the same for accurate comparison.

» Follow the same steps for the "Neonatal Mortality Rate"; fix the axis to the same whole number.

5 Filter the data

» Right-click on "WHO Region" in the Dimensions window.

» Select "Show Filter."

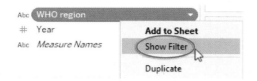

◄ Show Filter

Showing a Filter displays a type of selection menu that, when added to a report, allows end-users to interact with the fields on the Filters shelf. This feature permits a user to quickly and intuitively change data displayed in the report without having to select filters one at a time. Filters can be displayed as lists, dropdowns, or type-in fields, and can be customized to display data for maximum clarity and utility.

The "WHO Region" field now appears on the Filters shelf. The Filter displayed to the right of the chart permits display by WHO Region. The Filter display can be edited as desired.

» Hover over the Filter header and click the caret that appears.

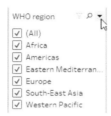

The menu that now appears offers several Filter-formatting options:

» Select the "Single Value (list)" option.

» Select "Africa" from the Filter display.

◄ Filter Options

The Filter Menu permits changing the style and function of a visible quick filter. It is possible to customize this type of filter's display format by choosing single vs. multi-select capabilities; displaying only relevant values based on other applied filters; and whether an "All" option is available.

6 Format the chart

Numbers in the columns shown are carried to one or two decimal places. To reduce the number of places:

» In the Measures window right-click "Life Expectancy at Birth."

» Select "Default Properties," then "Number Format..."

» Select "Number (Custom)."

» Change "Decimal places" to "0".

» Repeat these steps for "Neonatal Mortality Rate" and "Under-Five Mortality Rate."

» For "Health Expenditure per Capita," select "Currency (Custom)" and change "Decimal places" to "0."

To adjust the height of the X axis to display the complete title for each section:

» Hover the cursor exactly over the X axis line. When it changes to a bidirectional arrow, click and hold so that the solid axis line changes to a dotted one.

» Drag the line to the desired height.

To hide the "Country" row header:

» Right-click the header.

» Click "Hide Field Labels for Rows."

To change the size of the view:

» On the Toolbar, click the caret to the right of the "Standard" Fit option to open the drop-down menu.

» Select "Entire View."

Adjusting the Chart to the Workspace ▶

When a great deal of data is displayed, the chart may automatically size itself larger than the screen space. If this happens, scroll bars will appear. This may in some cases be necessary, but if the bars are unwanted, the report can be adjusted horizontally or vertically to make it fit. Using the "Fit Width," "Fit Height," or "Entire View" commands may affect the appearance, proportions, and/or display speed of the chart.

When "Entire View" is set as the Fit option, the display is legible for individual WHO regions. However, if "(All)" is selected on the WHO Region Quick Filter, the view compresses so much for full display that legibility is lost.

To avoid this problem, the "(All)" option must be removed from the Filter menu:

» Hover over the "WHO region" filter menu header and click the caret that appears at the right.

» Click "Customize."

» Click "Show 'All' Value" to uncheck the selection.

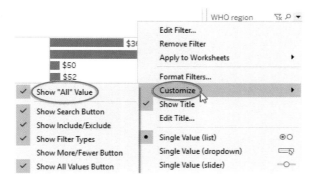

» From the adjusted "WHO Region" filter menu, select "Africa."

7 Create a set

As there are many countries to review in the four columns of data, color-coding the countries of interest is a way for the report-builder to help the end-user identify pertinent data quickly. To color-code selected rows of data, first create a Set, then drag it to Color on the Marks card.

» Hold down the Control key and click on "Mauritania" and "South Africa" to highlight. A Tooltip will appear.

» Hover over the "Set" icon until a caret appears.

» Click the caret and select "Create Set" from the submenu.

» Enter a title for the Set, "Mauritania/South Africa highlight."

» Click "OK."

◄ **Sets**

The Set feature can be used to capture or highlight a subset of the data. In this example, the Set is used to color-code the countries of interest to grab the audience's attention.

The new "Sets" field is now displayed in its own window below the Measures window.

》 Drag and drop the "Mauritania/South Africa highlight" Set to Color on the Marks card. The field aggregate is changed to IN/OUT of the set: IN = Mauritania and South Africa; OUT = all other countries.

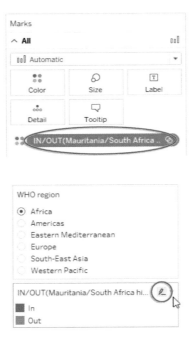

To edit the bar colors:

》 Click the caret to the right of the color legend header IN/OUT (see image above).

》 Select "Edit Colors."

》 Click the "In" Data Item to highlight, then click an Orange square.

》 Click the "Out" Data Item to highlight, then click a Blue square.

To hide the color legend:

» Hover over the color legend header until the caret appears.

» Click the caret.

» When a menu appears, click "Hide Card" at the bottom of it.

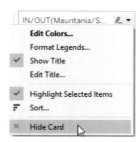

To redisplay the color legend, if desired:

» Click the "Analysis" option in the Menu bar.

» Click the "Legends" option, then select "Color Legend."

8 Add a title

» Double-click the Title Row at the top of the workspace.

» Enter the title, "World Bank Life Expectancy, Neonatal & Under-Five Mortality Rates, and Health Expenditure Analysis," then click "OK."

9 Rename the worksheet tab and save the worksheet

» Right-click the worksheet tab at the bottom of the workspace, then select "Rename."

» Enter an intuitive title , then click the "Save" icon on the Toolbar.

The final chart looks like this:

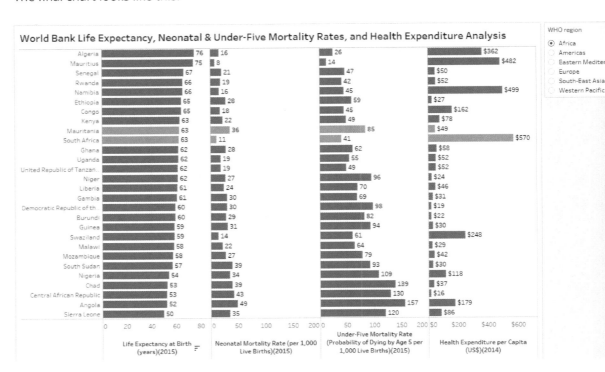

Insight: This Table Lens chart allows the viewer to consider potentially interesting relationships between and among life expectancy, neonatal and under-five mortality rates, and per capita health expenditures for people living in different countries for further study and investigation. For example, Mauritania and South Africa have the same life expectancy, yet Mauritania has higher mortality rates for neonates and children under five. Mauritania also has dramatically smaller per capita health expenditure ($49) than does South Africa ($570). Could this contribute to the high mortality rate? What other factors might be contributing?

HDVizoom™ ...to the Table Lens

1 Create new worksheet and connect to data

» At bottom of Tableau workspace, click icon for new worksheet

» In Data Pane, select "03 – WHO Life Expectancy, Mortality, & Health Expenditure" dataset

2 Create chart

» Drag and drop following Measures (in order below) onto Columns shelf:

- Life Expectancy at Birth (years) (2015)
- Neonatal Mortality Rate (per 1,000 Live Births) (2015)
- Under-Five Mortality Rate (Probability of Dying by Age 5 per 1,000 Live Births) (2015)
- Health Expenditure per Capita (US$) (2014)

» Drag and drop "Country" from Dimensions window onto Rows shelf

» Click "T" icon on Toolbar to add labels to bars

3 Sort data

» Click "Sort" icon once to sort descending

4 Edit axes

» Right-click "Under-Five Mortality Rate" axis

» Click "Edit Axis…"

» Under General tab, in dialog box Range, click Fixed radio button

» Round value in Fixed end box up to desired whole number, then click "OK"

» Follow same steps for "Neonatal Mortality Rate"; fix axis to same whole number

5 Filter data

» Right-click "WHO Region" in Dimensions window

» Select "Show Filter"

» Hover over Filter header and click caret that appears

» Select "Single Value (list)" option

» Select "Africa" from Filter display

6 Format chart

» In Measures window, right-click "Life Expectancy at Birth"

» Select "Default Properties," then "Number Format…"

» Select "Number (Custom)"

» Change "Decimal places" to 0

» Repeat same steps for Neonatal Mortality Rate and Under-Five Mortality Rate

» For "Health Expenditure per Capita" select "Currency (Custom)" and change decimal places to "0"

» Click and hold so that solid axis line changes to dotted one

» Drag line to desired height

» Right-click "Country" header

» Click "Hide Field Labels for Rows"

» On Toolbar, click caret on "Standard" Fit option to open drop-down menu

» Select "Entire View"

» Hover over "WHO region" filter menu header and click caret that appears at right

» Click "Customize"

» Click "Show 'All' Value" to uncheck selection

7 **Create set**

» Hold down Control key and click "Mauritania" and "South Africa" to highlight; Tooltip will appear

» Hover over "Set" icon until caret appears

» Click caret and select "Create Set"

» Enter title for Set, "Mauritania/ South Africa highlight, " then click "OK"

» Drag and drop "Mauritania/South Africa highlight" Set to Color on Marks card

» Click caret to right of color legend header IN/OUT

» Select "Edit Colors"

» Click "In" Data Item to highlight, then click to select Orange square

» Click "Out" Data Item to highlight, then click to select Blue square

8 **Add title**

» Double-click Title Row at top of workspace

» Enter title, "World Bank Life Expectancy, Neonatal & Under-Five Mortality Rates, and Health Expenditure Analysis" and click "OK"

9 **Rename worksheet tab and save worksheet**

» Right-click worksheet tab at bottom of workspace, then select "Rename"

» Enter intuitive title, then click "Save" on Toolbar

CHAPTER 9

Histogram

A Histogram is a type of vertical bar chart used to display the frequency distribution of data within an ordered (ordinal) range of values, arranged in intervals called "bins."

Each bin contains a uniform range of values. They reside very close to one another as a way of conveying that there is an order to the measure being displayed. Unlike bar charts, which rely on sorting for visual interpretation of data, Histograms cannot be rearranged. Some examples of the types of data displayed in a Histogram are age ranges (0-5, 6-11, 12-17), number of days (0-3, 4-7, 8-11), and time such as minutes or hours (0-1, 2-3, 4-5).

Visualization of data distribution in this way allows the viewer to look for peaks, valleys, and ranges in it, and to discover more than just the mean or median of the values. Because bar charts and Histograms can appear similar, and many people are unfamiliar with the concept of distribution, the design of the chart (including axis labels, titles, and distance between the bars) is as important as the data itself.

How To: Build a Histogram showing the age distribution of a clinic's patients.

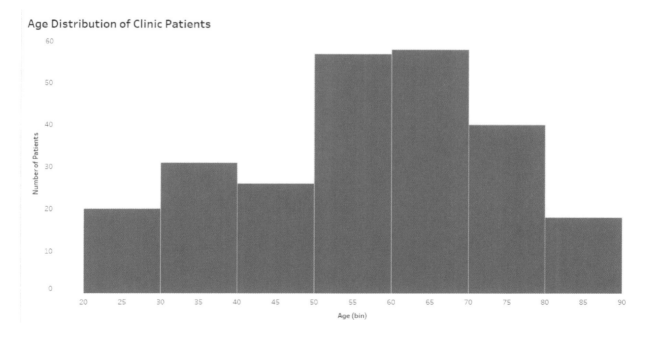

Data Source: *Mock clinic patient metrics*

About the Data: *250 mock adult patients from a hospital clinic were selected to have age, height, weight, and blood pressure recorded for comparison.*

1 Create a new worksheet and connect to the data

» At the bottom of the Tableau workspace, click the icon for a new worksheet.

» In the Data pane, select the "04 – Clinic Patient Metrics" dataset.

This dataset contains one Dimension (Patient ID) and several Measures, including "Age."

Displaying this data in any of the ways demonstrated so far permits only limited insights. For example, in the image below, patients are sorted by simple chronological age from youngest to oldest. This information is useful, but incomplete: knowing whether the target population skews older or younger, and whether that trend has changed, guides almost every important decision at the organizational level. A histogram can show (as other types of displays cannot) distribution across 10-year age ranges.

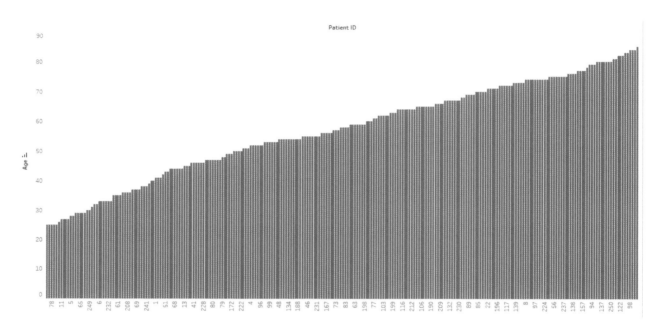

2 Create the chart

Using one Measure and the Show Me function quickly creates a Histogram.

» In the Measures window, click "Age" to highlight.

» Click the "Show Me" tab.

» Select the "Histogram" image.

» Click the "Show Me" tab again to close.

The chart looks like this:

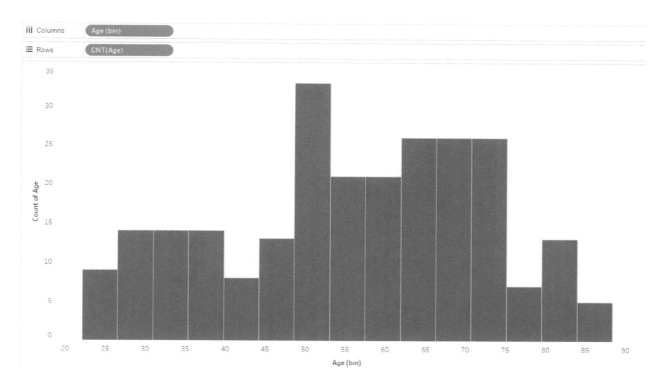

Tableau has created a new Dimension "Age (bin)" to provide the bins of equally-sized ranges required for a Histogram. The lengths of the bars represent the *count of records* containing the values within each of the bin ranges. The pill type is continuous to ensure correct bin order.

3 **Edit the bins**

» Right-click "Age (bin)" in the Dimensions window.

» Select "Edit..." from the menu.

Binning ▶

Tableau simplifies the process of breaking down a Measure into uniform bins by automatically creating a new field that breaks the Measure into equally spaced ranges. This new field, a binned version of the original one, appears as a Dimension because Bins are treated as discrete categories. (If desired, a Parameter can be used to dynamically change bin size for added interactivity.)

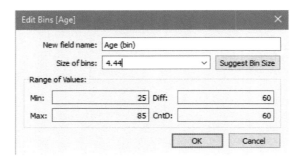

A dialog box appears with the "New field name" automatically created; this name may be customized if desired. Below the New field name is "Size of bins" with a calculated value that creates 15 bins. The drop-down menu allows the option of entering new values or creating new parameters.

» For this exercise, in the "Size of bins" field, enter the a new value of "10."

The bins will now group the number of patients by 10-year age ranges.

Best Practice

When creating bins, make sure to choose a size small enough to show detailed distribution, but not so small as to provide too much specificity. The Min, Max, and Diff values can aid in the selection of an appropriate bin range.

4 **Format the chart**

» Right-click the Y axis.

» Select "Edit Axis..."

Edit Axis ▶

Tableau automatically populates a chart axis with a header, number range, and tick marks. Right-clicking an axis and selecting Edit Axis... will present a menu of customizable axis options. On the General tab, Tableau automatically sets the axis range to account for the minimum and maximum values in the visualization. A fixed range with a static start and end may be selected, or alternative range settings may be considered. The title may be edited or removed; the axis scale may be Reversed or Logarithmic. Modify tick marks by using the Tick Marks tab.

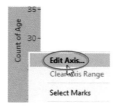

»   Change the Y axis title to "Number of Patients."

Best Practice

By default, Tableau bar and line graphs start at zero so as not to obscure bar or line length or distort the message in the data.

5 **Add a title**

»   Double-click the Title Row to open the Edit Title dialog box.

»   Add a title, "Age Distribution of Clinic Patients."

6 **Rename the worksheet tab and save the worksheet**

»   Right-click the worksheet tab at the bottom of the workspace, then select "Rename."

»   Enter an intuitive title, then click the "Save" icon on the Tool bar.

The final chart looks like this:

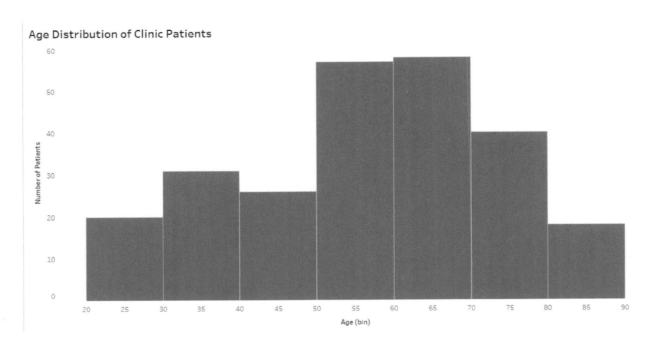

Age Distribution of Clinic Patients

Insight: The data displayed in this Histogram are negatively skewed, which makes it clear that the majority of clinic patients are in older age ranges (50 to 80).

▌▍ *HDVizoom*™...to the Histogram

1 Create new worksheet and connect to data

» At bottom of Tableau workspace, click icon for new worksheet

» In Data pane, select "04 – Clinic Patient Metrics" dataset

2 Create chart

» In Measures window, click "Age" to highlight

» Click "Show Me" tab

» Select Histogram image

» Click "Show Me" tab again to close

3 Edit bins

» Right-click "Age (bin)" in Dimensions window

» Select "Edit" from menu

» In Size of bins section, enter new value of "10"

4 Format chart

» Right-click Y axis

» Select "Edit Axis..."

» Change Y axis title to "Number of Patients"

5 Add title

» Double-click Title Row to open Edit Title dialog box

» Add title, "Age Distribution of Clinic Patients"

6 Rename worksheet tab and save worksheet

» Right-click worksheet tab at bottom of workspace, then select "Rename"

» Enter intuitive title, then click "Save" icon on Tool bar

CHAPTER 10

Line Charts

ines may be used in many different ways to visualize trends or distributions of data, or to forecast results. In the case of a Scatter Plot, a Line of Best Fit (sometimes called a trend line) may be used to display positive, negative, or loose correlations (or none at all) between variables. This chapter will guide the creation of a Line Chart to connect a series of data points over time in order to display the distribution and trend of the points.

How To: Build a Line Chart to compare viral surveillance results that are positive for influenza by months over a four-year time span.

Flu Viral Surveillance: % Respiratory Specimens Positive for Influenza
October -- September
For Flu Seasons 2013 - 2016

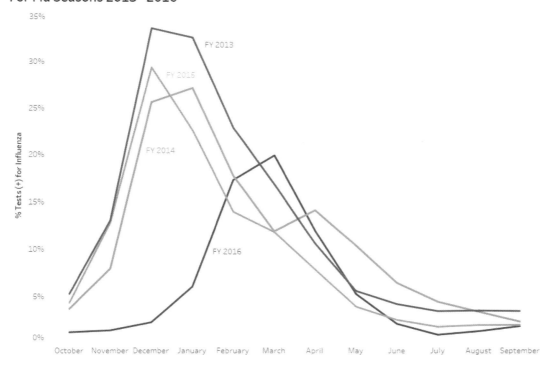

Data Source: *Centers for Disease Control and Prevention (CDC) Seasonal Flu Activity.*

About the Data: *National influenza viral surveillance results (percentage of positive influenza tests for respiratory specimens received at public health or clinical laboratories) by month for four flu seasons: Oct 2012–Sep 2013, Oct 2013–Sep 2014, Oct 2014–Sep 2015, and Oct 2015-Sep 2016. The Influenza Division at the CDC, working with state and local health departments, labs, hospitals, clinics and other healthcare facilities, collects and analyzes flu data year-round and presents the data through its weekly report, FluView.*

1 Create a new worksheet and connect to the data

» At the bottom of the Tableau workspace, click the icon for a new worksheet.

» In the Data pane, select the "05 - Flu Occurrences FY2013-FY2016" dataset.

In the Dimensions window, notice the Data Type icon to the left of the "Date" field. Tableau recognizes this field as containing Date values. Date fields in Tableau work in a hierarchy from the highest level of aggregation, Year, through Quarter, Month, and so on, to the lowest level of granularity of that date or date/time field (as displayed below).

Hierarchical Dates ▶   ⊞ Date

Dates in Tableau work in a hierarchical structure that enables the user to query reports at increasing levels of detail.

When a Date field is moved into the workspace, it will default to a discrete (blue) pill set at the highest level of aggregation, YEAR. A (+) sign will appear to the left of the text on the pill, indicating the presence of a hierarchy.

In the example below, clicking the (+) on the pill displays a new pill at the next lower level in the hierarchy. When the (+) is no longer visible on the pill, the lowest level of the hierarchy has been reached. Clicking on the now (-) sign will recompress the hierarchy.

Year of Date	Quarter of Date	Month of Date	Day of Date
2016	Q1	January	30
		February	27
		March	26
	Q2	April	30
		May	28
		June	25
	Q3	July	30
		August	27
		September	24

Both the Date level of aggregation and the pill type (discrete or continuous) can be changed. There are two ways to modify either of these categories:

Option 1: Right-click the Date pill present on the desired shelf. The context menu that appears displays two date- format sections, Date Part and Date Value.

Option 2: To move the Date pill out of the Dimensions window and onto the shelf, right-click and drag the pill from the window to the desired shelf. The Drop Field menu that appears displays the date format options Date Part and Date Value, as well as other aggregation options. This option serves as a shortcut to customizing the newly added pill.

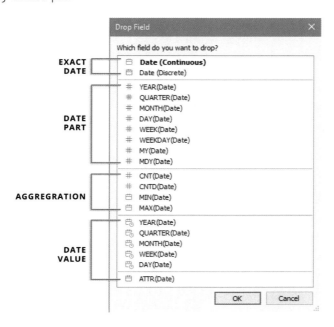

◀ **Date Defaults**

It is crucial to note that no matter which way dates are entered into the data source, Tableau views them all hierarchically, aggregating first by Year. If another level of aggregation is desired, choose between options 1 or 2, above.

Date Part and Date Value will display different views of the date.

Date Part	Date Value
Displays the "parts" of the date	Displays the "values" of the date

Date Example: **January 1, 2017**

Year	2017		**Year**	2017
Month	January		**Month**	January 2017
Day	1		**Day**	January 1, 2017

Pill defaults to discrete (blue)	Pill defaults to continuous (green)
⊞ MONTH(Date)	⊞ MONTH(Date)
Displays headers	Displays continuous axis

In this flu example line chart, viewing the flu occurrences trend over time is helpful; however, viewing the data by discrete months will allow for seasonal comparison across four different years. Option 1 (explained above) will therefore be used in the creation of the chart, but feel free to experiment with Option 2 if desired.

2 Create the chart

» Drag and drop the "% Tests (+) for Influenza" from the Measures window onto the Rows shelf.

» Drag and drop "Date" from the Dimensions window onto the Columns shelf.

» Right-click the "YEAR(Date)" pill and select "Month" from the Date Part section of the menu.

The chart now looks like this:

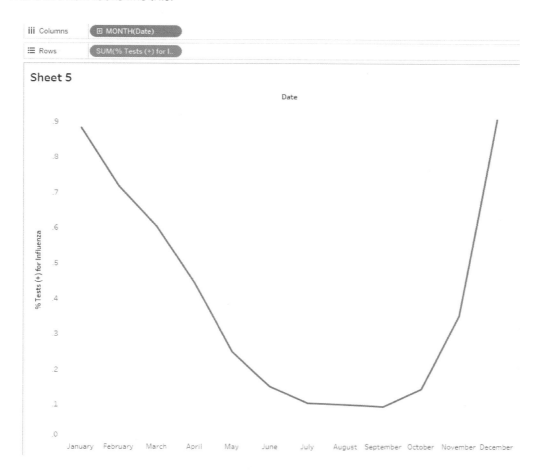

The line currently displays the aggregation of flu data for all four years. To disaggregate the date by year, and give each of the four flu seasons a unique line color for the chart,

» Drag and drop "Date" from the Dimensions window onto Color on the Marks card.

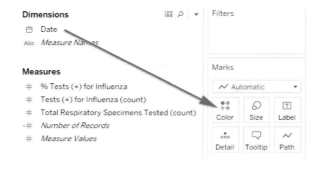

◄ **Marks Card – Color**

Dragging and dropping a Dimension or Measure onto Color on the Marks card creates a color key to that pill's data elements.

Options for discrete pills are clearly delineated hues, while continuous pill options are progressive/gradual shades.

If there is no pill on Color, default colors can still be changed by clicking "Color."

The chart now looks like this:

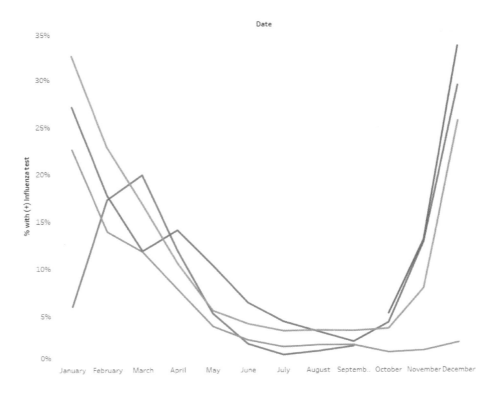

3 Format the chart

Notice that five lines are displayed on the chart. Flu season data starts in October, but the months for the current view start with January. It is more logical to display data from October through September instead of over a calendar year. To change month order,

》   Right-click "Date" in the Dimensions window.

》   Select "Default Properties."

》   Select "Fiscal Year Start."

》   Select "October."

◀ **Changing the Start of the Year:**

Tableau date fields default to January. Sometimes, as with fiscal-year reporting, the start date must be changed to a different month.

The chart now looks like this:

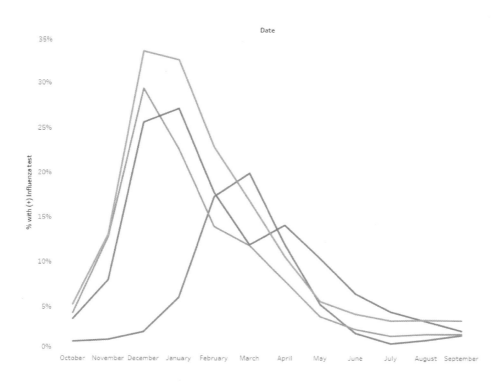

The reformatted chart makes clear that flu occurrences rise dramatically beginning in October and peak in the winter (roughly December through March).

To change the "% Tests (+) for Influenza" field from a decimal to a percentage:

» Right-click "% Tests (+) for Influenza" in the Measures window.

» From the context menu, select "Default Properties."

» Select "Number Format."

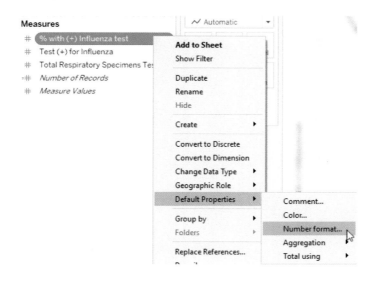

The Default Number Format dialog box appears.

» Select "Percentage."

» Change Decimal places to "0."

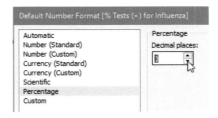

Tableau auto-generates a color for each line. To change these colors,

» Click the YEAR(Date) color-legend caret to open the sub-menu.

» Select "Edit Colors."

» Click the caret for the Color Palette drop-down, and select "Color Blind."

» Click the "Assign Palette" button to let Tableau assign colors from the color palette to the data items. Color selection may also be manually edited by clicking the data item to highlight it, then clicking a color in the palette to assign.

134

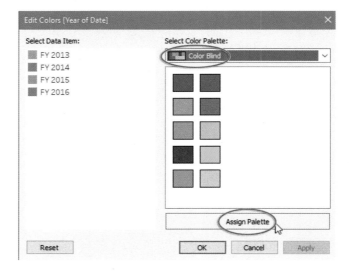

To hide the "Date" field label (since months are displayed at the bottom of the chart, this label is unnecessary),

» Right-click the field label "Date."

» Select "Hide Field Labels for Columns."

Add labels to the lines

» While holding down the "Control" key, drag and drop the "YEAR (Date)" pill (on the Marks card) onto Label. This action will place a copy of the "YEAR(Date)" pill that is on Color on Label.

The data marks for September are close together, so not all labels display fully. To display all four labels,

»   Click Label on Marks card.

»   When a menu appears, in the "Options" section at the bottom, click "Allow labels to overlap other marks."

The labels remain difficult to read. To move them,

»   Click a label to highlight it. The cursor, when placed over the label, should change to a plus sign.

»   Click the label and drag it to a location next to the corresponding line, which will then be auto-highlighted.

»   Follow the same steps for the other line labels.

To match the label colors with the line colors,

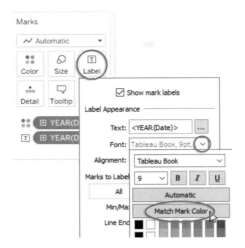

» Click "Label" on Marks card.

» Click the caret for the Font option.

» Click the "Match Mark Color" button.

4 Add a title

» Double-click the Title Row at the top of the workspace to edit it.

» Add the title

Flu Viral Surveillance: % Respiratory Specimens Positive for Influenza
October – September
For Flu Seasons 2013 - 2016

5 Rename the worksheet tab and save the worksheet

» Right-click the worksheet tab at the bottom of the workspace, then select "Rename."

» Enter an intuitive title, then Save.

The final chart looks like this:

Flu Viral Surveillance: % Respiratory Specimens Positive for Influenza
October -- September
For Flu Seasons 2013 - 2016

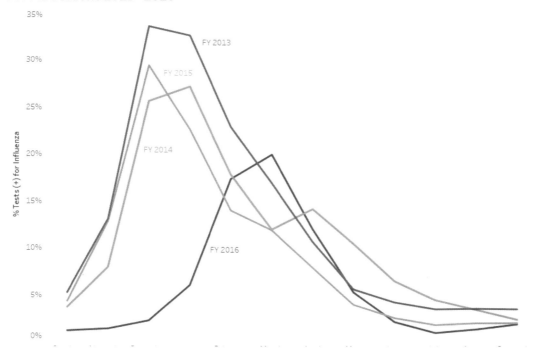

Insight: This chart enables the viewer to see that flu rates for FY2013 were highest during the winter months from December to January, with 34% of respiratory specimens testing positive for the virus. For FY2016, the rates peaked later in the season—February and March—and at a lower point (20%) than in the previous three seasons.

▌▌ *HDVizoom*™ ...to the Line Chart

1 **Create new worksheet and connect to data**

» At bottom of Tableau workspace, click icon for new worksheet

» In Data pane, select "05 - Flu Occurrences FY2013-FY2016" dataset

2 **Create chart**

» Drag and drop "% Tests (+) for Influenza" from Measures window onto Rows shelf

» Drag and drop "Date" from Dimensions window onto Columns shelf

» Right-click "YEAR (Date)" pill on Columns shelf and select "Month" from Date Part section of menu

» Drag and drop "Date" from Dimensions window onto Color on Marks card

3 **Format chart**

» Right-click "Date" in Dimensions window

» Select "Default Properties"

» Select "Fiscal Year Start"

» Select "October"

» Right-click "% Tests (+) for Influenza" in Measures window

» From context menu, select "Default Properties"

» Select "Number Format"

» Select "Percentage"

» Change Decimal places to "0"

» Click YEAR(Date) color legend caret to open sub-menu.

» Select "Edit Colors"

» Click caret for Color Palette drop-down and select "Color Blind"

» Click "Assign Palette" button to let Tableau assign colors from color palette

» Right-click field label "Date"

» Select "Hide Field Labels for Columns"

» While holding down "Control" key, drag and drop "YEAR (Date)" pill (on Marks card) onto Label

» Click "Label" on Marks card

» Click option at bottom of appearing menu "Allow labels to overlap other marks"

» Click line label to highlight

» Click label and drag to location next to corresponding line

» Follow same steps for other line labels

» Click "Label" on Marks card

» Click caret for Font option

» Click "Match Mark Color" button

4 **Add title**

» Double-click Title Row at top of workspace to edit

» Add title

» Flu Viral Surveillance: % Respiratory Specimens Positive for Influenza
October – September
For Flu Seasons 2013 - 2016

5 **Rename worksheet tab and save worksheet**

» Right-click worksheet tab at bottom of workspace, then select "Rename"

» Enter intuitive title then Save

Highlight Table/Heat Map

A Highlight Table/Heat Map encodes and displays quantitative values as color. One very familiar example is a weather map whose colors represent varying amounts of rainfall or degrees of temperature. But Highlight Tables/Heat Maps need not be limited to geographic data; they can also be structured as a matrix of cells, as in a table or crosstab view, that uses density of color to represent varying amounts or ranges of data.

This exercise will guide the creation of a Highlight Table/Heat Map in a crosstab view, using color in each of the cells to display and highlight the different values in the data.

How To: Build a Highlight Table/Heat Map displaying Flu Data over Time.

Flu Viral Surveillance: % Respiratory Specimens Positive for Influenza
October -- September
For Flu Seasons 2013 - 2016

	October	November	December	January	February	March	April	May	June	July	August	September
FY 2013	5%	13%	34%	33%	23%	17%	11%	6%	4%	3%	3%	3%
FY 2014	4%	8%	26%	27%	18%	12%	14%	10%	6%	4%	3%	2%
FY 2015	4%	13%	29%	23%	14%	12%	8%	4%	2%	2%	2%	2%
FY 2016	1%	1%	2%	6%	17%	20%	12%	5%	2%	1%	1%	2%

Data Source: Center for Disease Control and Prevention (CDC) Seasonal Flu Activity.

About the Data: National influenza viral surveillance results (percentage of positive influenza tests for respiratory specimens received at public health or clinical laboratory) by month for four flu seasons: Oct 2012–Sep 2013, Oct 2013–Sep 2014, Oct 2014–Sep 2015, and Oct 2015-Sep 2016. The Influenza Division at the CDC, working with state and local health departments, labs, hospitals, clinics and other healthcare facilities, collects and analyzes flu data year round and presents the data through its weekly report, FluView.

Note: This exercise assumes that a Line Chart was created in Chapter 10. If it was not, the user will be directed to Chapter 10 where data format changes are explained.

1 Create a new worksheet and connect to the data

» At the bottom of the Tableau workspace, click the icon for a new worksheet.

» In the Data pane, select the "05 - Flu Occurrences FY2013-FY2016" dataset.

2 Create the chart

» Drag and drop "Date" from the Dimensions window onto the Columns shelf.

» Right-click the "YEAR(Date)" pill on the Columns shelf.

» Change to Date Part "Month."

Note: if the displayed months begin with January and not October, go to Chapter 10 to learn how to change the start month.

» Drag and drop "Date" from the Dimensions window onto the Rows shelf.

» Keep the row "(YEAR)Date" pill formatted as a Date Part Year.

» Drag and drop "% Tests (+) for Influenza" from the Measures window onto Color shelf on the Marks card.

» Click the framed [T] Label icon on the Toolbar to add Flu Occurrence Rate percentages to the chart.

Note: If the Flu Occurrence Rate is not displaying as a percentage, go to Chapter 10 to learn how to format this rate as a percentage.

3 Format the chart

To adjust the width of the columns:

» Hover the cursor over the right border of the chart until it changes to a bi-directional arrow.

» Drag to an appropriate width to ensure that all month names are visible.

Color for this continuous data is displayed as a sequential color palette. To edit the color:

» Click the caret to the right of the "SUM(% Tests (+) for Influenza)" color legend to open a drop-down menu.

» Select "Edit Colors..."

From the Edit Colors dialog box,

» Click the caret to the right of "Automatic" to open a drop-down menu and display the Palette colors.

» Choose a color (for this example, Blue).

» Click "OK."

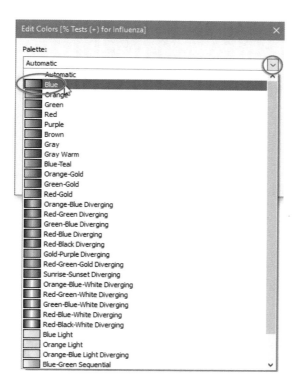

Best Practice

Tableau has a number of color gradients to convey the weight (density) of continuous data.

Sequential color: A single sequential color can be used to encode the weight of a measure: for example, very light blue for low weights, or very dark blue for high weights or data density.

Diverging color: A diverging gradient can be used to convey categorical shifts from a central point. For example, high rates of disease could be displayed in dark orange progressing to light orange as the rates get lower, then shifting to light blue, then to dark blue to contrast areas with significantly lower rates of disease.

> **Best Practice**
>
> *Darker and lighter hues of the same color in data visualization can convey different things to different people, depending on location and climate. For example, while those in the Eastern and Northern US may associate cold weather with the flu, those in the South and West may not. It is sensible to account for these regional differences.*

To hide the column and row headers:

» Right-click "Date" header.

» Click "Hide Field Labels for Columns."

» Right-click "Year of Date" header.

» Click "Hide Field Labels for Rows."

4 Add a title

» Double-click the Title Row to open the Edit Title dialog box.

» Enter the title, "Flu Viral Surveillance: % Respiratory Specimens Positive for Influenza October – September for Flu Seasons 2013 - 2016."

5 Rename the worksheet tab and save the worksheet

» Right-click the worksheet tab at the bottom of the workspace, then select "Rename."

» Enter an intuitive title, then cllick the "Save" icon on the Tool bar.

The final highlight table/heat map looks like this:

Flu Viral Surveillance: % Respiratory Specimens Positive for Influenza October -- September For Flu Seasons 2013 - 2016

	October	November	December	January	February	March	April	May	June	July	August	September
FY 2013	5%	13%	34%	33%	23%	17%	11%	6%	4%	3%	3%	3%
FY 2014	4%	8%	26%	27%	18%	12%	14%	10%	6%	4%	3%	2%
FY 2015	4%	13%	29%	23%	14%	12%	8%	4%	2%	2%	2%	2%
FY 2016	1%	1%	2%	6%	17%	20%	12%	5%	2%	1%	1%	2%

▲ **Refresher**

In the chart above, the months start with October and end in September because the Fiscal Year Start default in the Line Chart visualization was changed. This change also explains why the YEAR(Date) field displays as "FY 20xx."

Insight: The darker blue sections make it easy to see that during the winter months of December and January of FY2013 - FY2015, flu rates were at their highest as compared to FY2016, when the rates peaked later in the season.

▚ *HDVizoom*™...to the Highlight Table / Heat Map

Note: *This exercise assumes that a Line Chart was created in Chapter 10. If it was not, user will be directed in to Chapter 10 where format changes are explained*

1 Create new worksheet and connect to data

» At bottom of Tableau workspace, click icon for new worksheet

» In Data pane, select "05 - Flu Occurrences FY2013-FY2016" dataset

2 Create chart

» Drag and drop "Date" from Dimensions window onto Columns shelf

» Right-click "YEAR(Date)" pill on Columns shelf

» Change to Date Part "Month"

Note: *If displayed months begin with January and not October, go to Chapter 10 to learn how to change start month*

» Drag and drop "Date" from Dimensions window onto Rows shelf

» Keep row "(YEAR)Date" pill formatted as Date Part Year

» Drag and drop "% Tests (+) for Influenza" from Measures window onto Color on Marks card

» Click framed [T] Label icon in Toolbar to add Flu Occurrence percentages to chart

Note: *If Flu Occurrence is not displaying as a percentage, go to Chapter 10 to learn how to format this rate as a percentage*

3 Format chart

» Hover cursor over right border of chart until it changes to bi-directional arrow

» Drag to appropriate width to ensure all month labels are visible

» Click caret to right of "SUM(% Tests (+) for Influenza)" color legend to open drop-down menu

» Select "Edit Colors..."

» Click caret to open drop-down menu and display Palette colors

» Choose color (for this example, Blue)

» Click "OK"

» Right-click "Date" header

» Click "Hide Field Labels for Columns"

» Right-click "Year of Date" header

» Click "Hide Field Labels for Rows"

4 Add title

» Double-click Title Row to open Edit Title dialog box

» Double-click text and add title, "Flu Viral Surveillance: % Respiratory Specimens Positive for Influenza October -- September for Flu Seasons 2013 - 2016"

5 Rename worksheet tab and save worksheet

» Right-click worksheet tab at bottom of workspace, then select "Rename"

» Enter intuitive title, then click "Save" icon on Tool bar

CHAPTER 12

Small Multiples Chart

E dward Tufte popularized Small Multiples, which he described in *Envisioning Information* as "Illustrations of postage-stamp size...[sorted] by category or...label, sequenced over time like the frames of a movie, or ordered by a quantitative variable not used in the single image itself"(67).

Repeating a basic chart type in a grid formation, while altering a single condition for easy data comparison, creates a Small Multiple. If the reader can understand the first chart, the others are readily understood: thanks to carefully balanced parallel construction, all the charts convey the same message. The single differing value in each subsequent chart is easily compared to its fellows by a glance up, down, or across the charts. And because the charts are close together and visible at a single glance, the structure and patterns in complex data are clear and comprehensible.

As with any data display, a Small Multiple may be built using bars, lines, box plots, area charts, or even multiple maps, depending on the type of data to be communicated. The simplicity of the chart is paramount; therefore, keep measures, scales, sizes, and shapes consistent and proportionate to assure that the real story in the data is communicated.

How To: **Build a Small Multiple Line Chart to compare teenage obesity by gender and race over time.**

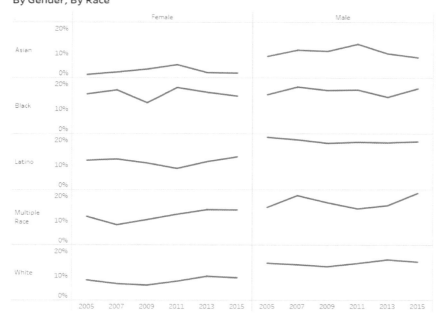

Data Source: *Centers for Disease Control and Prevention (CDC), National Center for Health Statistics (NCHS), 2005-2015 National Health and Nutrition Examination Survey (www.cdc.gov/nchs).*

About the Data: *The NCHS is a health statistics agency providing accurate and timely data to drive improvements in the health of adults and children in the US. The National Health and Nutrition Examination Survey (NHANES) captures data about the health and nutrition status of adults and children in the U.S. through interviews and physical examinations. This example uses the agency's survey data on the prevalence of obesity [body mass index (BMI) equal to or greater than 30] from 2005 to 2015 by gender and race.*

1 **Create a new worksheet and connect to the data**

» At the bottom of the Tableau workspace, click the icon for a New Worksheet.

» In the Data pane, select the "07 - Teenage Obesity Rates" dataset.

2 **Create the chart**

» Drag and drop "Race" from the Dimensions window onto the Rows shelf.

» Drag and drop "Prevalence (%)" from the Measures window onto the Rows shelf.

» Drag and drop "Gender" then "Date" from the Dimensions window onto the Columns shelf.

Scale ▶

To accurately compare Small Multiple charts, the axis scales must be consistent for all of them. If the scales of the charts need to be adjusted, right-click the Measure axis and adjust the range.

▲ **Dimension Order**

The order of multiple Dimensions on a row or column shelf affects how Measure data is divided. In the example above, the visualization would be markedly different if Date were positioned before Gender. Experiment with Dimension order to find the best visualization.

◀ **Wouldn't It Be Easier to Build This in Show Me?**

Tableau's Show Me functionality is a quick and powerful way to build charts with automated logic. If a customized layout is desired, however, Show Me is probably not the best choice. As is the case with Small Multiples, sometimes constructing a chart manually brings better results.

3 **Format the chart**

Format the y-axis values for Prevalence(%):

» Right-click "SUM(Prevalance(%))" pill on Rows shelf.

» Click "Format."

» Click the "Axis" tab.

» In the Scale section, click the caret for "Numbers."

» Select "Percentages" and change decimals to 0.

Hide the y-axis title "Prevalence (%):

» Right-click a Y axis.

» Select "Edit Axis..."

» In the Titles section of the dialog box, delete the title, then click "OK."

Hide field names:

» Right-click "Gender/Date."

» Click "Hide Field Labels for Columns."

» Right-click "Race."

» Click "Hide Field Labels for Rows."

4 Add a title

» Double-click the Title Row at the top of the workspace.

» Add title

Prevalence (%) of Teenage Obesity (BMI>=30)
2005 - 2015
By Gender, By Race

5 Rename the worksheet tab and save the worksheet

» Right-click the worksheet tab at the bottom of the workspace, then select "Rename."

» Enter an intuitive title.

» Click the "Save" icon on the Tool bar.

The final chart looks like this:

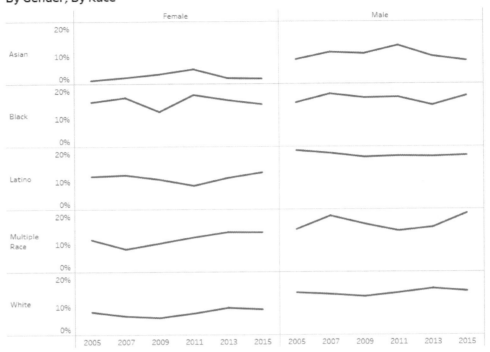

Insight: This Small Multiple Line Chart makes it possible to identify several interesting trends. It is very evident for example that Asian females consistently have the lowest prevalence of obesity for all races and genders, while Latino males consistently have the highest prevalence.

> **Best Practice**
>
> *A Small Multiple chart is created by stratifying one measure by two or more dimensions. In designing Small Multiples, focus more on clear and intuitive visualization, and less of following a specific formula.*

⊡ *HD*Vizoom™...to the Small Multiples Chart

1 Create new worksheet and connect to data

» At bottom of Tableau workspace, click icon for new worksheet

» In Data pane, select "07 – Teenage Obesity Rates" dataset

2 Create chart

» Drag and drop "Race" from Dimensions window onto Rows shelf

» Drag and drop "Prevalence (%)" from Measures window onto Rows shelf

» Drag and drop "Gender" then "Date" from Dimensions window onto Columns shelf

3 Format chart

» Right-click "SUM(Prevalence (%))" pill on Rows shelf

» Click "Format"

» Click "Axis" tab

» In Scale section, click caret for "Numbers"

» Select "Percentages" and change decimals to 0

» Right-click Y axis

» Select "Edit Axis"

» In Titles section of dialog box, delete title, then click "OK"

» Right-click "Gender/Date"

» Click "Hide Field Labels for Rows"

» Right-click "Race"

» Click "Hide Field Labels for Rows"

4 Add title

» Double-click Title Row at top of workspace

» Add title

Prevalence (%) of Teenage Obesity (BMI >= 30)
2005–2010
By Gender, By Race

5 Rename worksheet tab and save worksheet

» Right-click worksheet tab at bottom of workspace, then select "Rename"

» Enter intuitive title

» Click "Save" icon on Tool bar

149

CHAPTER 13

Deviation Charts

A Deviation Chart displays the way sets of quantitative values differ from reference or primary sets of values. Examples are the differences between actual expenses compared to budgeted ones, or between state childhood immunization rates compared to national rates. A Deviation Chart can show the reference (for example, an expense budget) as the anchor or constant over time (regardless of how it may change), while showing how the other value (for example, actual expenses) differs from it. This flexibility allows the easy monitoring of such information as: "Are we over or under budget, and by how much?" or "Are we meeting or missing target, and by how much?" Deviation Charts answer directly and simply the basic but crucial question, "Is one measure more or less than another measure?"

13.1 Deviation Bar Charts

How To: Build a Deviation Bar Chart to compare budgeted and actual full-time employees (FTE) in five different hospital departments.

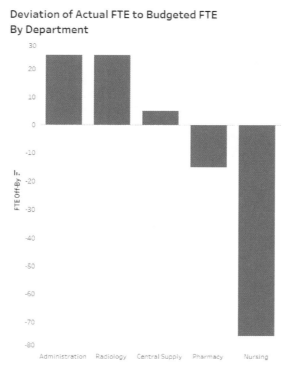

Deviation of Actual FTE to Budgeted FTE
By Department

Data Source: Mock hospital data

About the Data: We created mock hospital data on the difference between the budgeted and actual numbers of full-time equivalents (FTE) for five major hospital departments.

1 **Create a new worksheet and connect to the data**

» At the bottom of the Tableau workspace, click the icon for a new worksheet.

» In the Data pane, select the "08 – Department FTE Counts" dataset.

2 **Create a calculated field**

The dataset documents budgeted FTEs vs. actual FTEs. For a Deviation Chart, the difference between budgeted and actual FTEs is required and must be calculated.

» Right-click "Actual FTE" in the Measures window.

» Select "Create" from the menu that appears, then select "Calculated Field..."

Calculated Fields ▶

Calculated Fields can be used to create simple aggregations such as MIN, MAX, and AVG; construct IF / THEN and CASE / WHEN statements; perform date-field and string manipulation; and a host of other functions. This book covers some basic, common Calculated Fields in Chapter 26.

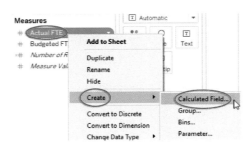

The Calculated Field dialog box appears.

» Replace "Calculation 1" in the Name field with "FTE Off By."

Best Practice:

The Calculated Field needs an intuitive name to make it easy to find in a list of Dimensions or Measures.

In the Formula section of this dialog box, assemble a calculation that subtracts Budgeted FTE from Actual FTE. The previous right-click on Actual FTE populated that field in the Formula section.

» Type a minus sign (-) to the right of the "Actual FTE" field.

» Complete the formula by dragging and dropping the "Budgeted FTE" field from the Measures window to the right of the minus sign (-) in the Formula window.

» Click "OK."

◄ **Auto-Complete**

Start typing a formula and Tableau displays a list of options (functions, operators, field names, parameters, and sets) for completing the formula.

▲ Non-Aggregate (Row-Level) Calculation

This formula is considered a "non-aggregate" or "row-level" calculation because no aggregation function (SUM, AVG, etc.) has been entered before each Measure name. As a result, when a non-aggregate measure field is placed in the workspace, Tableau applies the default aggregation (SUM). This can be edited, as needed, by right-clicking the pill and selecting the appropriate level of aggregation.

The = sign to the left of the newly created "FTE Off By" measure indicates that this field contains a user-defined calculation.

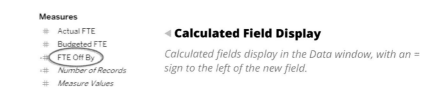

◄ **Calculated Field Display**

Calculated fields display in the Data window, with an = sign to the left of the new field.

3 Create the chart

» Drag and drop the newly created "FTE Off By" from the Measures window onto the Rows shelf.

» Drag and drop "Department" from the Dimensions window onto the Columns shelf.

The chart now looks like this:

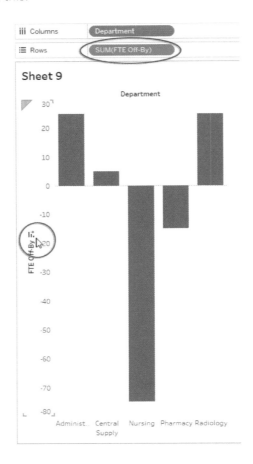

Calculated Field Aggregation ▷

Calculated Fields that are Measures need a level of aggregation, as does any other measure. Aggregation can happen at one of two points: it can be specified within a calculation formula; or, if it is not, Tableau aggregates when the Measure is dragged and dropped onto the view.

4 **Format the chart**

The default sort is alphabetical order by Department. To rank the data from highest to lowest value instead:

» Hover over the Y axis title, "FTE Off By" (see image above). The Sort icon appears.

» Click the icon until the data is displayed in the desired rank.

Delete the Department field label.

» Right-click "Department" header.

» Click "Hide Field Labels for Columns."

Widen the chart to display complete department names.

» Hover over the right border of the chart until the cursor changes to a bi-directional arrow.

» Click and drag the border to the desired width.

5 **Add a title**

» Double-click the Title Row to open the Edit Title dialog box.

» Enter the title, "Deviation of Actual FTE to Budgeted FTE by Department."

6 **Rename the worksheet tab and save the worksheet**

» Right-click the worksheet tab at the bottom of the workspace, then select "Rename."

» Enter an intuitive title, then click the "Save" icon on the Tool bar.

The final chart looks like this:

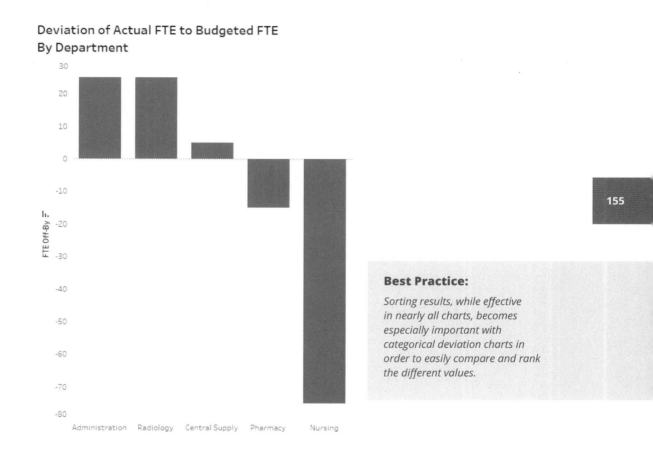

Deviation of Actual FTE to Budgeted FTE
By Department

Best Practice:

Sorting results, while effective in nearly all charts, becomes especially important with categorical deviation charts in order to easily compare and rank the different values.

Insight: This Deviation Bar Chart enables the viewer to easily determine that Nursing is significantly below the budgeted number of FTEs, whereas Administration and Radiology have more staff than budgeted.

155

▐▖▌ *HDVizoom*™ ...to the Deviation Bar Chart

1 Create new worksheet and connect to data

» At bottom of Tableau workspace, click icon for new worksheet

» In Data pane, select "08 – Department FTE Counts" dataset

2 Create Calculated Field

» Right-click "Actual FTE" in Measures window

» Select "Create" from menu, then select "Calculated Field..."

» Replace "Calculation 1" in Name field with "FTE Off By"

» In Formula section, type minus sign (-) to right of "Actual FTE" field

» Complete formula by dragging and dropping "Budgeted FTE" from Measures window to right of minus sign (-) in Formula window

3 Create chart

» Drag and drop newly created "FTE Off By" from Measures window onto Rows shelf

» Drag and drop "Department" from Dimensions window onto Columns shelf

4 Format chart

» Hover over Y axis title "FTE Off By" to view Sort icon

» Click icon until data is displayed in desired rank

» Right-click "Department" header

» Click "Hide Field Labels for Columns"

» Hover over right border of chart until cursor changes to bi-directional arrow

» Click and drag border to desired width

5 Add title

» Double-click Title Row to open Edit Title dialog box

» Enter title, "Deviation of Actual FTE to Budgeted FTE by Department"

6 Rename worksheet tab and save worksheet

» Right-click worksheet tab at bottom of workspace, then select "Rename"

» Enter intuitive title, then click "Save" icon on Toolbar

13.2 Deviation Line Charts

As described in the previous section, Deviation Bar Charts, directly expressing the differences between two sets of values creates a Deviation chart. This example shows how a Deviation Line Chart is an efficient way to compare change over time.

How To: Build a Deviation Line Chart of a hospital emergency department's percent change of patient volume by month, 2016 compared with 2015.

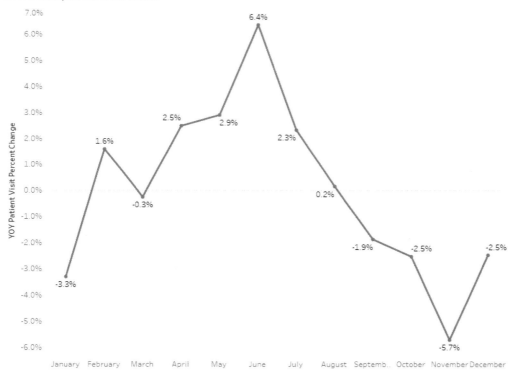

Percent Change of Hospital Emergency Department Patient Volume by Month 2016 compared with 2015

157

Data source: de-identified hospital data

About the data: represents the number of patients seen in a hospital's emergency department by month for a two-year period.

1 Create a new worksheet and connect to the data

» At the bottom of the Tableau workspace, click the icon for a new worksheet.

» In the Data pane, select the "09 - Patient Volume YOY Change" dataset.

2 Create the calculated fields

The dataset currently contains two fields: Date and Patient Visits. The Deviation chart should depict the percent change in the number of patients seen in 2016 compared to those seen in the previous year for each month. Four Calculated Fields need to be created: one for patients seen in each of two years; one for the numeric difference; and one for the percent difference.

» Right-click "Date" in the Dimensions window.

» Select "Create," then select "Calculated Field..." from the menus.

» Enter a field title "Patient Visits for 2016."

For this formula, the number of patient visits for the year 2016 only needs to be calculated. A conditional calculation is used here:

```
IF "condition X" is true, THEN return "Y"
```

IF the Date field shows the year 2016, then return Patient Visits for that year; otherwise, the field will return a null value (ELSE NULL).

» Enter the formula:

```
IF YEAR([Date]) = 2016
THEN [Patient Visits]
ELSE NULL
END
```

» Click "OK."

List of Functions ▶

Click the small gray caret on the right border of the calculation window to view a list of available functions. Click a Function to view its definition. Double-click the Function to populate it in the formula.

View the data to see how this calculation worked. The new field "Patient Visits for 2016" lists only the Patient Visits for each month of the year 2016. The values for 2015 in the new field are Null.

Date	Patient Visits	Patient Visits for 2016
1/31/15	2,541	Null
2/28/15	2,312	Null
3/31/15	2,358	Null
4/30/15	2,401	Null
5/31/15	2,231	Null
6/30/15	2,357	Null
7/31/15	2,352	Null
8/31/15	2,614	Null
9/30/15	2,462	Null
10/31/15	2,616	Null
11/30/15	2,590	Null
12/31/15	2,514	Null
1/31/16	2,457	2,457
2/28/16	2,349	2,349
3/31/16	2,352	2,352
4/30/16	2,461	2,461
5/31/16	2,296	2,296
6/30/16	2,507	2,507
7/31/16	2,407	2,407
8/31/16	2,618	2,618
9/30/16	2,416	2,416
10/31/16	2,550	2,550
11/30/16	2,442	2,442
12/31/16	2,452	2,452

Follow the same steps above to create a calculated field for "Patient Visits for 2015," using "2015" instead of "2016" in the formula.

These two calculated fields restrict the Patient Visits data to 2016 and 2015 only.

A field is needed to calculate the difference between "Patient Visits for 2016" and "Patient Visits for 2015."

» Right-click "Patient Visits for 2016."

» Select "Create," then select "Calculated Field…" from the sub-menu.

» Enter a title for the field: "YOY Patient Visit Difference."

» Enter the formula:

```
SUM([Patient Visits for 2016]) - SUM([Patient Visits for 2015])
```

| YOY Patient Visit Difference | 09 - Patient Volume YOY Change |

SUM([Patient Visits for 2016]) - SUM([Patient Visits for 2015])

» Click "OK."

The SUM function used in this operation is called an "Aggregate Calculation." It is used here because of the null values in many rows of the new fields (see image above).

Note

It is important to understand how Non-Aggregate and Aggregate calculations behave.

Non-Aggregate calculations evaluate each row in a data source then calculate the *row-level* results.

The Non-Aggregate Calculation for "YOY Patient Visit Difference" would be:

```
[Patient Visits for 2016] - [Patient Visits for 2015]
```

The calculation is performed on a single row of data at a time. It's important to remember that performing row-level calculations with null values produces a "null" answer and can significantly affect results.

Date	Patient Visits for 2015		Patient Visits for 2016		
1/31/15	2,541	–	null	=	null
2/28/15	2,312	–	null	=	null
3/31/15	2,358	–	null	=	null
4/30/15	2,401	–	null	=	null
5/31/15	2,231	–	null	=	null
6/30/15	2,357	–	null	=	null
7/31/15	2,352	–	null	=	null
8/31/15	2,614	–	null	=	null
9/30/15	2,462	–	null	=	null
10/31/15	2,616	–	null	=	NULL
11/30/15	2,590	–	null	=	null
12/31/15	2,514	–	null	=	null
1/31/16	null	–	2,457	=	null
2/28/16	null	–	2,349	=	null
3/31/16	null	–	2,352	=	null
4/30/16	null	–	2,461	=	null
5/31/16	null	–	2,296	=	null
6/30/16	null	–	2,507	=	null
7/31/16	null	–	2,407	=	null
8/31/16	null	–	2,618	=	null
9/30/16	null	–	2,416	=	null
10/31/16	null	–	2,550	=	null
11/30/16	null	–	2,442	=	null
12/31/16	null	–	2,452	=	null
				SUM	**NULL**

When this field is placed in the workspace, the aggregation is automatically performed.

Aggregate calculations apply to *all rows* in a partition (grouping of values based on the Dimensions in the view).

The Aggregate Calculation for "YOY Patient Visit Difference" is:

```
SUM([Patient Visits for 2016]) - SUM([Patient Visits for 2015])
```

The aggregation of each field is performed first (summing all rows for each field), then the calculation is performed.

Date	Patient Visits for 2015	Patient Visits for 2016		
1/31/15	2,541	null		
2/28/15	2,312	null		
3/31/15	2,358	null		
4/30/15	2,401	null		
5/31/15	2,231	null		
6/30/15	2,357	null		
7/31/15	2,352	null		
8/31/15	2,614	null		
9/30/15	2,462	null		
10/31/15	2,616	null		
11/30/15	2,590	null		
12/31/15	2,514	null		
1/31/16	null	2,457		
2/28/16	null	2,349		
3/31/16	null	2,352		
4/30/16	null	2,461		
5/31/16	null	2,296		
6/30/16	null	2,507		
7/31/16	null	2,407		
8/31/16	null	2,618		
9/30/16	null	2,416		
10/31/16	null	2,550		
11/30/16	null	2,442		
12/31/16	null	2,452		
	29,348	– 29,307	=	**41**

The final calculated field displays the percent change from 2015 to 2016.

» Right-click the calculated field just created, "YOY Patient Visit Difference."

» Select "Create," then "Calculated Field" from the sub-menu.

» Enter a new title: "YOY Patient Visit Percent Change."

For this formula, the field "YOY Patient Visit Difference" should be divided by the field "Patient Visits for 2015."

However, if the formula is written as:

        SUM([YOY Patient Visit Difference]) / SUM([Patient Visits for 2015])

a syntax error appears. Tableau provides information to identify the error in the formula. In this example, YOY Patient Visit Difference has already been aggregated and cannot therefore be further aggregated.

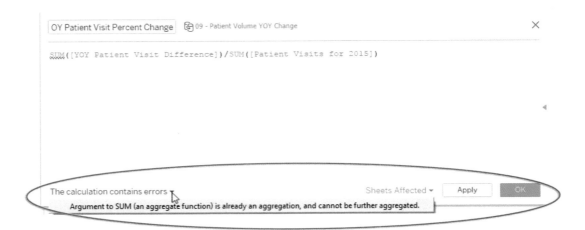

▲ Avoiding Errors in Calculated Fields

Tableau's formula editor has built-in coloring and validation to help avoid syntax errors. Such an error is highlighted with a red squiggly line, which generates directions for fixing the errors when clicked. The caret at the end of the error statement, when clicked, can also provide additional information to fix the error. A valid calculation is identified in gray text at the bottom of the formula window.

To write this formula correctly:

» Enter:

        [YOY Patient Visit Difference] / SUM([Patient Visits for 2015])

» Click "OK."

Since this field is a percentage, the number format needs to change.

- » Right-click the new calculated field "YOY Patient Visit Percent Change."
- » Select "Default Properties."
- » Select "Number Format."
- » Select "Percentage."
- » Decrease Decimal places to "1."

3 Create the chart

- » Drag and drop "YOY Patient Visit Percent Change" from the Measures window onto the Rows shelf.
- » Right-click and drag "Date" from the Dimensions window to the Columns shelf.
- » Select "MONTH(Date)" from the Drop Field menu box, then click "OK."
- » Click the framed [T] Label icon on the Toolbar to add labels to the line.

The chart now looks like this:

▲ The Effect of Dimensions on Aggregate Calculations

Dimensions affect how aggregate calculations perform. When the Dimension "MONTH(Date)" is added to the workspace, the calculation is partitioned to each Month. The example here examines how the calculation for the month of January is performed.

Date	Patient Visits for 2016	Patient Visits for 2015	YOY Patient Visit Difference	Patient Visits for 2015	YOY Patient Visit Percent Change
1/31/15	null	2,541			
1/31/16	2,457	null			
	2457 − 2541		= -84	/2541	-0.033

4 **Format the chart**

  » Right-click the header "Date."

  » Select "Hide Field Labels for Columns."

5 Add a title

» Double-click the Title Row to open the Edit Title dialog box.

» Enter the title, "Percent Change of Hospital Emergency Department Patient Volume by Month, 2016 compared with 2015."

6 Rename the worksheet tab and save the worksheet

» Right-click the worksheet tab at the bottom of the workspace, then select "Rename."

» Enter an intuitive title, then click the "Save" icon on the Toolbar.

The final chart looks like this:

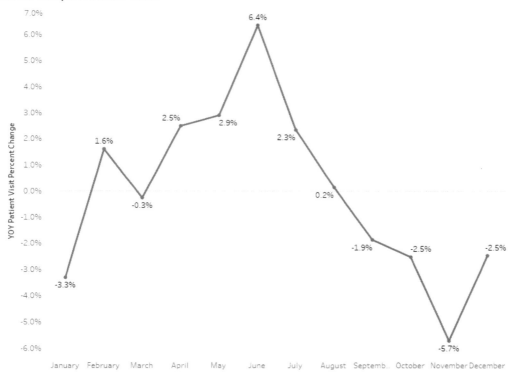

Percent Change of Hospital Emergency Department Patient Volume by Month 2016 compared with 2015

Insight: In 2016, the Emergency Department's actual patient volume was highly variable compared with 2015. In six of the months displayed, the number of patients visiting the ED was lower than in 2015, from -0.3% in March to -5.7% in November. In the other six months of the year, patient numbers were higher than in 2015, from 0.2% in August to 6.4% in June.

▐▌ *HDVizoom*™ ...to the Deviation Line Chart

1 **Create new worksheet and connect to data**

» At bottom of Tableau workspace, click icon for new worksheet

» In Data pane, click "09 - Patient Volume YOY Change" dataset

2 **Create Calculated Fields**

» Right-click "Date" in Dimensions window

» Select "Create," then "Calculated Field" from menus

» Enter field title, "Patient Visits for 2016"

» Enter formula:

```
IF YEAR([Date]) = 2016
THEN [Patient Visits]
ELSE NULL
END
```

» Click "OK"

» Follow same steps to create calculated field for "Patient Visits for 2015," using "2015" instead of "2016" in formula

» Right-click "Patient Visits for 2016"

» Select "Create," then "Calculated Field" from menus

» Enter new title, "YOY Patient Visit Difference"

» Enter:

```
SUM([Patient Visits for 2016])
- SUM([Patient Visits for
2015])
```

» Click "OK"

» Right-click calculated field "YOY Patient Visit Difference"

» Select "Create," then "Calculated Field" from menus

» Enter new title "YOY Patient Visit Percent Change"

» Enter "[YOY Patient Visit Difference] / SUM([Patient Visits for 2015])"

» Click "OK"

» Right-click new calculated field "YOY Patient Visit Percent Change"

» Select "Default Properties"

» Select "Number Format"

» Select "Percentage"

» Decrease Decimal places to "1"

3 **Create chart**

» Drag and drop "YOY Patient Visit Percent Change" from Measures window onto Rows shelf

» Right-click and drag "Date" from Dimensions window onto Columns shelf

» Select "MONTH(Date)" from Drop Field menu box, then click "OK"

» Click framed [T] Label icon on Toolbar

4 **Format chart**

» Right-click header "Date"

» Select "Hide Field Labels for Columns"

5 **Add title**

» Double-click Title Row to open Edit Title dialog box

» Enter title, "Percent Change of Hospital Emergency Department Patient Volume by Month, 2016 compared with 2015"

6 **Rename worksheet tab and save worksheet**

» Right-click worksheet tab at bottom of workspace, then select "Rename"

» Enter intuitive title, then click "Save" icon on Toolbar

CHAPTER 14

Sparklines

Edward Tufte coined the term "Sparkline" in his book *Beautiful Evidence*: "These little data lines, because of their active quality over time, are named *sparklines* – small, high-resolution graphics usually embedded in a full context of words, numbers, images. Sparklines are *datawords*: data-intense, design-simple, word-sized graphics" (47).

Typically displayed without axes or coordinates, Sparklines present trends and variations associated with some measurement of frequent "sparks" of data in a simple and condensed way. They can be small enough to insert into a line of text, or several Sparklines may be grouped as elements of a Small-Multiple chart.

How To: Build Sparklines displaying a patient's vital signs over a 24-hour period.

24-Hour Patient Vital Signs

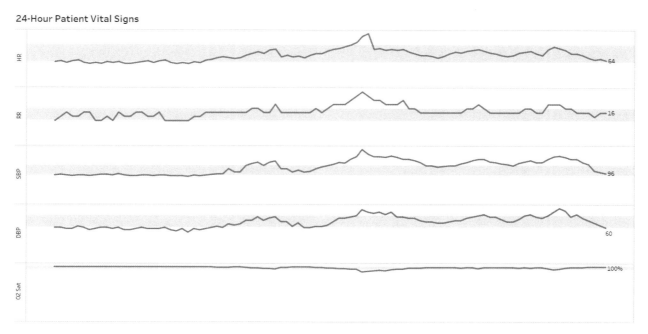

Data Source: Mock patient's vital-sign data

About the Data: A single patient's vital signs – heart rate, respiratory rate, blood pressure (systolic and diastolic), and oxygen saturation – recorded every 15 minutes for a 24-hour period.

1 Create a new worksheet and connect to the data

» At the bottom of the Tableau workspace, click the icon for a new worksheet.

» In the Data pane, select the "10 – Patient 24-Hour Vital Signs" dataset.

2 Create the chart

» Drag and drop "Date/Time" from the Dimensions window onto the Columns shelf.

» Drag and drop the following from the Measures window onto the Rows shelf, in the order shown:

- "Heart Rate"
- "Respiratory Rate"
- "Systolic BP"
- "Diastolic BP"
- "Oxygen Saturation"

The chart initially looks like this:

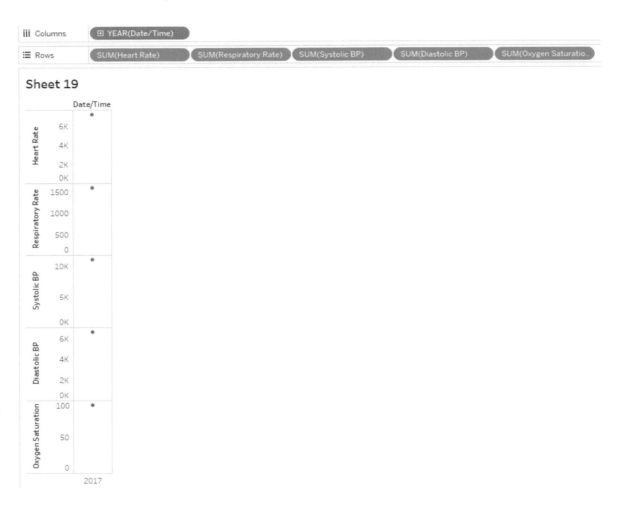

▲ Sparkline Creation

This visualization was created with five separate Measures. It is also possible to create a Sparkline that graphs a single Measure stratified by multiple values in a Dimension. For example, 24-hour Heart Rate values could be compared across several days of the week.

3 Format the axis Date/Time

The Date/Time pill on the Columns shelf is default-formatted as "Year." In this instance, having the exact date/time is more useful, as the database lists the time in 15-minute intervals.

» Right-click the "YEAR(Date/Time)" pill on the Columns shelf.

» Select "Exact Date." This will automatically change the date field to "Continuous."

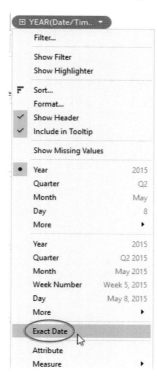

The chart now looks like this:

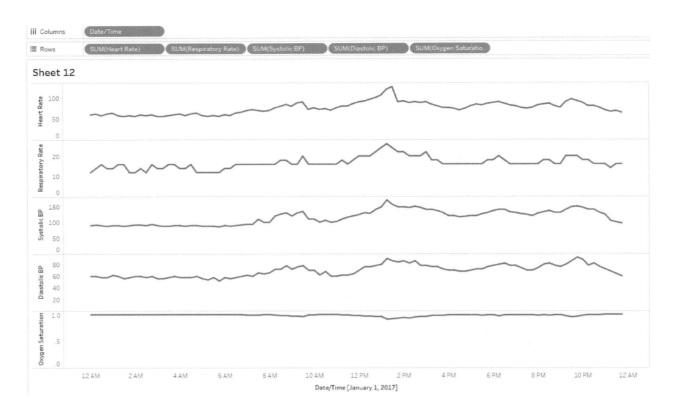

4 Add Reference Bands

Reference Lines or Bands help quickly identify trends outside of normal range. Reference Bands will now be added to each of the displayed vital signs in the Sparkline.

These normal ranges will be added to each respective Reference Band:

- Heart Rate: 60-100

- Respiratory Rate: 12-18

- Systolic Blood Pressure: 90-120

- Diastolic Blood Pressure: 60-80

- Oxygen Saturation: 95-100%

» Click the Analytics tab at the top of the Side Bar.

» Locate "Reference Band" in the Custom section and drag it into the workspace.

» A dialog box appears. Drop the Reference Band into the Pane column for SUM(Heart Rate).

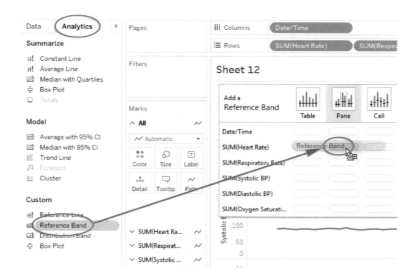

» The "Edit Reference Line, Band, or Box" dialog box appears.

» Band From:

  • Value: click the caret and select "Constant," then enter "60" for the value.

  • Label: "None."

» Band To:

  • Value: click the caret and select "Constant," then enter "100" for the value.

  • Label: "None."

» Fill: select a light gray shade.

» Click "OK."

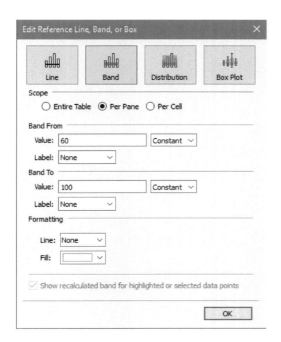

◀ Reference Lines and Bands

A Reference Line or Band can be added to any continuous axis to incorporate additional data into a visualization. The Bands can be added using a constant integer (as in this example) or can be incorporated from a Measure. A Measure to be used as a Reference Line must first be present in the worksheet. If the Reference Line is created from a Measure already in the worksheet (for example, an average of a line chart already built), then the field will automatically appear on the Value drop-down list on the Reference Line menu. If, however, the field is not present, it can be added to Details on the Marks card so that it will populate on the Value drop-down list. To add a static number (such as standard ranges for vital signs), make sure that "Constant" is selected on both drop-down menus to the right of the Value fields.

◀ Scope of Reference Lines and Bands

The number of Dimensions on shelves affects Scope. With no Dimensions present, all areas (Table, Pane, Cell) display the same reference line value. Adding one Dimension to the Measure causes the Table Reference Line value to display differently from that for Pane or Cell. Two or more Dimensions will cause the Table, Pane, and Cell to each display different values.

» Follow the same steps for the remaining vital signs, using the ranges listed above.

• For "Oxygen Saturation," enter 0.95 and 1 for the values.

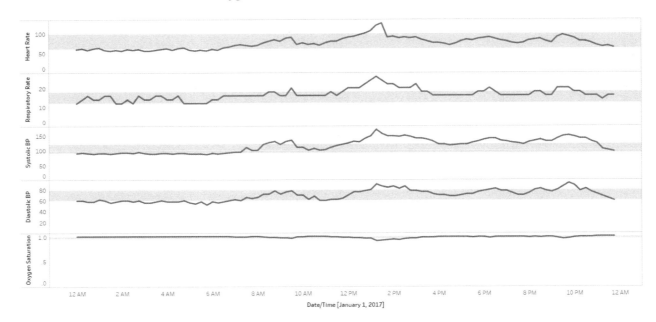

5 Format the chart

To format Oxygen Saturation as a percentage:

» Click the "Data" tab to return to the Dimensions/Measures windows.

» Right-click "Oxygen Saturation" in the Measures window.

» Select "Default Properties."

» Select "Number Format."

» Change to "Percentage" and "0" decimal places.

To remove the gridlines:

» Right-click the middle of the chart.

» Select "Format."

» At the top of the Format window, select the icon of 3 horizontal lines to format lines.

» Select the "Rows" tab.

» Click the caret to the right of "Grid Lines" and change to "None."

Best Practice

Sparkline formatting is designed to be as simple as possible to save real estate and to clearly emphasize general trends with no distracting detail. Sparklines can be displayed with additional information if needed, and it may make sense to retain certain elements (headers or axes) for clarity.

To remove the X and Y axes:

- » Right-click the X axis.
- » Uncheck the "Show Header" box.

To view the headers along the Y axis but remove the tick marks:

- » Right-click the Y axis for "Heart Rate."
- » Select "Edit Axis."
- » In the General tab, edit the Title to an abbreviation (Heart Rate = HR).
- » Select the "Tick Marks" tab.
- » Change Major and Minor tick marks to "None."

◄ Tick Marks

The second tab on the "Edit Axis" screen provides options for adjusting tick-mark spacing. Major tick marks are typically identified by a number; minor tick marks are not. Tableau will automatically space tick marks by default, but the marks can be spaced manually by using the "Fixed" option or removed entirely.

- » Follow the same steps for each Y axis. Abbreviate Respiratory Rate "RR", Systolic BP "SBP", Diastolic BP "DBP", and Oxygen Saturation "O2 Sat."
- » Hover the cursor over the Y axis line until it changes to a bidirectional arrow. Drag to the left to set an appropriate width for the labels.

The chart now looks like this:

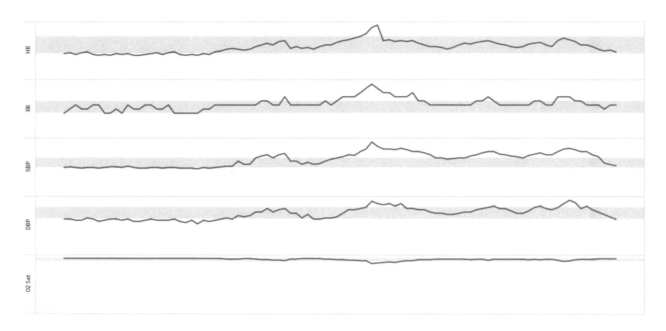

Value Labels applied to the last mark of each line add clarity.

» On the Marks card, click the "All" tab to format the labels on all the lines.

» Click "Label."

» Check the box next to "Show mark labels."

» In the Marks to Label section, select "Line Ends."

» In the Options section, uncheck the box for "Label start of line."

Best Practice

Depending on the message to be conveyed by the data, a Min/Max or Most Recent label may be more useful than labeling the Line Ends. If trends over time are the important message, no label is needed.

6 Add a title

» Double-click the Title Row at the top of the workspace to open the Edit Title dialog box.

» Enter the title, "24-Hour Patient Vital Signs."

7 Rename the worksheet tab and save the worksheet

» Right-click the worksheet tab at the bottom of the workspace, then select "Rename."

» Enter an intuitive title, then click the "Save" icon on the Toolbar.

The final Sparkline chart looks like this:

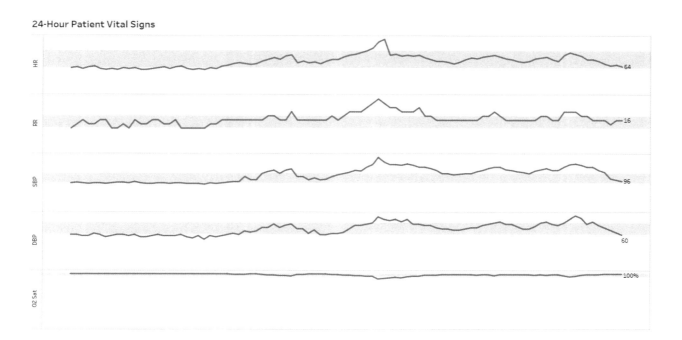

Insight: There is a certain point at which all patient vital signs fall outside normal range. What could be the possible cause?

This insight demonstrates a particular strength of Sparklines: how well it works in tandem with data in a table to demonstrate significant change over time.

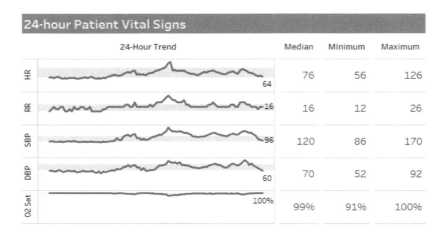

▲ **Combining Sparklines and Data Tables**

The Median, Minimum, and Maximum columns in this display are individual worksheets placed side-by-side on a dashboard. Each was built by placing the Measure Names pill on the Rows shelf and the Measure Values pill on Label on the Marks card. Rearrange the pills on the Measure Values shelf to the appropriate order and remove extraneous pills. Right-click each pill in the Measure Values shelf and change the level of aggregation to Median, Minimum, or Maximum as appropriate.

▌▎ *HDVizoom*™...to the Sparkline Chart

1 **Create new worksheet and connect to data**

» At bottom of Tableau workspace, click icon for new worksheet

» In Date pane, select "10 – Patient 24-Hour Vital Signs" dataset

2 **Create chart**

» Drag and drop "Date/Time" from Dimensions window onto Columns shelf

» Drag and drop following from Measures window onto Rows shelf, order shown:

• "Heart Rate"

• "Respiratory Rate"

• "Systolic BP"

• "Diastolic BP"

• "Oxygen Saturation"

3 **Format axis date/time**

» Right-click "YEAR (Date/Time)" pill on Columns shelf

» Select "Exact Date"

4 **Add Reference Bands**

Normal ranges to be added:

• Heart Rate: 60-100

• Respiratory Rate: 12-18

• Systolic Blood Pressure: 90-120

• Diastolic Blood Pressure: 60-80

• Oxygen Saturation: 95-100%

» Click Analytics tab at top of Side Bar

» Locate "Reference Band" in Custom section and drag it into workspace

» In dialog box, drop Reference Band into Pane column for SUM(Heart Rate)

In "Edit Reference Line, Band, Box" dialog box:

» Band From:

• Value: select "Constant," then enter value of "60"

• Label: "None"

» Band To:

• Value: select "Constant," then enter value of "100"

• Label: "None"

» Fill: select a light gray shade

» Click "OK"

» Follow same steps for remaining vital signs, using ranges listed above

For "Oxygen Saturation," use values 0.95 and 1

5 **Format chart**

» Click "Data" tab to return to Dimensions/Measures window

» Right-click Measure "Oxygen Saturation"

» Select "Default Properties"

» Select "Number Format"

» Change to "Percentage" and "0" decimal places

» Right-click middle of chart

» Select "Format"

» At top of Format window, select icon of 3 horizontal lines to format lines

» Select "Rows" tab

» Click caret to right of "Grid Lines" and change to "None"

» Right-click X axis

» Uncheck "Show Header" checkmark

» Right-click Y axis for "Heart Rate"

» Select "Edit Axis"

» In General tab, edit Title to abbreviation (Heart Rate = HR)

» Select "Tick Marks" tab

» Change Major and Minor tick marks to "None"

» Follow same steps for each Y axis, abbreviating Respiratory Rate "RR", Systolic BP "SBP", Diastolic BP "DBP", and Oxygen Saturation "O2 Sat"

» Hover cursor over Y axis line until it changes to bidirectional arrow. Drag line to left to set appropriate width for labels

» On Marks card, click "All" tab to format labels on all lines

» Click "Label"

» Check box next to "Show mark labels"

» In Marks to Label section, select "Line Ends"

» In Options section, uncheck box for "Label start of line"

6 Add title

» Double-click Title Row at top of workspace to open Edit Title dialog box

» Enter title, "24-Hour Patient Vital Signs"

7 Rename worksheet tab and save worksheet

» Right-click worksheet tab at bottom of workspace, then select "Rename"

» Enter intuitive title, then cllick "Save" icon on Toolbar

CHAPTER 15

Area Chart

An Area Chart is an extension of a line chart. In an Area Chart, the space between each line and the next line is filled with a color to emphasize the magnitude of change in the measure over time. This chart visually displays a part-to-whole relationship where a set of layers for multiple categories flows along the corresponding time series. Since both line and Area Charts can be used to facilitate trend analysis, it is better to use the Area Chart when there is a summation relationship between the data sets. An Area Chart is not the best way to show specific values along the line, but it can clearly show total values to effectively display the way a dimension contributes to an overall trend.

How To: Build an Area Chart to display the change in amounts of US healthcare expenditures from 1980 to 2015.

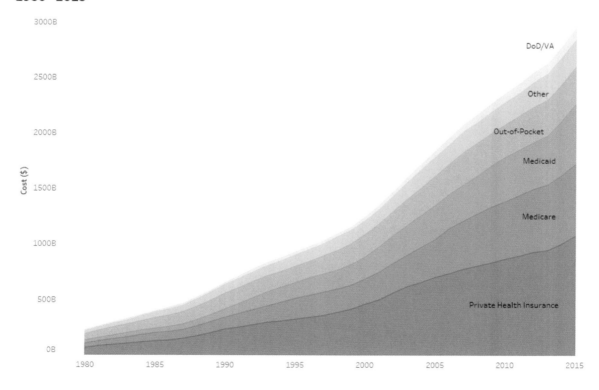

US Healthcare Expenditures by Type of Service/Source of Funds
1980 - 2015

Data Source: *Centers for Medicare and Medicaid Services*

About the Data: *The data for this exercise is from the dataset "National Health Expenditures by Type of Service and Source of Funds: Calendar Years 1980 to 2015."*

1 **Create a new worksheet and connect to the data**

» At the bottom of the Tableau workspace, click the icon for a new worksheet.

» In the Data pane, click the "11 - US Healthcare Expenditures" dataset.

2 **Create the chart**

» While holding down the Control key, select "Date" in the Dimensions window and "Cost ($)" in the Measures window.

» Go to the "Show Me" palette and select "area charts (continuous)."

» Click the "Show Me" tab again to close.

Tableau offers two types of Area Charts: Continuous and Discrete. Both appear on the Show Me menu. Discrete fields display data organized by row or column headers; Continuous fields display data along axes. Because the dataset in use contains data for every year from 1980 to 2015, a continuous Area Chart is the better choice here.

3 **Color the chart**

The resulting chart displays the sum of the Cost by Date. It must be disaggregated by Type of Service/Source of Funds.

» Drag and drop "Type of Service/Source of Funds" from the Dimensions window onto Color on the Marks card.

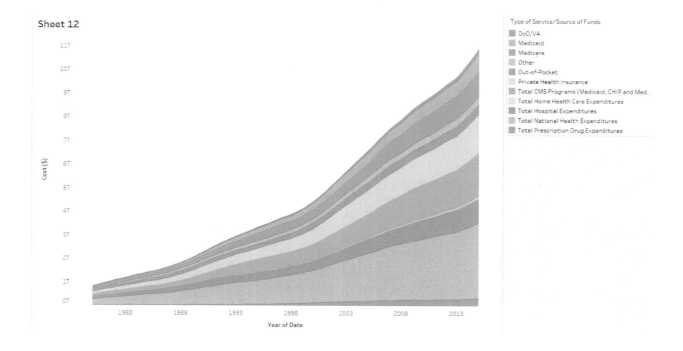

4   Analyze the data

Notice that the Y axis' top range is 11 trillion, and that the color legend lists different types of services as well as totals of different categories. Examine the data more closely to determine the next steps.

» Click the View Data icon to the right of the Dimensions header in the Dimensions window.

The misleadingly large costs are caused by overlapping categories and row-level totals in the dataset. National Health Expenditures is the only category of interest. Filtering resolves this problem.

>> Click the "X" at the top right of the View Data window to close the window.

5 Filter the data

Data can be filtered from the Filter shelf by inclusion or exclusion. Decide which filter method to use after evaluating what will happen if the data set is updated with new values. The two filtering activities shown here describe filtering by inclusion and then by exclusion, and illustrate the choices made in each case.

>> Drag and drop "Categories" from the Dimensions window onto the Filters shelf.

>> Click the "National Health Expenditures" checkbox, then click "OK."

Filter by Inclusion ▶

It is important to include only the desired data values in the report. To do so, include only "National Health Expenditures," thus ensuring that new values will not populate when the data is refreshed. For example, if "Hospice Expenditures" is later added to the Category field and the dataset is then renewed, the inclusion method will prevent the new data from interfering with the current report.

>> Drag and drop "Type of Service/Source of Funds" from the Dimensions window onto the Filters shelf.

The Dimension "Type of Service/Source of Funds" is already in the view (on Color on the Marks card); as a result, many of the boxes are already checked. Unchecked boxes result from the filter applied to the Categories field. The National Health Expenditures categories filter at a higher level. The new filter ("Type of Service...") is necessary to filter out "Totals" for row level Types of Service/Source of Funds.

» Click the "None" button to remove all checkmarks.

» Click the "Exclude" checkbox.

» Click all checkboxes for "Total..." fields, then click "OK."

◄ Filter by Exclusion

If a filtered value will never be needed, exclude it to ensure that other values will nonetheless populate when the data is refreshed. For example, if the category "DoD/VA" is replaced in the dataset by "DoD" and "VA," the exclusion method will ensure that the two new fields are present in the report.

The chart now looks like this:

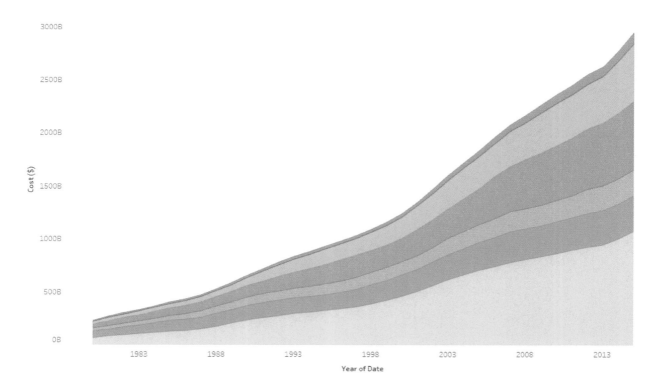

6 Format the chart

Alphabetical order is Tableau's default sort for Type of Service/Source of Funds. However, sorting by lowest cost to highest is more useful here.

» Right-click "Type of Service/Source of Funds" pill on Color on the Marks card.

» Select "Sort..."

A Sort dialog box appears.

» For "Sort order," select "Ascending."

» For "Sort by," select "Field," then "Cost($)."

» Under "Aggregation," select "Sum."

» Click "OK."

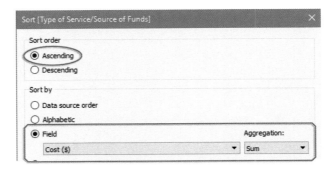

Visual Cue for Sort ▶

A sorted pill displays the Sort icon, so it's easy to tell if sorts have been applied in the current view. To clear the sort, right-click the sorted pill and select "Clear Sort." Alternatively, on the Toolbar, click the caret to the right of the Clear Sheet icon and select "Clear Sorts."

To edit the colors:

» Hover the cursor over the Color Legend header and click the caret that appears on the right.

» Select "Edit Colors..."

» Click the caret for the Select Color Palette menu, then change the color to Blue.

» Click the "Assign Palette" button to assign colors to all data items.

» Click "OK."

184

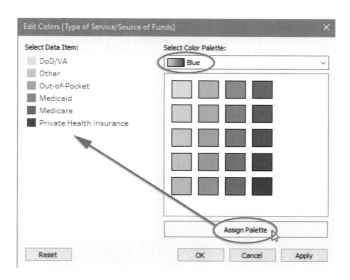

Add labels to each colored area:

» Drag and drop the "Type of Service/Source of Funds" from the Dimensions window onto Label on the Marks card.

Because of area segment size constraints, not all labels are displayed. To see them all:

» Click Label on the Marks card.

» Click Options "Allow labels to overlap other marks."

Allow Labels to Overlap Other Marks ▷

*In compressed visualizations, Tableau makes its best guess about what data labels will fit into a readable format. Choosing **Allow labels to overlap other marks** forces Tableau to display every labeled value. On charts where fields overlap, one solution is to manually reposition the labels where possible.*

To reposition the labels on each part of the area chart:

    »   Click a label. When the cursor changes to a +, click the label again to drag to and drop on the desired chart position.

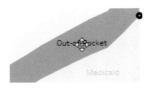

The chart now looks like this:

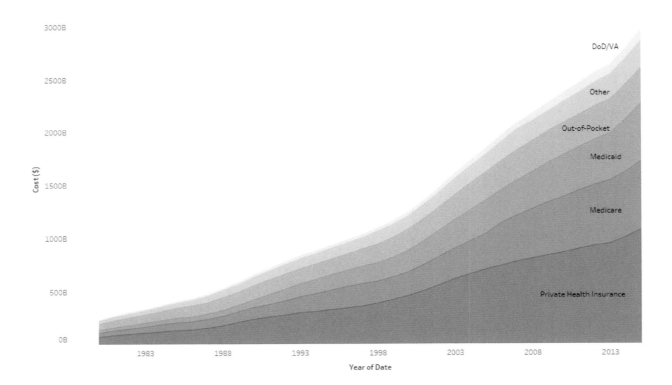

The years on the X axis can be edited for easier reading; the title is redundant, and can be removed.

>> Right-click the X axis.

>> Select "Edit axis...".

>> Highlight and delete the Title "Year of Date."

>> Click the "Tick Marks" tab at the top of the dialog box.

>> In the "Major tick marks" section, click "Fixed"

>> Change "Every:" to "5 years."

>> Navigate to the bottom of the dialog box and uncheck "Include times."

>> Change "Tick Origin:" to "1/1/80" by typing over the values for M/D/YY

>> Click "OK."

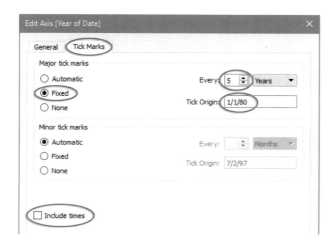

7 Add a title

>> Double-click the Title Row to open the Edit Title dialog box.

>> Enter the title, "US Healthcare Expenditures by Type of Service/Source of Funds 1980 – 2015."

8 Rename the worksheet tab and save the worksheet

>> Right-click the worksheet tab at the bottom of the workspace, then select "Rename."

>> Enter an intuitive title, then click the "Save" icon on the Tool bar.

The final Area Chart looks like this:

US Healthcare Expenditures by Type of Service/Source of Funds
1980 - 2015

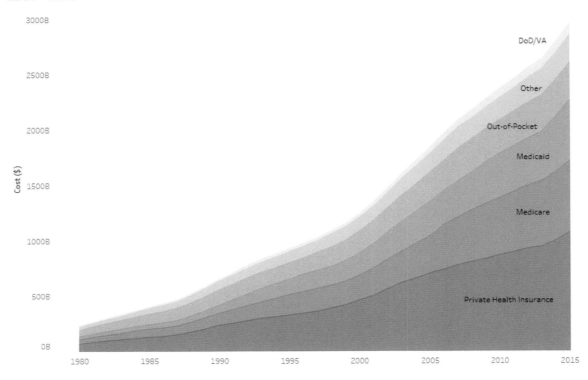

Insight: This Area Chart makes it clear that healthcare costs have risen dramatically in the last 30 years, with Private Health Insurance, Medicare, and Medicaid showing the biggest increases.

HD*Vizoom*™ ...to the Area Chart

1 Create new worksheet and connect to data

» At bottom of Tableau workspace, click icon for new worksheet

» In Data pane, click "11 – US Healthcare Expenditures" dataset

2 Create chart

» While holding down Control key, select "Date" in Dimensions window and "Cost ($)" in Measures window

» Go to "Show Me" palette and select "area charts (continuous)"

» Click "Show Me" tab again to close

3 Color chart

» Drag and drop "Type of Service/Source of Funds" from Dimensions window onto Color on Marks card

4 Analyze data

» Click View Data icon to right of Dimensions header in Dimensions window

» Click "X" at top right of View Data window to close window

5 Filter data

» Drag and drop "Categories" from Dimensions window onto Filters shelf

» Click "National Health Expenditures" checkbox, then click "OK"

» Drag and drop "Type of Service/ Source of Funds" from Dimensions window onto Filters shelf

» Click "None" button to remove all checkmarks

» Click "Exclude" checkbox

» Click all checkboxes for "Total..." fields, then click "OK"

6 Format chart

» Right-click "Type of Service/Source of Funds" pill on Color on Marks card

» Select "Sort..."

» For "Sort order," select "Ascending"

» For "Sort by," select "Field," then "Cost($)"

» Under "Aggregation," select "Sum"

» Click "OK"

» Hover cursor over Color Legend header and click caret that appears on right

» Select "Edit Colors..."

» Click caret for Select Color Palette menu, then change color to Blue

» Click "Assign Palette" button to assign colors to all data items

» Click "OK"

» Drag and drop "Type of Service/ Source of Funds" from Dimensions window onto Label on Marks card

» Click Label on Marks card

» Click Options "Allow labels to overlap other marks"

» Click label. When cursor changes to +, click label again to drag to and drop on desired chart position

» Right-click X axis

» Select "Edit axis..."

» Highlight and delete Title "Year of Date"

» Click "Tick Marks" tab at top of dialog box

» In "Major tick marks" section, click "Fixed"

» Change "Every:" to "5 years"

189

» Navigate to bottom of dialog box and uncheck "Include times"

» Change "Tick Origin:" to "1/1/80" by typing over values for M/D/YY

» Click "OK"

7 **Add title**

» Double-click Title Row to open Edit Title dialog box

» Enter title, "US Healthcare Expenditures by Type of Service/ Source of Funds 1980 – 2015"

8 **Rename worksheet tab and save worksheet**

» Right-click worksheet tab at bottom of workspace, then select "Rename."

» Enter intuitive title, then click "Save" icon on Toolbar

CHAPTER 16

Scatter Plot – Regression Line

A Scatter Plot is a chart of plotted points that show the relationship between two sets of data. Scatter Plots are useful for comparison/correlation of two measures and/or display of outliers in the data. Data are displayed as a collection of points (called "marks" in Tableau), each having the value of one variable determining the position on the X axis and the value of the other variable determining the position on the Y axis. A "line of best fit" (also called a "Trend Line" in Tableau) can be drawn to highlight the correlation between the variables. Another useful aspect of a Scatter Plot is its ability to show nonlinear relationships between variables.

A Scatter Plot may show that a relationship exists, but does not and cannot prove that one variable is affecting the other. There could be a third factor causing changes in either variable, or both; or some other systemic cause. Or the apparent relationship could be just a chance event. In any case, the Scatter Plot can suggest that two things are related, and if so, how they move together.

How To: Build a Scatter Plot to examine any possible relationship between clinic patients' BMI (Body Mass Index) and their systolic blood pressure.

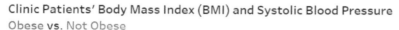

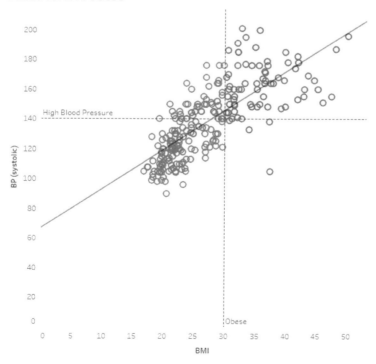

Clinic Patients' Body Mass Index (BMI) and Systolic Blood Pressure
Obese vs. Not Obese

Data Source: Mock patient weight and systolic blood pressure data

About the Data: 250 mock adult patients from a hospital clinic visit were selected to record their height, weight, and systolic blood pressure measurements for comparison.

1 Create a new worksheet and connect to the data

» Open a new worksheet.

» In the Data pane, select the "04 - Clinic Patients Metrics" dataset.

2 Create the chart

The dataset contains height and weight figures for each patient. A BMI can be calculated from these two measures. The formula to calculate a BMI is (body weight in kg) / (body height in meters)^2.

» Right-click "Weight(kg)" in the Measures window.

» Click "Create" to open a sub-menu.

» Select "Calculated field…"

Building a Calculated Field ▶

Building a Calculated Field based on a specific field (Dimension or Measure) automatically populates the Calculation window with that field. Starting with a specific field makes this process shorter and easier.

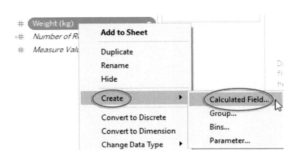

» Edit the field name to "BMI."

» In the formula window, enter:

```
[Weight (kg)]/([Height(cm)]/100)^2
```

» Click "OK."

» While holding down the Control key, click:
  • Dimensions: "Patient ID"
  • Measures: "BMI"
  • Measures: "BP (systolic)"

» Click the "Show Me" tab and select the highlighted "Scatter Plot."

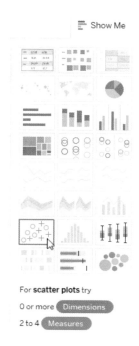

For **scatter plots** try

0 or more Dimensions

2 to 4 Measures

» Click the "Show Me" tab again to close the tab.

The chart now looks like this:

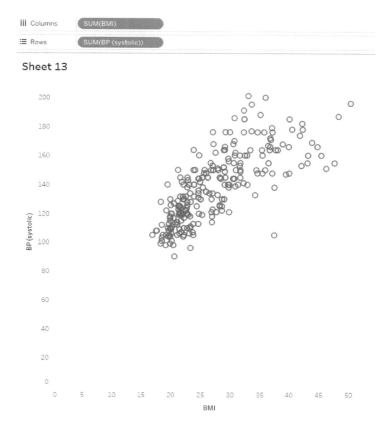

Best Practice

What variable goes on what axis?

The Independent variable, sometimes referred to as the "Possible Cause Variable" goes on the X axis. The Dependent variable, sometimes referred to as the "Response Variable," goes on the Y axis. If the terms "Independent" and "Dependent" get confusing, try to associate the X axis with the "possible cause" and the Y axis with the "possible effect." In this example, the "possible cause" is Body Mass Index (BMI) and the "possible effect" is elevated Blood Pressure.

3 Add a Trend Line

» Click the Analytics Tab in the Side Bar.

» Locate "Trend Line" under Model. Click and drag onto worksheet. An option menu appears.

» Drag Trend Line across "Linear," then drop it onto the highlighted "Linear" icon.

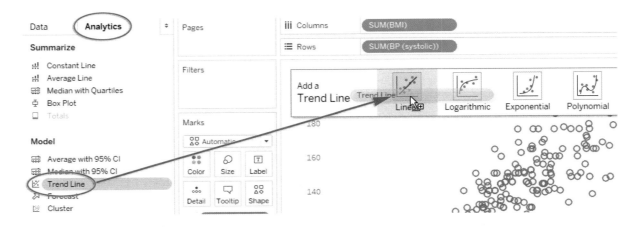

A Linear Trend Line is now present with corresponding Confidence Interval lines.

Tableau Trend Lines can be customized in many ways. For this example, the Confidence Intervals will be removed:

» Right-click the Trend Line. On the menu that appears:

» Click "Edit Trend Line…"

» In the dialog box that appears, uncheck the box "Show Confidence Bands."

Trend Lines ▶

"Describe Trend Line" and "Describe Trend Model" display statistical values, such as R-Squared and p-value, evaluating the reliability and predictive value of the trend line plot.

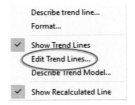

Tableau also offers on-the-fly analysis to custom-select marks of interest. To activate the Toolbar for this feature:

» Click "Worksheet" on the Menu Bar.

» Click "Show View Toolbar."

» Select "Show on Hover."

» Hover the cursor over the top left section of the Scatter Plot chart to display the View Toolbar.

» Click the caret and select the lasso option.

» Select a small number of scatter plot marks. The Trend Line will adjust for the selected marks.

» Click anywhere in the worksheet to discontinue the custom lasso.

4 Add Reference Lines

Obesity is defined as a BMI >= 30 kg/m2. High Blood Pressure is defined as a Systolic BP > 140 (and a Diastolic BP > 90). Reference Lines set to these values can help determine which patients fall in both categories. To add Reference Lines:

» With the Analytics tab in the Data pane selected, drag "Reference Line" into the workspace.

» In the dialog box that appears, drop the Reference Line onto the junction of "SUM(BMI)" and "Table."

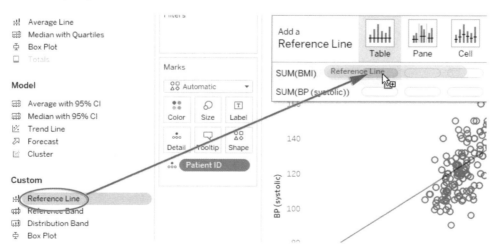

» In the "Edit Reference Line, Band, or Box" dialog box, edit as follows:

In the Line section,

- Value: click the caret and select "Constant," then enter "30" for the value.
- Label: click the caret and select "Custom." In the blank field that appears, enter "Obese."

In the Formatting section,

- Line: select dashed; the thinnest line option; and a lighter shade of gray.

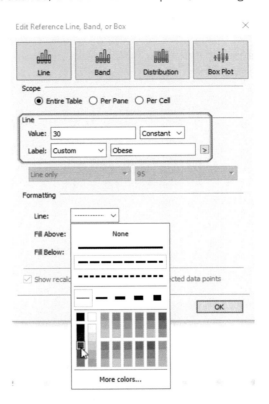

» Follow these steps again to add a second Reference Line, this one for SUM(BP(systolic)).

- Set the value to "140" and label the line "High Blood Pressure."

The chart now looks like this:

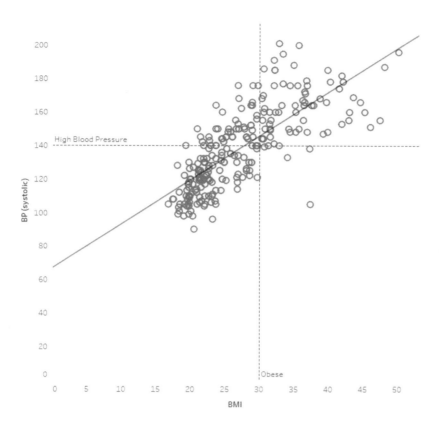

5 Color-encode select data

Color-encode the marks for BMI >= 30 to more easily identify the obesity cohort. To make the distinction between patients with a BMI >= 30 and those with a BMI < 30, use a calculated field:

»   Right-click "BMI" in the Measures window.

»   Click "Create..." then select "Calculated Field."

»   Enter the field name "Obese?."

»   Enter the following calculation: **[BMI] >= 30**

»   Then click "OK."

◄ Boolean Calculations

Use Boolean calculations instead of logical ones whenever possible for better performance. While a logical calculation of "IF [BMI] >=30 THEN "Obese" ELSE "Not Obese" END" would work, the resulting performance would be slower.

The "Obese?" calculated field is now a new field in the Dimensions window. Notice that the data type icon is "=T/F", indicating a Boolean data type.

» Drag and drop "Obese?" from the Dimensions window onto Color on the Marks card. One color is assigned to the "True" cohort (patients with BMI >= 30); another color to the "False" cohort (patients with BMI < 30).

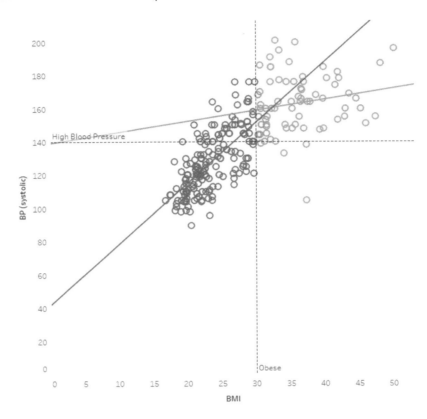

Each group of patients now has a corresponding trend line. To have just one trend line representing the whole sample population:

» Right-click either trend line.

» Select "Edit Trend Lines…"

» Uncheck the box "Allow a trend line per color."

» Click "OK."

To edit the colors:

» Hover over the Color Legend header until a caret appears at the right side of the header.

» Click the caret.

» Select "Edit Colors."

» Click the caret for "Select Color Palette" and choose "Color Blind."

» Click the Data Item "False" to highlight and select the medium-dark gray color.

» Click the Data Item "True" to highlight and select the dark orange color.

» Click "OK."

The color legend labels currently read "False" and "True." Changing the labels to "Obese" and "Not Obese" is clearer. To edit the labels:

» Right-click the "Obese?" calculated field in the Dimensions window.

» Select the "Aliases..." option.

» Click "False" under the "Value (Alias)" column, then change to "Not Obese." Note that an asterisk appears in the Has Alias column once the name has been changed.

» Click "True" under the "Value (Alias)" column and change to "Obese."

» Click "OK."

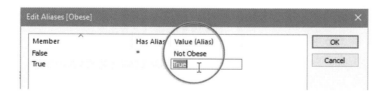

6 Add a title

» Enter the title, "Correlation of Clinic Patients' Body Mass Index (BMI) and Systolic Blood Pressure Obese vs. Not Obese"

» Highlight "Obese" and click the caret for the color icon.

» Select "More Colors."

» Click the "Pick Screen Color" button.

» Hover cursor over the "Obese" color in the color legend, then click to save the color.

» Follow the same steps to edit the font color for "Not Obese."

7 Rename the worksheet tab and save the worksheet

» Right-click the worksheet tab at the bottom of the workspace, then select "Rename."

» Enter an intuitive title, then click the "Save" icon on the Tool bar.

The final chart looks like this:

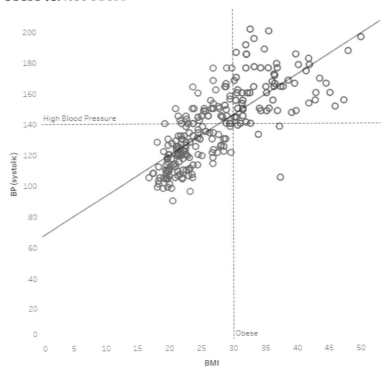

Clinic Patients' Body Mass Index (BMI) and Systolic Blood Pressure
Obese vs. Not Obese

Insight: This Scatter Plot chart displays what seems to be a positive correlation between BMI and Systolic blood pressure.

HDVizoom™ ...to the Scatter Plot

1 Create new worksheet and connect to data

» Open new worksheet

» In Data pane, select "04 – Clinic Patients Metrics" dataset

2 Create chart

» Right-click "Weight (kg)" in Measures window

» Click "Create" to open sub-menu

» Select "Calculated Field"

» Edit field name to "BMI"

» In formula window, enter:

`[Weight(kg)]/([Height(cm)]/100)^2`

» Click "OK"

» While holding down Control key, click:

- Dimensions: "Patient ID"
- Measures: "BMI"
- Measures: "BP (systolic)"

» Click "Show Me" tab and select highlighted "Scatter Plot"

» Click "Show Me" tab again to close

3 Add Trend Line

» Click Analytics Tab in Side Bar

» Locate "Trend Line" under Model. Click and drag onto worksheet

» Drag Trend Line across "Linear," then drop it onto highlighted "Linear" icon

» Right-click Trend Line to display sub-menu

» Click "Edit Trend Line..."

» In dialog box that appears, uncheck box "Show Confidence Bands"

» Click "Worksheet" on Menu Bar

» Click "Show View Toolbar"

» Select "Show on Hover"

» Hover cursor over top left section of Scatter Plot chart to display View Toolbar

» Click caret and select Lasso option

» Select small number of scatter plot marks to view readjustment of Trend Line

» Click anywhere on worksheet to discontinue custom lasso

4 Add Reference Lines

» Select Analytics tab in Data pane

» Drag "Reference Line" into workspace

» In dialog box that appears, drop Reference Line onto junction of "SUM(BMI)" and "Table"

» In "Edit Reference Line, Band, or Box" dialog box, edit as follows:

In Line section,

- Value: click caret and select "Constant," then enter "30" for value
- Label: click caret and select "Custom." In blank field that appears, enter "Obese"

In Formatting section,

- Line: select dashed; thinnest line option; and lighter shade of gray

» Follow steps again to add second Reference Line, this one for SUM(BP(systolic))

- Set value to "140" and label line "High Blood Pressure"

5 Color-encode select data

» Right-click "BMI" in Measures window

» Click "Create" then select "Calculated Field"

» Enter field name "Obese?"

» Enter calculation: [BMI] >= 30

» Click "OK"

» Drag and drop "Obese?" from Dimensions window onto Color on Marks card. One color is assigned to "True" cohort (BMI >= 30), another color to "False" cohort (BMI < 30)

» Right-click either trend line

» Select "Edit Trend Lines..."

» Uncheck box "Allow trend line per color"

» Click "OK"

» Hover over Color Legend header until caret appears at right side of header

» Click caret

» Select "Edit Colors..."

» Click caret for "Select Color Palette" and choose "Color Blind"

» Click Data item "False" to highlight and select medium-dark gray color

» Click Data item "True" to highlight and select dark orange/brown color

» Click "OK"

» Right click "Obese?" calculated field in Dimensions window

» Select "Aliases..." option

» Click "False" under "Value (Alias)" column and change to "Not Obese"

» Click "True" under "Value (Alias)" column and change to "Obese"

» Click "OK"

6 **Add title**

» Enter title, "Correlation of Clinic Patients' Body Mass Index (BMI) and Systolic Blood Pressure Obese vs. Not Obese"

» Highlight "Obese" and click caret for color icon

» Select "More Colors"

» Click "Pick Screen Color" button. Hover cursor over "Obese" color in color legend then click to save color

» Follow same steps to edit font color for "Not Obese"

7 **Rename worksheet tab and save worksheet**

» Right-click worksheet tab at bottom of workspace, then select "Rename"

» Enter intuitive title, then click "Save" icon on Tool bar

Intermediate Charts

CHAPTER 17

Box-and-Whisker Plot

A Box-and-Whisker Plot illustrates the distribution of a data set, highlighting the spread of percentiles: minimum value; 25th, 50th, and 75th percentiles; and maximum value. "Boxes" enclose the middle 50% of the data, known as the middle two quartiles of the distribution. "Whiskers" are the lines that encode the top and bottom range of data values. The whiskers can be placed at a location to display the most widely separated data points in the distribution of the data or at a location that is 1.5 times further out than the width of the adjoining box, known as the interquartile range (IQR).

Although Box-and-Whisker Plots look similar to Bar Charts, they are very different. Whereas a Bar Chart encodes and displays a single value, a Box-and-Whisker Plot features a range of values from lowest to highest, and allows comparison of the distribution of those values to other value ranges and distributions.

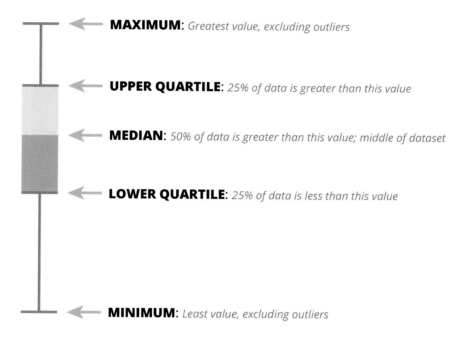

MAXIMUM: *Greatest value, excluding outliers*

UPPER QUARTILE: *25% of data is greater than this value*

MEDIAN: *50% of data is greater than this value; middle of dataset*

LOWER QUARTILE: *25% of data is less than this value*

MINIMUM: *Least value, excluding outliers*

How To: Build a Box-and-Whisker Plot chart showing the distribution of cardiovascular patients' ages by race.

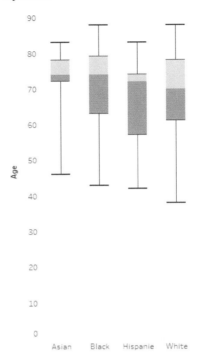

Age Distribution of Cardiovascular Clinic Patients By Race

Data Source: *De-identified hospital data*

About the Data: *Age and race of selected hospital clinic patients being examined for cardiovascular disease.*

1 Create a new worksheet and connect to the data

» At the bottom of the Tableau workspace, click the icon for a new worksheet.

» In the Data pane, select the "12 - Clinic Patient Demographics" dataset.

2 Create the chart

» Holding down the Control key, click:
- "Pt ID" in the Dimensions window.
- "Race" in the Dimensions window.
- "Age" in the Measures window.

» Click the "Show Me" tab.

» Select the "Box-and-Whisker Plot" icon.

» Click "Show Me" again to close the tab.

The chart initially looks like this:

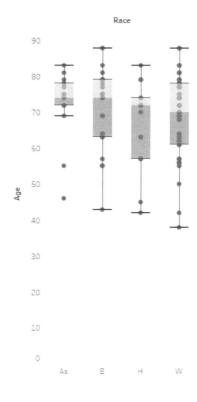

◀ Box-and-Whisker Creation

The Show Me button creates a basic Box-and-Whisker Plot based on the data selected. Individual marks (blue dots) plot each patient's age on the vertical axis. All elements of the visualization, including the blue dots, are controlled through the Edit Reference Line, Band, or Box menu.

3 Format the whiskers

Tableau automatically formats the whiskers to be 1.5 times the Interquartile Range (IQR). For this particular chart, the whiskers should contain maximum and minimum age values for patients. To edit:

» Right-click the Y axis.

» Select "Edit Reference Line."

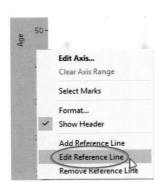

» For "Plot Options, Whiskers extend to," click the caret on the drop-down menu and select "Maximum extent of the data."

» Check the box "Hide underlying marks (except outliers)."

» In the "Formatting" section, format the chart with desired colors.

Best Practice

Showing individual underlying marks often clutters the visualization, so they can be suppressed.

Box-and-Whisker Customization ▶

The Edit Reference Line dialog box enables customization of the style, fill, border, and whisker formatting on the Box Plot menu.

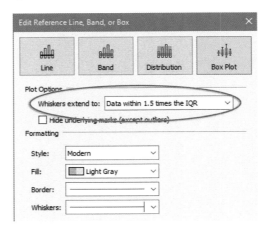

The chart now looks like this:

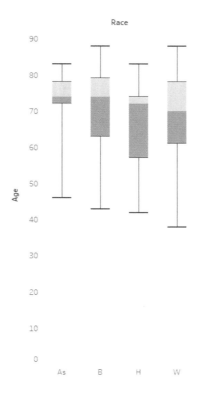

4 Format the chart

To clarify and streamline the display of Aliases:

» Right-click the "Race" pill on the Columns shelf.

» Select "Edit Aliases" from the context menu.

» Click in the "Value (Alias)" column to highlight.

» Type the full name of each race, then click "OK".

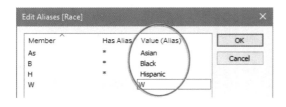

◀ **Edit Aliases**

Dimension headers may be changed by assigning Aliases. This change does not affect the underlying data, but does propagate the Alias through all worksheets in the workbook using that Dimension. This feature permits clarifying display data without the need to alter underlying information. Note that every Alias value must have a unique name.

To remove the Header:

» Right-click the "Race" header at the top of the chart.

» Select "Hide Field Labels for Columns."

5 Add a title

» Double-click the Title Row to open the Edit Title dialog box.

» Enter the title, "Age Distribution of Cardiovascular Clinic Patients by Race."

6 Rename the worksheet tab and save the worksheet

» Right-click the worksheet tab at the bottom of the workspace, then select "Rename."

» Enter an intuitive title, then click the "Save" icon on the Toolbar.

The final chart looks like this:

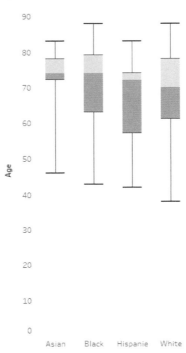

Age Distribution of Cardiovascular Clinic Patients By Race

Insight: The Box-and-Whisker Plot makes clear the distribution of age by race of cardiovascular patients. Here in particular, it is apparent that while overall age range is very similar in Asian and Hispanic patients, the middle 50% of Asian patients are much older (72-78) than the middle 50% of Hispanic patients (57-74).

▋▙ *HDVizoom*™...to the Box-and-Whisker Plot Chart

1 Create new worksheet and connect to data

» At bottom of Tableau workspace, click icon for new worksheet

» In Data pane, select "12 - Clinic Patient Demographics" dataset

2 Create chart

» Holding down Control key, click:
- "Pt ID" in Dimensions window
- "Race" in Dimensions window
- "Age" in Measures window

» Click "Show Me" tab

» Select "Box-and-Whisker Plot" icon

» Click "Show Me" again to close

3 Format whiskers

» Right-click "Y axis"

» Select "Edit Reference Line"

» For "Plot Options, Whiskers extend to," click caret of drop-down menu and change to "Maximum extent of the data"

» Check box for "Hide underlying marks (except outliers)"

» In Formatting section, format with desired colors

4 Format chart

» Right-click "Race" pill on Columns shelf

» Select "Edit Aliases" from context menu

» Click in "Value (Alias)" column to highlight

» Type full name of each race, then click "OK"

» Right-click "Race" header at top of chart

» Select "Hide Field Labels for Columns"

5 Add title

» Double-click Title Row to open Edit Title dialog box

» Enter title, "Age Distribution of Cardiovascular Clinic Patients by Race"

6 Rename worksheet tab and save worksheet

» Right-click worksheet tab at bottom of workspace, then select "Rename"

» Enter intuitive title, then click "Save" icon on Toolbar

211

CHAPTER 18

Maps

Maps are an intuitive and increasingly widely used way to visualize data, especially if location is crucial to the problems being analyzed. Geographic Maps are simply scatter plots that use longitude and latitude as X and Y coordinates and maps as background images.

There are two types of Maps: Symbol and Filled. Size- and/or color-encoded shapes represent data on Symbol Maps. A Filled Map, sometimes called a choropleth map, is a modification of a traditional marks map. Its study areas are filled with the measure of interest, and colors are used with different hues or diverging progression to assist in identifying areas of the measure performance. Filled Maps are the most common way to map regional data.

Tableau geocodes at the following levels: Country/Region; State/Province; City; Congressional District (U.S.); County; CBSA (Core-Based Statistical Area)/MSA (Metropolitan Statistical Area); Area Code (U.S.); ZIP Code/Postcode; and Airport (International Air Transport Association [IATA] and International Civil Aviation Organization [ICAO]), and NUTS Europe (Nomenclature of Territorial Units for Statistics). Overlaying demographic data adds useful information from the U.S. Census, such as median income, population, and race.

18.1 Filled Maps

How To: Build a Filled Map for U.S. Cancer Mortality Rates to show states that have the highest and lowest rates. (Instructions for Symbol Map conversion begin on page 222.)

2013 Cancer Mortality Rates (per 100,000) by State
All Cancers, All Patients

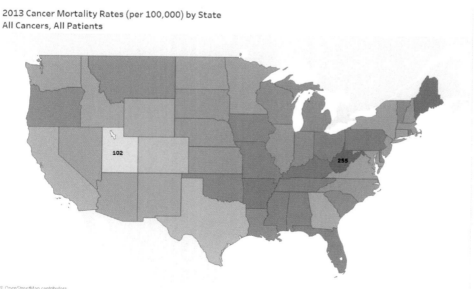

© OpenStreetMap contributors

Data Source: National Cancer Institute (www.cancer.gov).

About the Data: 2013 cancer death rates by state (all types of cancer, per 100,000 people).

1 Create a new worksheet and connect to the data

» At the bottom of the Tableau workspace, click the icon for a new worksheet.

» In the Data pane, select the "13 - Cancer Death Rates by State" dataset.

2 Create the chart

» Holding down the Control key, click "State" in the Dimensions window and "Crude Death Rate" in the Measures window.

» Click the "Show Me" tab and select "Filled Map."

» Click "Show Me" again to close.

3 Highlight continental United States

For this display, the area under study will be limited to the continental United States.

» To select this area only, hover the cursor in the top left corner of the Map workspace to display a column of icons.

» Click the bottom (caret) icon, then choose the Rectangular Selection icon.

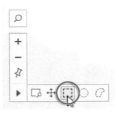

Map Options ▶

View Toolbar: this toolbar enables viewer interactivity with the map and can be customized.

Show/Hide View Toolbar: Click Worksheet on the Menu bar, then select Show View Toolbar.

Edit Icons in View Toolbar: Click Map on the Menu bar, then select Map Options. The Map Options menu enables customization of what appears on the View Toolbar. There is also an option to display map scale.

214

» Place the cursor in the upper left hand corner of the continental US map. While holding the left mouse button down, draw the cursor diagonally across the US, toward Florida to generate a box.

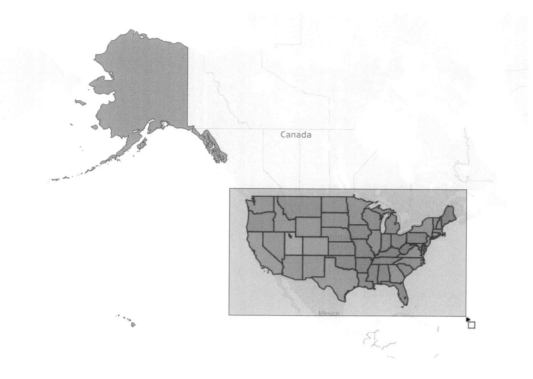

» Once the box covers the entire continental US, release the mouse button. The borders of the continental US are now highlighted and a small menu appears.

◄ Refresher

Using the Keep Only or Exclude options creates a filter. In this example, the filter is by state.

» On this menu, select "Keep Only."

The map now looks like this, with the range in mortality rate represented by color variation.

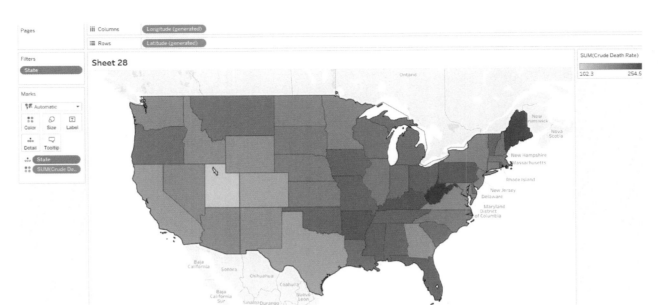

▲ Tableau Map Creation

Tableau must identify a Dimension as geographic to use it for maps; once it has done so, it automatically geocodes the data. When the data has been loaded, Tableau determines geographic fields using field names such as city, state, zip code, or airport codes. It will also generate latitude/longitude for those fields. Tableau places a global icon next to the field name in the Data window and, by default, displays a background map downloaded from the Internet behind the X/Y coordinate map marks. The resulting fields can overlay the data on live maps to analyze it spatially.

4 Format the chart

To identify the states with the highest and lowest death rates:

» Click "Label" on the Marks card.

» Click the "Show mark labels" checkbox.

» In the Marks to Label section, select "Min/Max."

» In the Scope section, select "Table."

» In the Label Appearance section, click the caret to the right of Font. Change the font to Tableau Semibold, 10-point. Click the Bold icon.

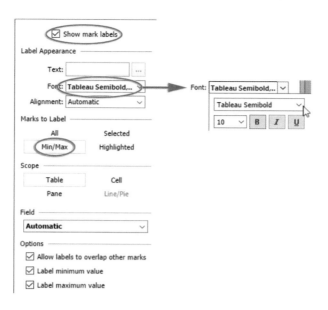

Remove the decimal places from the number values:

» Right-click "Crude Death Rate" in the Measures window.

» Click "Default Properties."

» Click "Number Format."

» Select "Number (Custom)."

» Decrease Decimal places to "0."

Edit the map color:

» Hover over the header for the color legend until a caret appears at the right corner.

» Click the caret.

» Select "Edit Colors" from the submenu.

» Click the caret for the Palette color drop-down menu.

» Select the color "Blue," then click "OK."

The map currently displays unneeded state and country labels. To remove these:

» Click "Map" on the Menu bar.

» Select "Map Layers" from the submenu.

The Side Bar is replaced with the Map Layers pane; this feature allows formatting of the Map background and layers such as Country and State names and borders.

» In the "Map Layers" section, click to remove the checkmarks in all boxes except "Base."

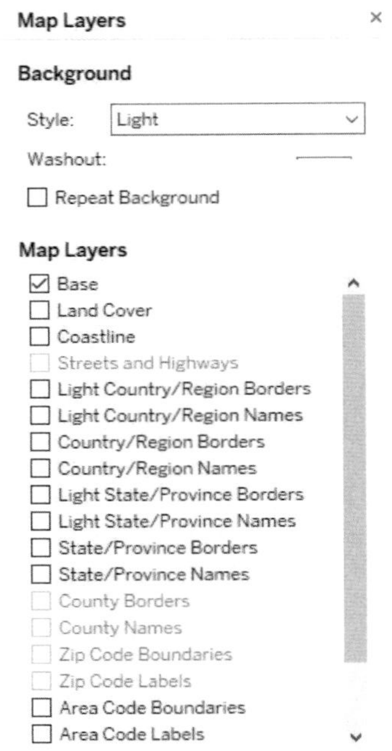

Map Layers   ×

Background

Style: Light ⌄

Washout: —

☐ Repeat Background

Map Layers

☑ Base
☐ Land Cover
☐ Coastline
☐ Streets and Highways
☐ Light Country/Region Borders
☐ Light Country/Region Names
☐ Country/Region Borders
☐ Country/Region Names
☐ Light State/Province Borders
☐ Light State/Province Names
☐ State/Province Borders
☐ State/Province Names
☐ County Borders
☐ County Names
☐ Zip Code Boundaries
☐ Zip Code Labels
☐ Area Code Boundaries
☐ Area Code Labels

Customizing Maps ▶

Tableau can customize maps in a variety of ways. Aspects of Backgrounds, Map Layers, and Data Layers can be added, removed, or modified.

5   **Add a title**

   »   Double-click the Title Row to open the Edit Title dialog box.

   »   Enter the title, "2013 Cancer Mortality Rates (per 100,000) by State, All Cancers, All Patients."

6   **Rename the worksheet tab and save the worksheet**

   »   Right-click the worksheet tab at the bottom of the workspace, then select "Rename."

   »   Enter an intuitive title, then click the "Save" icon on the Tool bar.

The final Filled Map looks like this:

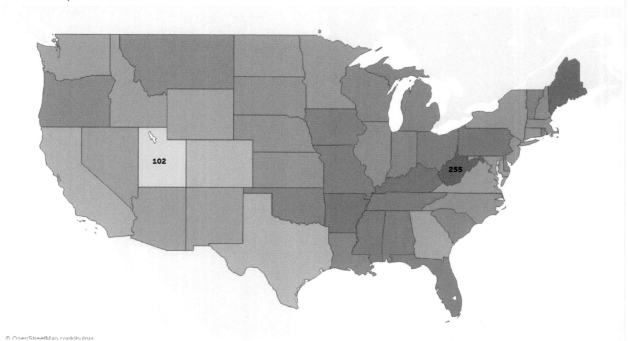

2013 Cancer Mortality Rates (per 100,000) by State
All Cancers, All Patients

102

255

© OpenStreetMap contributors

Insight: On this Filled Map, Utah is the lightest shade of blue because it had the lowest rate of cancer deaths in 2013 (102 per 100,000), and West Virginia is the darkest shade because it had the highest cancer death rate that year (255 per 100,000).

18.2 Symbol Maps

S ymbol Maps can offer additional insight that Filled Maps cannot through the use of Data Layers. The same data displayed in the Filled Map above is here shown on a Symbol Map, with an additional Data Layer (in this example, Per Capita Income).

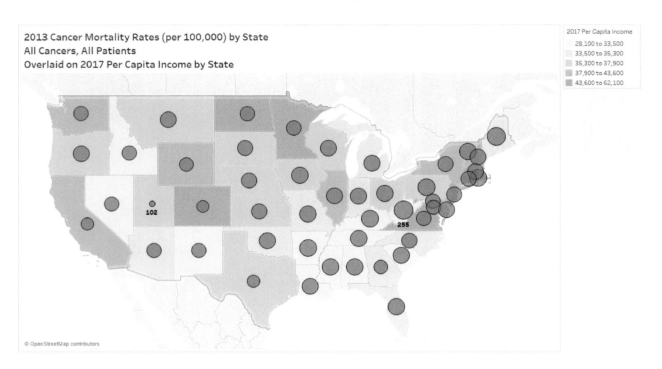

2013 Cancer Mortality Rates (per 100,000) by State
All Cancers, All Patients
Overlaid on 2017 Per Capita Income by State

2017 Per Capita Income
- 28,100 to 33,500
- 33,500 to 35,300
- 35,300 to 37,900
- 37,900 to 43,600
- 43,600 to 62,100

© OpenStreetMap contributors

1 **Duplicate the worksheet**

» Right-click the Filled Map worksheet tab at the bottom of the worksheet.

» Select "Duplicate Sheet" from the menu.

2 **Convert the map**

To create this Symbol Map from the previous Filled Map,

» Click the "Show Me" tab.

» Select "Symbol Map."

» Click "Show Me" again to close.

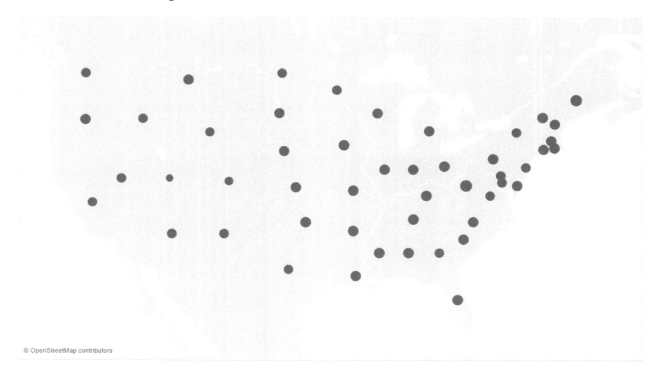

© OpenStreetMap contributors

3 Format the map

Because this map uses symbols to encode the data, state and country outlines are needed.

» Click "Map" on the Menu bar.

» Select "Map Layers."

» In the Map Layers section, click the box for "Light State/Province Borders."

The size of the blue circles encodes the Crude Death Rate by state, but the size range is so small that the symbols initially appear to be the same. To adjust them:

» Click the caret to the right of the "SUM(Crude Death Rate)" size legend to open the drop-down menu.

» Select "Edit Sizes..." A dialog box appears.

» Under "Sizes vary:" choose "By range" on the drop-down menu.

» Adjust "Mark size range:" as desired (both ends of the slider are adjustable).

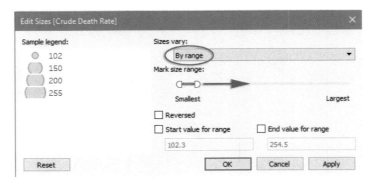

» Click "Size" on the Marks card.

» Adjust the slider to the right so that all symbols increase in size (and Utah's symbol is a bit more visible).

» Click "Color" on the Marks card.

» Under Effects, change the Border to Black (or the preferred color).

» If the symbols are too bright, adjust Opacity to preference (this example is at 60%).

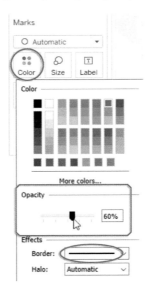

Best Practice

Adding a border to the marks on a Symbol Map with many overlapping marks can often help improve readability.

To add a Label to the states with the highest and lowest rates:

» Drag and drop "Crude Death Rate" from the Measures window onto Label on the Marks card.

» Click "Label" to open.

» Change the font to "Tableau Semibold," 10-point, and add Bold.

» In the Marks to Label section, select "Min/Max."

» In the Scope section, select "Table."

The map now looks like this:

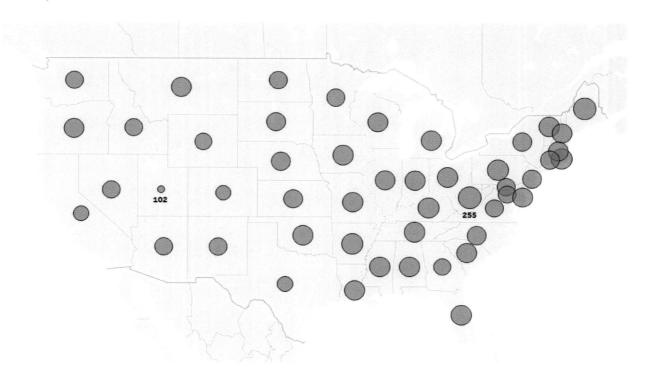

4 Add the Data Layer

Data Layers can add another level of interest to the map with categories such as US Population, US Population By Race, US Occupations, US Households, and US Housing information. To add a Data Layer:

» Click "Map" on the Menu bar.

» Select "Map Layers."

» Locate "Data Layer" below the Map Layers section of the window and click the caret to its right to open the drop-down menu.

» Select "Per Capita Income."

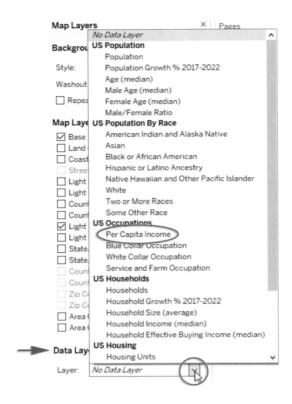

- Next to "By:" select "State."
- Next to "Using:" select "Blue-Green Sequential."

Best Practice

It is not recommended to use a Data Layer with a Filled Map because the two encoded colors conflict and are hard to interpret accurately.

5 Edit the title

» Adjust title to include information on the added data layer: "Overlaid on 2017 Per Capita Income by State"

6 Rename the worksheet tab and save the worksheet

» Right-click the worksheet tab at the bottom of the workspace, then select "Rename."

» Enter an intuitive title, then click the "Save" icon on the Toolbar.

The final map looks like this. Although comparing Cancer Mortality data from 2013 and Per Capita Income from 2017 is not ideal, the title and legend have been labeled with the year to clarify the difference. (The most recently available cancer mortality data was for 2013.)

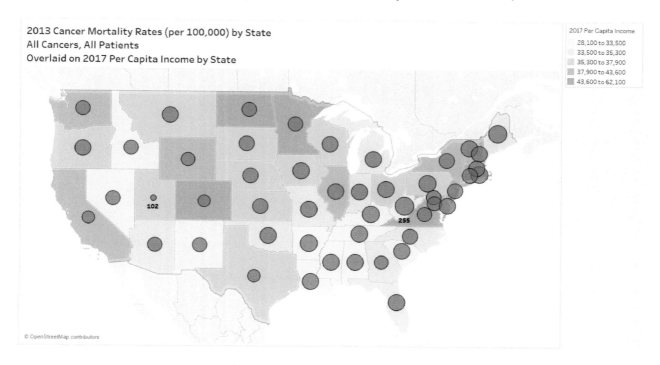

2013 Cancer Mortality Rates (per 100,000) by State
All Cancers, All Patients
Overlaid on 2017 Per Capita Income by State

2017 Per Capita Income
28,100 to 33,500
33,500 to 35,300
35,300 to 37,900
37,900 to 43,600
43,600 to 62,100

© OpenStreetMap contributors

Insight: West Virginia has a cancer rate (255 deaths per 100,000) more than twice the Utah rate (102 deaths per 100,000) and a per capita income range ($28,100 to $33,500) lower than Utah's ($35,300 to $37,900).

▌▍ *HDVizoom*™ ...to Filled and Symbol Maps

1 Create new worksheet and connect to data

» At bottom of Tableau workspace, click icon for new worksheet

» In Data pane, select "13 - Cancer Death Rates by State" dataset

2 Create chart

» Holding down Control key, click "State" in Dimensions window and "Crude Death Rate" in Measures window

» Click "Show Me" tab and select "Filled Map"

» Click "Show Me" again to close

3 Highlight continental United States

» To select this area only, hover cursor in top left corner of Map workspace to display column of icons

» Click bottom (caret) icon, then choose Rectangular Selection icon

» Place cursor in upper left hand corner of continental US map. While holding left mouse button down, draw cursor diagonally across US toward Florida, to generate a box

» Once box covers entire continental US, release mouse button

» On menu that appears, select "Keep Only"

4 Format chart

» Click "Label" on Marks card

» Click "Show mark labels" checkbox

» In Marks to Label section, select "Min/Max"

» In Scope section, select "Table"

» In Label Appearance section, click caret to right of Font. Change font

to Tableau Semibold, 10-point. Click Bold icon

» Right-click "Crude Death Rate" in Measures window

» Click "Default Properties"

» Click "Number Format"

» Select "Number (Custom)"

» Decrease Decimal places to "0"

» Hover over header for color legend until caret appears at right corner

» Click caret

» Select "Edit Colors" from submenu

» Click caret for Palette color drop-down menu

» Select color "Blue," then click "OK"

» Click "Map" on Menu bar

» Select "Map Layers" from submenu

» In "Map Layers" section, click to remove checkmarks in all boxes except "Base"

5 Add title

» Double-click Title Row to open Edit Title dialog box

» Enter title, "2013 Cancer Mortality Rates (per 100,000) by State, All Cancers, All Patients"

6 Rename worksheet tab and save worksheet

» Right-click on worksheet tab at bottom of workspace, the select "Rename"

» Enter intuitive title, then click "Save" on Toolbar

Conversion to Symbol Map

1 Duplicate worksheet

» Right-click Filled Map worksheet tab at bottom of worksheet

» Select "Duplicate Sheet" from menu

2 Convert map

» Click "Show Me" tab

» Select "Symbol Map"

» Click "Show Me" again to close

3 Format map

» Click "Map" on Menu bar

» Select "Map Layers"

» In Map Layers section, click box for "Light State/Province Borders"

» Click caret to right of "SUM(Crude Death Rate)" size legend to open drop-down menu

» Select "Edit Sizes..."

» Under "Sizes vary:" choose "By range" on drop-down menu

» Adjust "Mark size range:" as desired (both ends of slider are adjustable)

» Click "Size" on Marks card

» Adjust the slider to right so that all symbols increase in size (and Utah's symbol is a bit more visible)

» Click "Color" on Marks card

» Under Effects, change Border to Black (or the preferred color)

» If symbols are too bright, adjust Opacity to preference (this example is at 60%)

» Drag and drop "Crude Death Rate" from Measures window onto Label on Marks card

» Click "Label" to open

» Change font to "Tableau Semibold," 10-point, and add Bold

» In Marks to Label section, select "Min/Max"

» In Scope section, select "Table"

4 Add Data Layer

» Click "Map" on Menu bar

» Select "Map Layers"

» Locate "Data Layer" below Map Layers section of window and click caret to its right to open drop-down menu

» Select "Per Capita Income"

• Next to "By:" select "State"

• Next to "Using:" select "Blue-Green Sequential"

5 Edit title

» Adjust title to include information on added data layer: "Overlaid on 2017 Per Capita Income by State"

6 Rename worksheet tab and save worksheet

» Right-click on worksheet tab at bottom of workspace, the select "Rename"

» Enter intuitive title, then click "Save" on Tool bar

227

CHAPTER 19

Bullet Graph

Designed by Stephen Few, a Bullet Graph is a variation of the bar chart that provides a multi-faceted display of data in a linear design, eliminating the need for meters or gauges. The Bullet Graph features three elements: a primary performance measure, a target, and a range for context. The graph compares the performance measure, represented by a horizontal bar, to another value, represented by a vertical line, and relates performance to quantitative ranges. These ranges are displayed as varying intensities of a single hue such as gray, to make them clearly visible to colorblind users.

The following diagram displays the different parts of a Bullet Graph:

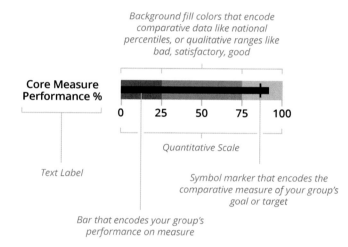

How To: Build a Bullet Graph displaying a Physician Group's performance on HEDIS Measures for Comprehensive Diabetes Care compared to a target goal and quantitative performance (poor, fair, good).

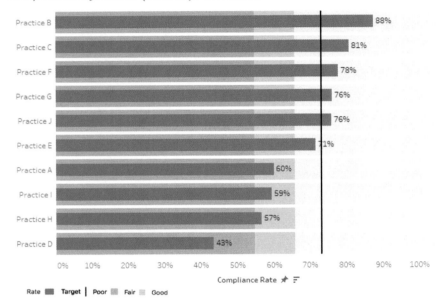

2016 Compliance Rates of Physician Group Practices
For HEDIS Measure: Comprehensive Diabetes Care
Component: Eye Exam (Retinal) Performed

HEDIS Measure Components
- ◉ Eye Exam (Retinal) Performed
- ○ Hemoglobin A1c (HbA1c) Control (< 8.0%)
- ○ Hemoglobin A1c (HbA1c) Testing
- ○ Medical Attention for Nephropathy

Rate ■ Target │ Poor ■ Fair ■ Good

Data Source: *mock physician group data for HEDIS measure "Comprehensive Diabetes Care" and mock target and quantitative performance ranges*

About the Data: *The Healthcare Effectiveness Data and Information Set (HEDIS) is a set of performance measures designed to provide consumers and regulators with information to reliably compare competing managed-care health plans. HEDIS measures form a report card that evaluates a health plan's success in providing preventive care via the physicians in a plan's provider network.*

1 **Create a new worksheet and connect to the data**

» At the bottom of the Tableau workspace, click the icon for a new worksheet.

» In the Data pane, select the "14 – HEDIS Comprehensive Diabetes Care" dataset.

2 Create the chart

» While holding down the Control key, click:
  - "Physician Group" in the Dimensions window
  - "Compliance Rate" in the Measures window
  - "Target" in the Measures window

» Click the "Show Me" tab and select "Bullet Graph."

» Click the Show Me tab again to close.

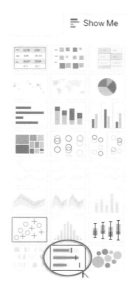

The chart initially looks like this:

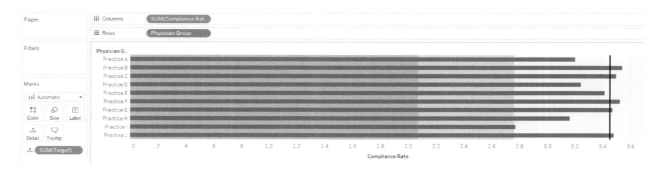

▲ Bullet Graph Creation

The Show Me feature automatically (1) adds any Dimension to the Rows shelf to divide data according to categories; (2) adds one Measure to the Columns shelf to serve as the primary metric (blue bar); (3) adds one Measure to Details of the Marks card to create the target and distribution reference lines.

If after these steps Tableau has created a Bullet Graph that is the inverse of what was intended, the two Measure fields can be switched by right-clicking on the X axis and selecting Swap Reference Line Fields.

231

3 **Filter the data**

The bars currently represent the aggregation of the four component measures of HEDIS Comprehensive Diabetes Care for each Physician Group. A filter menu can be added for the end-user to select the desired measure for viewing.

>> Right-click "HEDIS Measure Components" in the Dimensions window.

>> Select "Show Filter" from the sub-menu. The filter will appear to the right of the Bullet Graph.

>> Hover the cursor over the filter menu header and click the caret that appears in the top right corner.

>> Select the "Single Value (list)" option.

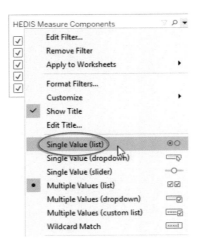

>> Click the filter menu header caret again.

>> Click "Customize."

>> Click the "Show 'All' Value" option to remove the checkmark.

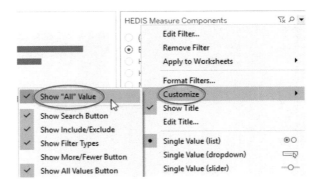

The chart now looks like this:

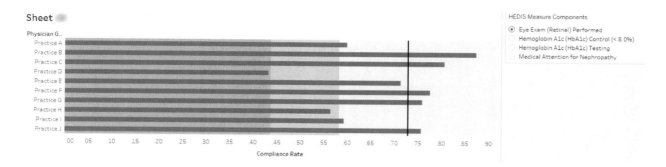

4 Edit the chart components

To add labels to the bars:

》 Click the framed "T" icon on the Toolbar to add labels.

The Rate and Target Measures should be expressed as percentages.

》 Right-click "Compliance Rate" in the Measures window.

》 Select "Default Properties," then "Number Format."

》 Select "Percentage."

》 Change the Decimal places to "0."

》 Repeat these steps for the "Target" field in the Measures window.

The shading of the Reference Bands in this chart encodes comparative data, such as percentages, quartiles, etc. In this case, Reference Bands need to be set at 75% and 90%.

》 Right-click the "X axis."

》 Select "Edit Reference Line."

》 Select "60%,80% of Average Target."

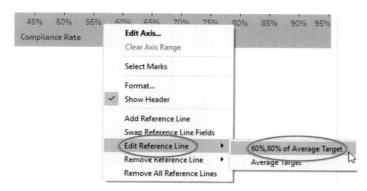

By displaying 75% and 90% (instead of 60% and 80%) of the target value for each Core Measure, the Reference Bands will make clearer both quantitative and qualitative performance as compared to target.

> » Ensure that the "Distribution" box is selected. ("Distribution" refers to a grouping of Reference Bands.)
>
> » For Scope, select "Per Cell."
>
> » For Computation, click the caret to the right of Value.
> - On the drop-down menu, select "Percentages."
> - Change Percentages to "75,90"
> - On the second drop-down menu below "Percent of," click the caret and select "Maximum."
>
> » Under Formatting, change Fill to "Gray."
>
> » Click "OK."

Reference Distribution ▶

Use the Distribution button at the top of the Edit Reference... dialog box to encode confidence intervals, percentiles, standard deviations, and more. The choice of Distribution over Band permits layering of additional calculations without the need to create new calculated fields.

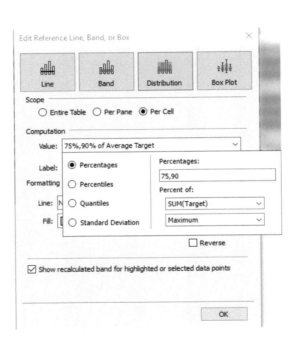

The chart now looks like this:

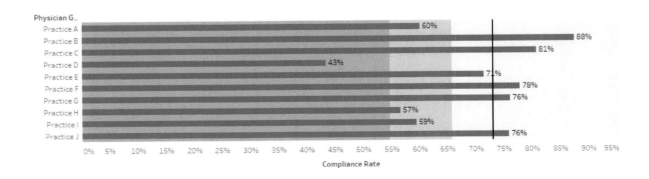

The background shades of gray indicate qualitative scale:

- Dark gray = Poor
- Medium gray = Fair
- Light gray = Good

5 Format the chart

To make the horizontal bars thicker:

» On the Menu bar, click "Format."

» Click "Cell Size."

» Select "Taller" from the submenu.

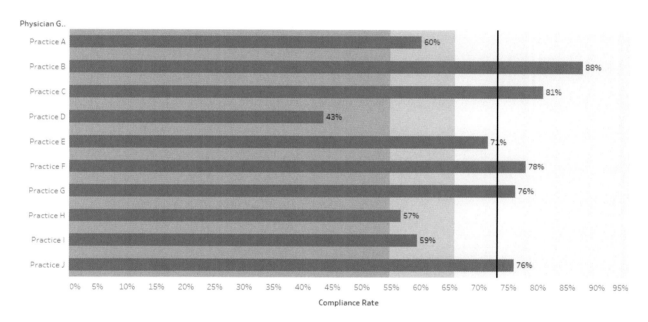

▲ **Cell Sizing**

Cell Size can be adjusted in small increments by using the Format menu or by dragging a Row or Column border.

To increase white space between horizontal bars:

» In the Menu bar, click the "Format" button again.

» Select "Borders."

» Select the "Rows" tab.

» In the "Row Divider" section, click "Pane."

» Select the image of the widest line and change the color to "White."

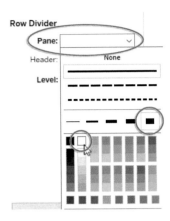

Using Row Dividers to Create Spacing ▷

Tableau does not have a feature specifically designed to create spacing between reference lines, bands, or distributions. To enhance readability by increasing this space, insert a thick white row.

Sort the Physician Groups from highest to lowest.

> » Click the Sort descending icon on the Toolbar.

The label "Physician Group" appears in the title, so the field label can be hidden.

> » Right-click "Physician Group" field label.

> » Click "Hide Field Labels for Rows."

Test the filter by selecting each of the options. Notice the adjustment of the X axis as different HEDIS Measure Components are selected. The axis must have a fixed value to ensure accurate comparison. To lock the axis:

> » Right-click the X axis and select "Edit Axis."

> » Under the "General" tab, in the Range section, click the "Fixed" radio button.

> » Change the Fixed end value to "1.05" (to allow room for labels on high-percentage bars).

6 Add a title

> » Double-click the Title Row to open the Edit Title dialog box.

> » Enter the title, "2016 Compliance Rates of Physician Group Practices for HEDIS Measure: Comprehensive Diabetes Care Component: "

The title can be formatted to reflect the filter selection.

> » With the cursor in the space after "Component:", click the "Insert" button.

> » Select "HEDIS Measure Components" from the sub-menu.

> » Highlight the inserted "<HEDIS Measure Components>" text and change the font color to dark blue.

7 Rename the worksheet tab and save the worksheet

» Right-click the worksheet tab at the bottom of the workspace, then select "Rename."

» Enter an intuitive title, then click the "Save" icon on the Toolbar.

The final chart looks like this:

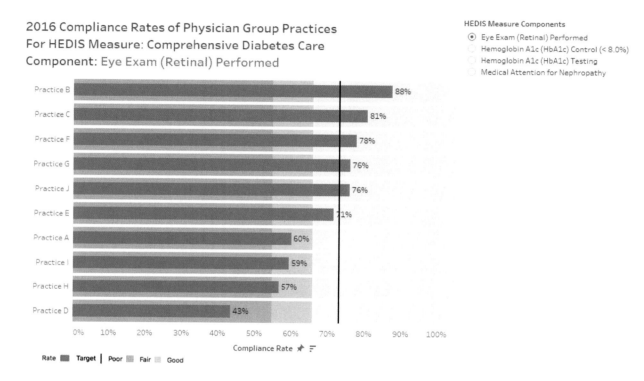

▲ Custom Color Key

It is not currently possible to create a customized color key based on background shading from within Tableau. Use any image software (Photoshop or Paint) to create a a color key, then save it as an image. The above view was created in a dashboard; the image was added as an Object and floated below the chart. This topic is covered in the Dashboard chapter.

Insight: This Bullet Graph allows the viewer to see Physician Group compliance rates for a selected Comprehensive Diabetes Care measures (horizontal blue bars). For the selected measure component "Eye Exam (Retinal) Performed," five practices are above target (B, C, F, G, and J). Practice E is below target but still within the "Good" range. A, I, and H are below target, in the "Fair" range, while Practice D is below target, in the "Poor" range.

◼️ *HDVizoom*™ ...to the Bullet Graph

1 **Create new worksheet and connect to data**

» At bottom of Tableau workspace, click icon for new worksheet

» In Data pane, select "14 – HEDIS Comprehensive Diabetes Care" dataset

2 **Create chart**

» While holding down Control key, click:

- "Physician Group" in Dimensions window

- "Compliance Rate" in Measures window

- "Target" in Measures window

» Click "Show Me" tab and select "Bullet Graph"

» Click "Show Me" tab again to close

3 **Filter data**

» Right-click "HEDIS Measure Components" in Dimensions window

» Select "Show Filter" from sub-menu

» Hover cursor over filter menu header and click caret that appears in top right corner

» Select "Single Value (list)" option

» Click filter menu header caret again

» Click "Customize"

» Click "Show 'All' Value" option to remove checkmark

4 **Edit chart components**

» Right-click "Compliance Rate" in Measures window

» Select "Default Properties," then "Number Format"

» Select "Percentage"

» Change Decimal places to "0"

» Repeat steps for "Target" field in Measures window

» Right-click "X axis"

» Select "Edit Reference Line"

» Select "60%,80% of Average Target"

» Ensure "Distribution" box is selected

» For Scope, select "Per Cell"

» For Computation, click caret to right of Value

- On drop-down menu, select "Percentages"

- Change Percentages to "75,90"

- In second drop-down menu below "Percent of," click caret and select "Maximum"

» Under Formatting, change Fill to "Gray"

» Click "OK"

5 **Format chart**

» On Menu bar, click "Format"

» Select "Cell Size"

» Select "Taller" from submenu

» In Menu bar, click "Format" button again

» Select "Borders"

» Select "Rows" tab

» In "Row Divider" section, click "Pane"

» Select image of widest line and change color to "White"

» Click Sort descending icon on Toolbar

» Right-click "Physician Group" field label

» Click "Hide Field Labels for Rows"

» Right-click X axis and select "Edit Axis"

» Under General tab, in Range section, click "Fixed" radio button

» Change Fixed end value to "1.05"

6   **Add title**

» Double-click Title Row to open Edit Title dialog box

» Enter title, "2016 Compliance Rates of Physician Group Practices for HEDIS Measure: Comprehensive Diabetes Care Component: "

» With cursor in space after "Component:" click "Insert" button

» Select "HEDIS Measure Components" from sub-menu

» Highlight inserted "<HEDIS Measure Components>" text and change font color to dark blue

7   **Rename worksheet tab and save worksheet**

» Right-click worksheet tab at bottom of workspace, then select "Rename"

» Enter intuitive title, then click "Save" icon on Toolbar

CHAPTER 20

Table Calculations

Table Calculations are computations applied to the values visibly present on a worksheet. They are dependent on the amount, type, and orientation of data present. Table Calculations can be used to generate running totals, year-over-year comparisons, percent of totals, index calculations, and much more. Table Calculations can be added to the view using either predefined quick calculations or by specifying a custom definition.

Two examples of predefined Quick Table Calculations are shown below.

20.1 Percent of Total

This Table Calculation computes a percent of total—in this case, of full-time equivalent (FTE) employees among hospital departments. The sum value of all the bars must equal 100%, conveying a part-to-whole relationship for each hospital department.

Department FTE - Percent of Total

Nursing	47.5%
Administration	25.3%
Radiology	15.8%
Pharmacy	6.3%
Central Supply	5.1%

Data Source: Mock hospital data

About the Data: Mock hospital data based on actual numbers of full-time employees (FTE) for five major hospital departments.

1 Create a new worksheet and connect to the data

» At the bottom of the Tableau workspace, click the icon for a new worksheet.

» In the Data pane, select the "08 - Department FTE Counts" dataset.

2 Create the chart

» Drag and drop "Department" from the Dimensions window to the Rows shelf

» Drag and drop "Actual FTE" from the Measures window to the Columns shelf.

» Click the Sort Descending icon on the Toolbar.

» Click the [T] icon on Toolbar to add labels.

The bar chart now looks like this:

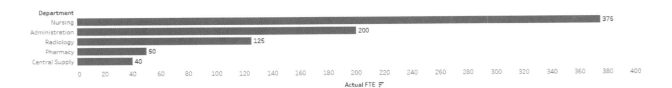

The labels for each bar identify the raw number of employees. The objective is to compare the Percent of Total Actual FTE for each department.

3 **Perform a Quick Table Calculation**

» Right-click the "SUM(Actual FTE)" pill on the Columns shelf.

» Click "Quick Table Calculation."

» Select "Percent of Total."

Quick Table Calculation ▶

In generating a Quick Table Calculation, Tableau makes its best guess as to how it should compute the results. For Percent of Total Calculation, it can perform the calculation on each row of data down the table, across the table, or by specifying a particular field.

Grayed-Out Table Calculations ▶

Since table calculations are dependent on the source worksheet view, some of the predefined quick calculations may be unavailable if the worksheet view does not support the calculation. If this is the case, the unavailable calculations will be visible in the menu, but will be grayed out.

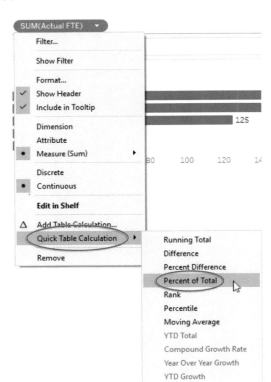

» Right-click the "SUM(Actual FTE)" pill again.

» Click "Compute using" from the drop-down menu.

Tableau computes this Percent of Total calculation using Table (Down). In this example, "Compute using Table (Down)" works because each department is oriented down the worksheet; however, a more precise method is to compute using "Department."

» Select "Department."

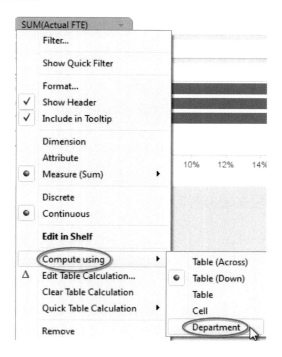

Best Practice

While using Table (Down) and Table (Across) to compute table calculations may work, it is a better practice to explicitly tell Tableau what field or fields to use to perform the calculation. This ensures that if column orientation is later changed or dimensions are added, the Tableau calculation will still use only the fields chosen for its computation.

» Right-click "SUM(Actual FTE)Δ" pill on the Columns shelf.

» Select "Format."

» Select the "Pane" tab.

» In the Default section, click the caret to the right of "Numbers."

» Select "Percentage" and decrease Decimal places to "1."

4 Format the chart

» Right-click the "Department" header.

» Select "Hide Field Labels for Rows."

» Right-click the X axis.

» Uncheck "Show Header."

5 Confirm the calculation

To double-check the calculation, display a Grand Total showing that the percentages add up to 100%.

» Click the "Analytics" tab at the top of the Data/Analytics pane.

» Click and drag "Totals" onto the workspace. An option display will appear.

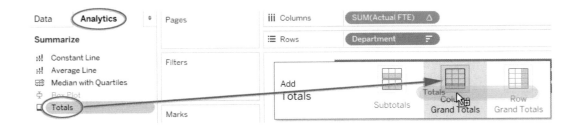

» Drop "Totals" onto the "Column Grand Totals" image.

» Confirm that the Grand Total equals 100%.

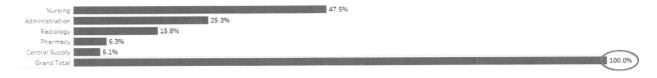

To remove the Grand Total:

» Click "Analysis" in the Menu bar.

» Click "Show Column Grand Totals" to unselect.

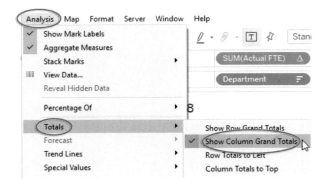

6 **Add a title**

» Double-click the Title Row to open the Edit Title dialog box.

» Enter the title, "Department FTE – Percent of Total."

244

7 **Rename the worksheet tab and save the worksheet:**

>> Right-click the worksheet tab at the bottom of the workspace, then select "Rename."

>> Enter an intuitive title, then click the "Save" icon on the Toolbar.

The final chart looks like this:

Department FTE - Percent of Total

Insight: Using the percent of total table calculation makes it easy to see that Nursing constitutes 47.5%, or nearly half, of the full-time employees of these five hospital departments.

▐▌ *HDVizoom*™...to Percent of Total

1 Create new worksheet and connect to data

» At bottom of Tableau workspace, click icon for new worksheet

» In Data pane, select "08 - Department FTE Counts" dataset

2 Create chart

» Drag and drop "Department" from Dimensions window to Rows shelf

» Drag and drop "Actual FTE" from Measures window to Columns shelf

» Click the Sort Descending icon on Toolbar

» Click [T] icon on Toolbar to add labels

3 Perform Quick Table Calculation

» Right-click "SUM(Actual FTE)" pill on Columns shelf

» Click "Quick Table Calculation"

» Select "Percent of Total"

» Right-click "SUM(Actual FTE)"

» Click "Compute using" from drop-down menu

» Select "Department"

» Right-click "SUM(Actual FTE)∆" pill on Columns shelf

» Select "Format"

» Select "Pane" tab

» In Default section, click caret to right of "Numbers"

» Select "Percentage" and decrease Decimal places to "1"

4 Format chart

» Right-click "Department" header

» Select "Hide Field Labels for Rows"

» Right-click X axis

» Uncheck "Show Header"

5 Confirm calculation

» Click "Analytics" tab at top of Data/Analytics pane

» Click and drag "Totals" onto workspace

» Drop "Totals" onto "Column Grand Totals" image

» Click "Analysis" in Menu bar

» Click "Totals"

» Click "Show Column Grand Totals" to unselect

6 Add title

» Double-click Title Row to open Edit Title dialog box

» Enter title, "Department FTE – Percent of Total"

7 Rename worksheet tab and save worksheet

» Right-click worksheet tab at bottom of workspace, then select "Rename"

» Enter intuitive title, then click "Save" icon on Toolbar

20.2 Running Total

ARunning Total Table Calculation computes a cumulative total along a specified dimension. This report presents the progression of groups of motor vehicle incident deaths from 2006 to 2015 across regions.

Running Total of Motor Vehicle Incident Deaths
For Years 2006 - 2015, by US Region

	Midwest	Northeast	South	West
2006	8,928	5,350	21,197	9,841
2007	17,808	10,402	42,044	19,007
2008	25,757	15,040	61,204	27,050
2009	32,863	19,352	78,735	34,317
2010	40,306	23,886	95,392	41,015
2011	47,497	28,430	112,033	47,942
2012	55,045	32,937	129,364	54,971
2013	62,252	37,283	145,937	62,214
2014	69,245	41,327	162,805	69,707
2015	76,661	45,448	180,890	77,842

Data Source: *CDC Wonder*

About the Data: *CDC Wonder, developed by the Centers for Disease Control and Prevention (CDC), is an integrated information and communication system for public health. It provides the public with access to data from the CDC, to help promote information-driven decisions. The data for this exercise is from the dataset Multiple Cause of Death, by Census Region, where the underlying cause of death is from the UDC – ICD-10 113 Cause list: Motor vehicle accidents, for the years 2006 – 2015.*

1 Create a new worksheet and connect to the data

» At the bottom of the Tableau workspace, click the icon for a new worksheet.

» In the Data pane, select the "18 – Motor Vehicle Incident Deaths" dataset.

2 Create the chart

» Drag and drop "Census Region" from the Dimensions window onto the Columns shelf.

» Drag and drop "Date" from the Dimensions window onto the Rows shelf.

» Drag and drop "Motor Vehicle Incident Deaths" from the Measures window onto Label on the Marks card.

» Hover the cursor over the right border of the chart until it changes to a bi-directional arrow. Click and drag to adjust width until column headers are fully visible.

3 Show Grand Totals

» Click the "Analytics" tab in the Data/Analytics pane.

» Drag "Totals" onto the workspace to open an image display.

» Drop "Totals" onto the "Column Grand Totals" image.

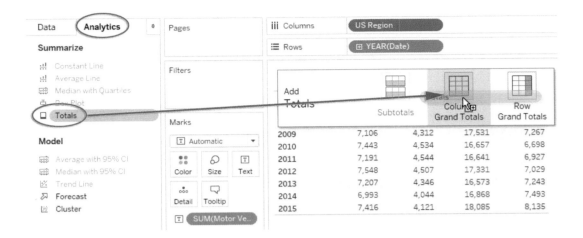

Best Practice

Although adding a Grand Total is not necessary in creating a Running Total Table Calculation, it is a good idea to include one while building the chart, so that the accuracy of the calculation can easily be checked. This Grand Total will be removed for the finished visualization.

The table now looks like this:

		US Region		
Year of Date	Midwest	Northeast	South	West
2006	8,928	5,350	21,197	9,841
2007	8,880	5,052	20,847	9,166
2008	7,949	4,638	19,160	8,043
2009	7,106	4,312	17,531	7,267
2010	7,443	4,534	16,657	6,698
2011	7,191	4,544	16,641	6,927
2012	7,548	4,507	17,331	7,029
2013	7,207	4,346	16,573	7,243
2014	6,993	4,044	16,868	7,493
2015	7,416	4,121	18,085	8,135
Grand Total	76,661	45,448	180,890	77,842

Totals ▸

Totals can also be created from the Analysis tab on the Menu bar. Additional options are available here, including formatting and location | placement choices.

4 Perform the Quick Table Calculations

To generate the Running Total:

» Right-click the "SUM(Motor Vehicle Incident Deaths)" pill on the Marks card.

» Click "Quick Table Calculation."

» Select "Running Total."

◀ Running Total Aggregation

Tableau's Running Total Calculation defaults to a running sum. Manually editing the Table Calculation permits changing the aggregation to a running average, minimum, or maximum, as needed.

» Right-click the "SUM(Motor Vehicle Incident Deaths)" pill again.

» Click "Compute Using."

» Select "Date."

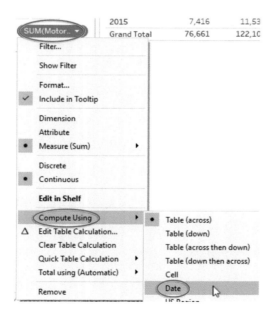

◀ Refresher

*As discussed in the previous section, Tableau makes its best guess as to how to compute the Table Calculation. In this case, Tableau chose to calculate a running total along Table (Across); this choice, however, does not yield the desired result which is By Year. This total can be adjusted accordingly with the **Compute Using** menu option.*

To double-check the Running Total:

» Drag and drop "Motor Vehicle Incident Deaths" from the Measures window onto the Workspace to make it easy to compare the new Table Calculation to the original measure.

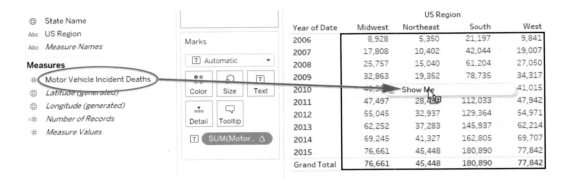

» Drag and drop the "Measure Names" pill from the Rows shelf to the Columns shelf.

The chart now looks like this:

	US Region							
	Midwest		Northeast		South		West	
Year of Date	Motor Vehicle ..	Running Sum of ..	Motor Vehicle ..	Running Sum of ..	Motor Vehicle ..	Running Sum of ..	Motor Vehicle ..	Running Sum of ..
2006	8,928	8,928	5,350	5,350	21,197	21,197	9,841	9,841
2007	8,880	17,808	5,052	10,402	20,847	42,044	9,166	19,007
2008	7,949	25,757	4,638	15,040	19,160	61,204	8,043	27,050
2009	7,106	32,863	4,312	19,352	17,531	78,735	7,267	34,317
2010	7,443	40,306	4,534	23,886	16,657	95,392	6,698	41,015
2011	7,191	47,497	4,544	28,430	16,641	112,033	6,927	47,942
2012	7,548	55,045	4,507	32,937	17,331	129,364	7,029	54,971
2013	7,207	62,252	4,346	37,283	16,573	145,937	7,243	62,214
2014	6,993	69,245	4,044	41,327	16,868	162,805	7,493	69,707
2015	7,416	76,661	4,121	45,448	18,085	180,890	8,135	77,842
Grand Total	76,661	76,661	45,448	45,448	180,890	180,890	77,842	77,842

Best Practice

Temporarily adding the original field (Numeric Value) next to the Table Calculation (Running Sum of Numeric Value) confirms that the running total is calculating as intended. Under Midwest, for example, adding the 2007 Motor Vehicle Incident Deaths (8,880) to the 2006 Running Sum (8,928) confirms that the 2007 Running Sum (17,808) is correct. Notice that the last Running Sum row for Midwest for 2015 is 76,661, the same as the Grand Total. Once the correct calculation has been confirmed, the Motor Vehicle Incident Deaths field (without the table calculation) can be removed.

» Drag the "SUM(Motor Vehicle Incident Deaths)" pill (without the calculation symbolized by the triangle) off the Measure Values shelf.

5 Format the chart

Hide Headers and Column Field Label:

» Right-click the "Year of Date" header.

» Select "Hide Field Labels for Rows."

» Right-click "US Region" header.

» Select "Hide Field Labels for Columns."

Hide Grand Total:

» Click "Analysis" on the Menu bar.

» Click "Totals."

» Click "Show Column Grand Totals" to remove.

6 Add a title

» Double-click the Title Row to open the Edit Title dialog box.

» Enter the title, "Running Total of Motor Vehicle Incident Deaths For Years 2006 – 2015 by US Region."

7 Rename the worksheet tab and save the worksheet

» Right-click the worksheet tab at the bottom of the workspace, then select "Rename."

» Enter an intuitive title, then click the "Save" icon on the Toolbar.

The final chart looks like this:

Running Total of Motor Vehicle Incident Deaths For Years 2006 - 2015, by US Region

	Midwest	Northeast	South	West
2006	8,928	5,350	21,197	9,841
2007	17,808	10,402	42,044	19,007
2008	25,757	15,040	61,204	27,050
2009	32,863	19,352	78,735	34,317
2010	40,306	23,886	95,392	41,015
2011	47,497	28,430	112,033	47,942
2012	55,045	32,937	129,364	54,971
2013	62,252	37,283	145,937	62,214
2014	69,245	41,327	162,805	69,707
2015	76,661	45,448	180,890	77,842

Insight: In this Running Total table calculation, it is clear that from 2006 to 2015, it was damned unsafe to be driving in the South!

251

▐▌ *HDVizoom*™ ...to the Running Total

1 Create new worksheet and connect to data

» At bottom of Tableau workspace, click icon for new worksheet

» In Data pane, select "18 – Motor Vehicle Incident Deaths" dataset

2 Create chart

» Drag and drop "Census Region" from Dimensions window onto Columns shelf

» Drag and drop "Date" from Dimensions window onto Rows shelf

» Drag and drop "Motor Vehicle Incident Deaths" from Measures window onto Label on Marks card

» Hover cursor over right border of chart until it changes to bi-directional arrow. Click and drag to adjust width until column headers are fully visible

3 Show Grand Totals

» Click "Analytics" tab in Data/Analytics pane

» Drag "Totals" onto workspace to open image display

» Drop "Totals" onto "Column Grand Totals" image

4 Perform Quick Table Calculation

» Right-click on "SUM(Motor Vehicle Incident Deaths)" pill on Marks card

» Click "Quick Table Calculation"

» Select "Running Total"

» Right-click on "SUM(Motor Vehicle Incident Deaths)" again

» Click "Compute Using"

» Select "Date"

» Drag and drop "Motor Vehicle Incident Deaths" from Measures window onto Workspace

» Drag and drop "Measure Names" from Rows shelf to Columns shelf

» Drag and drop "SUM(Motor Vehicle Incident Deaths)" pill (without calculation symbolized by triangle) off Measure Values shelf

5 Format chart

» Right-click "Year of Date" header

» Select "Hide Field Labels for Rows"

» Right-click "US Region" header

» Select "Hide Field Labels for Columns"

» Click "Analysis" on Menu bar

» Click "Totals"

» Click "Show Column Grand Totals" to remove checkmark

6 Add title

» Double-click Title Row to open Edit Title dialog box

» Enter title, "Running Total of Motor Vehicle Incident Deaths For Years 2006 – 2015 by US Region"

7 Rename worksheet tab and save worksheet

» Right-click worksheet tab at bottom of workspace, then select "Rename"

» Enter intuitive title, then click "Save" icon on Toolbar

252

CHAPTER 21

Pareto Chart

areto Analysis is a decision-making technique used to identify a limited number of metrics that produce the most significant overall effect. It uses the Pareto Principle, also known as the 80/20 rule—the idea that 80% of a project's benefit can be achieved by doing 20% of the work or, conversely, that 80% of problems can be traced to 20% of causes. In healthcare, Pareto Charts can be applied to the design of medical processes in order to identify errors and incidents, or to analyze performance data in health organizations. The objective of a Pareto Chart is to separate a few major problems from the many possible ones, so that improvement efforts can be focused based on data rather than on perception.

In Tableau, a Pareto Chart is created in multiple steps, including table calculations. Essentially, a bar chart and a line chart are built and turned into a Dual Axis chart, where the line is the running total viewed as a percentage of the total.

How To: Build a Pareto Chart to identify where to focus improvement efforts for laboratory testing.

Root Causes of Repeat Laboratory Samples

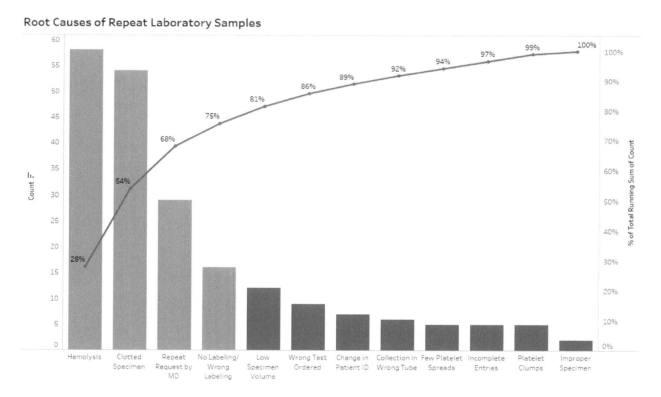

Data Source: *De-identified hospital laboratory data*

About the Data: *Problems with samples of blood, urine, and other specimens from patients sent for analysis in a hospital laboratory required a re-sampling of the specimens. This data contains a list and count of the reasons that the specimens had to be re-sampled.*

1 **Create a new worksheet and connect to the data**

» At the bottom of the workspace, click the icon for a new worksheet.

» In the Data pane, select "15 - Repeat Lab Samples" dataset.

2 **Create the chart**

» Drag and drop "Root Cause of Repeat of Lab Samples" from the Dimensions window onto the Columns shelf.

» Drag and drop "Count" from the Measures window onto the Rows shelf.

» Click the "Sort descending" icon on the Tool bar.

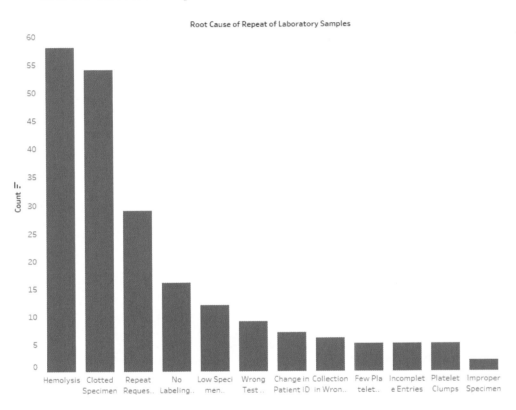

Root Cause of Repeat of Laboratory Samples

3 **Perform table calculations**

» Right-click "SUM(Count)" pill on the Rows shelf.

» In the context menu, select "Add Table Calculation."

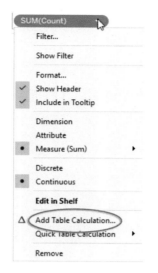

◀ Add Table Calculation

Specifications for a Table Calculation can be added by using either Add Table Calculation or Quick Table Calculation. Choosing Add Table Calculation brings up a menu from which the type of calculation, the method of computation, or other custom details can be chosen. Quick Table Calculation automatically provides the computation and other details.

The Table Calculation dialog box appears, and the chart automatically adjusts to the default Calculation Type, "Difference From."

In the Table Calculation dialog box:

» In the Calculation Type section, click the caret to the right of the default selection "Difference From."

» Change the Calculation Type to "Running Total."

» In the Compute Using section, select "Specific Dimensions."

Since the only Dimension is "Root Cause of Repeat Laboratory Samples," it is automatically checked.

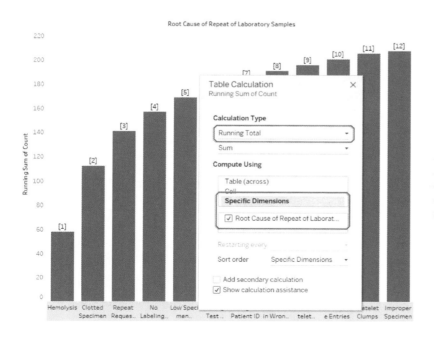

◀ Real-Time Table Calculations

Table Calculation changes made from the dialog box are displayed instantly. Yellow highlighting and corresponding bracketed numbers indicate what direction the calculation is computing along. The Show calculation assistance check box controls this display, also in real-time.

» Click the box near the bottom of the dialog box for "Add Secondary Calculation." This will expand the Table Calculation dialog box to add that calculation.

» In the Secondary Calculation Type section, click the caret to the right of the default selection "Difference From."

» Change to "Percent of Total."

» In the Compute Using section, select "Specific Dimensions." The only Dimension in the menu (Root Cause of Repeat Laboratory Samples) will be checked.

Perform a Secondary Table Calculation ▸

Adding a secondary Table Calculation works just like adding a primary one. The results computed take into account the computations already performed in the Primary Calculation Type settings. In this example, a Percent of Total calculation is being added as a secondary calculation to a Running Total calculation. This means that instead of displaying a running sum of the raw numbers from the Count field, the calculation will compute a running percent of the Count going from left to right across the worksheet Running Total and Moving Calculation are the only table calculations that can have a secondary calculation; the others are considered to be terminal calculations.

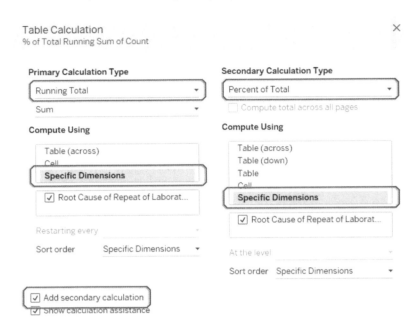

» To close the dialog box, click the "X" in the top right corner.

To change the bars to a line:

» In the Marks card, click the caret to the right of "Automatic" mark type.

» Select "Line."

This is the "Pareto" part of the chart.

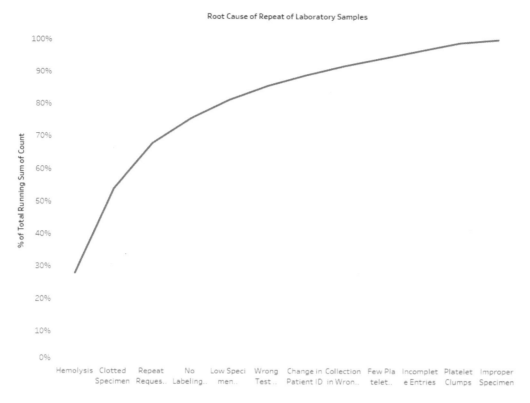

Root Cause of Repeat of Laboratory Samples

▲ **Refresher**

In order to create this Pareto Line, the results in the original bar chart were sorted so that root causes appear from largest on the left to smallest on the right. Combining this display with the Percent of Total Running Sum table calculation creates the Pareto Line. Proof of its accuracy is provided by the gradual progress towards 100% along the horizontal axis.

4 **Create the Dual Axis chart**

» Drag and drop "Count" from the Measures window onto the Rows shelf to the right of the "SUM(Count)Δ" pill already on the shelf. (The Δ symbol on the other SUM(Count) field denotes a Table Calculation.) Two line charts are created: "Percent of Total Running Sum of Count" and "Count."

» Click the "SUM(Count)" pill just added to the Row shelf, highlighting it to display its own Marks card.

» Click the caret to the right of Line to display the drop-down menu.

» Change Line to "Bar."

Refresher ▶

Tableau makes its best guess as to what visualization works with the data in the worksheet. If its choice is not acceptable, the chart type can always be changed by using the "Show Me" button or by manually choosing a different chart type on the Marks card.

The chart now looks like this:

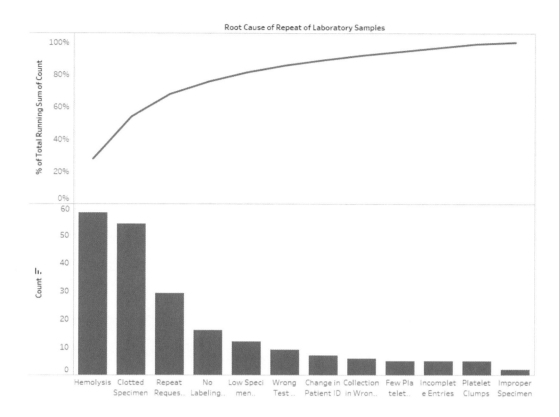

To swap the two Row fields:

» Drag the first pill to the right of the second pill so that the bar chart is on top in the view.

This makes the bar chart the primary axis on the left and the Pareto line the secondary axis on the right.

» Right-click the "SUM(Count)Δ" pill on the Rows shelf.

» Select "Dual Axis" from the context menu.

Dual Axis Charts ▷

The presence of two measures on the Rows or Columns shelf offers the possibility of creating a Dual Axis chart. Selecting "Dual Axis" causes Tableau to place the two charts one on top of the other, with a second axis appearing on the right or top of the chart depending on its orientation. These two charts do not have to be of the same type. The Dual Axis technique can overlay lines on a scatter plot, bars on an area chart, or a geographic symbol map on a filled map. This technique can also be used to plot two separate fields on the same axis with the same chart type.

When units of the two axes are similar (and the data types are the same), the latter should be synchronized on the same scale (by right-clicking the secondary axis and selecting Synchronize Axis). It may sometimes be impossible to do this if the formats of the two axes (for example, Count and Percent) are incompatible.

Tableau automatically orients the two charts so that one chart is in front of the other. This order can be changed by right-clicking one of the dual axes and selecting Move Marks to Front/Back.

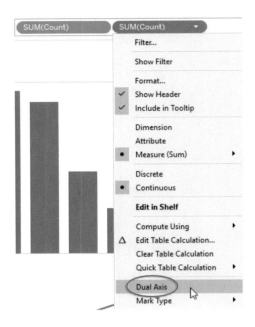

This will overlay the Pareto line on the bar chart and add the corresponding axis for the line to the right side of the chart.

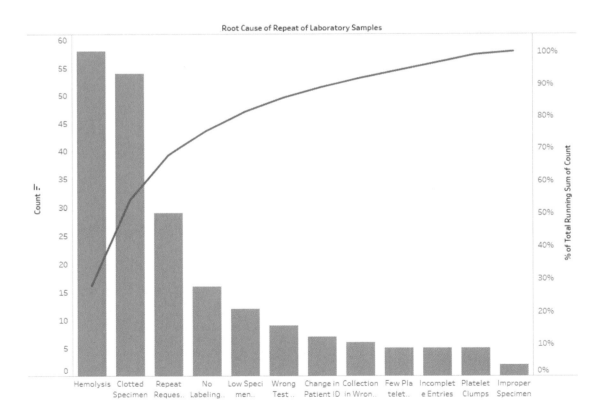

Display the Percent of Total Running Sum to help identify the root causes that collectively contribute to 80% of the repeat laboratory samples. To add the percentages to the line:

» Click the "SUM(Count)Δ" pill on the Rows shelf to highlight the Line view on the Marks card.

» While holding down the Control key, drag and drop the "SUM(Count)Δ" pill from the Rows shelf onto Label on the Marks card.

» Right-click the "SUM(Count)Δ" pill on the Marks card.

» Select "Format" from the drop-down menu.

» With the Pane tab selected, click the caret to the right of "Numbers" in the Default section.

» Select "Percentage" and change Decimal places to "0."

To arrange the values above the line:

» Click the caret to the right of "Alignment" in the Default section of the Format pane.

» In the Vertical alignment section, click the icon farthest to the right to position the percentages above the line.

The chart now looks like this:

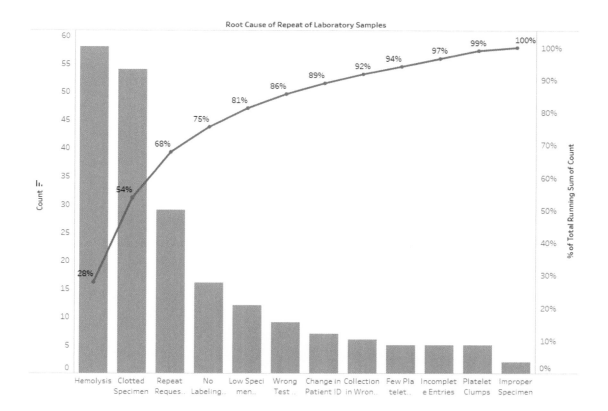

5 Highlight 80% contribution with color

Visual interest can be added to this classic Pareto chart by using a calculated field to color-code the laboratory errors that contributed 80% of repeat draws.

» Click the "SUM(Count)" pill on the Rows shelf to highlight the label header on the Marks card.

» While holding down the Control key, drag and drop "SUM(Count) Δ" from the Rows shelf to Color on the Marks card.

Refresher ▶

Holding the Control key while dragging and dropping a pill will copy it to a new location.

Dual Axis Visual Cue ▶

Tableau changes the oval pill shape of the two measures to flat edges, denoting the Dual Axis chart.

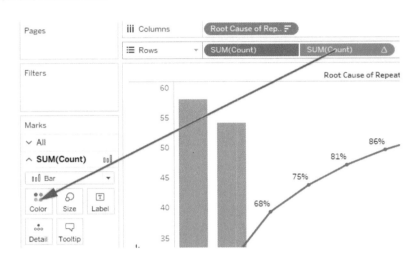

The chart color changes intentionally to a color gradient because "SUM(Count) Δ" is a continuous measure.

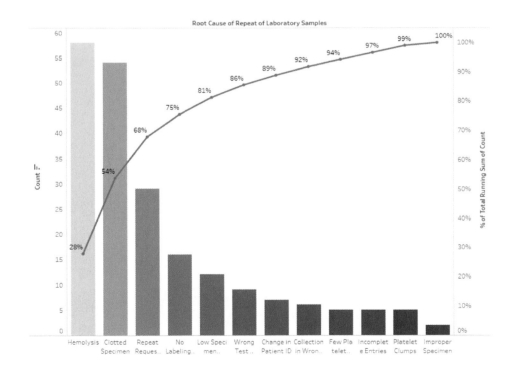

» Right-click "SUM(Count)Δ" on Color on the Marks card.

» Select "Edit in Shelf" from the menu that appears.

» Add the following to the end of the formula displayed in the pill: "<=.8." This will distinguish the counts below or equal to 80% from those greater than 80%.

Interactive Editing ▶

Pressing Ctrl and Enter while in the Edit in Shelf function applies the formula within the pill while leaving the Edit window open for further editing if necessary.

)) / TOTAL(SUM([Count]))<=.8

◀ **Customize Table Calculations**

When Table Calculations are selected, Tableau writes a calculated field formula in the background. Clicking on the Edit in Shelf button permits the user to edit this formula as needed (scroll left to view the entire calculation). Pressing the Enter saves the change to the formula in the pill.

To save the formula as a new calculated field in the Measures window, hold down Ctrl, then drag and drop the edited pill to the Measures window. Rename with an intuitive title.

The calculation is now a Boolean value. Notice it is a discrete pill on Color on the Mark card, creating a color palette, not a color gradient. Bar colors now highlight the root causes contributing to 80% of the repeat labs, separating them from those contributing to the remaining 20%.

6 Format the Chart

To edit the Line color:

» Click the caret to the right of the "Measure Names" color legend.

» Select "Edit Colors."

» Change the color palette to "Color Blind."

» Click the Data item "% of Total Running Sum of Count" to highlight.

» Select the gray square on the Color Palette.

» Click "OK."

Widen the columns enough to make complete headers visible:

» From the Fit selection box on the Toolbar, click "Fit Width."

» Hover the cursor over the X axis until a vertical bi-directional arrow appears. Click and drag the axis to the appropriate height to view full label names.

To hide the Column header:

» Right-click the column header "Root Cause of Repeat Laboratory Samples."

» Select "Hide Field Labels for Columns."

7   Add a title

»   Double-click the Title Row to open the Edit Title dialog box.

»   Enter the title, "Root Causes of Repeat Laboratory Samples," then click "OK."

8   Rename the worksheet tab and save the worksheet

»   Right-click the worksheet tab at the bottom of the workspace, then select "Rename."

»   Enter a descriptive title, then click the "Save" icon on the Toolbar.

The final chart looks like this:

Root Causes of Repeat Laboratory Samples

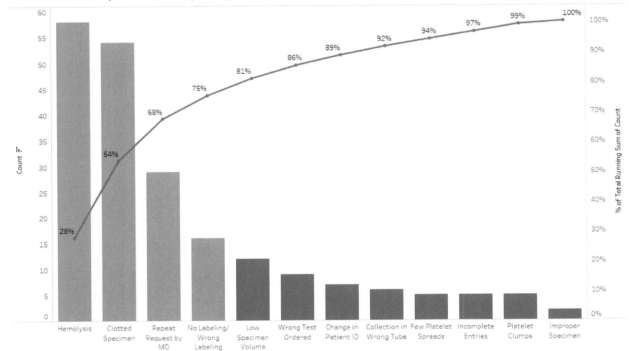

Insight: 80% of the repeat laboratory samples (shown in orange) have just four root causes: Hemolysis, Clotted Specimen, Repeat Request by MD, and No Labeling/Wrong Labeling.

HDVizoom™...to the Pareto Chart

1 Create new worksheet and connect to data

» At bottom of workspace, click icon for new worksheet

» In Data pane, select "15 - Repeat Lab Samples" dataset

2 Create chart

» Drag and drop "Root Cause of Repeat of Lab Samples" from Dimensions window onto Columns shelf

» Drag and drop "Count" from Measures window onto Rows shelf

» Click "Sort descending" icon on Tool bar

3 Perform table calculations

» Right-click "SUM(Count)" pill on Rows shelf

» In context menu, select "Add Table Calculation"

» In Table Calculation dialog box, Calculation Type section, click caret to right of default selection "Difference From"

» Change Calculation Type to "Running Total"

» In Compute Using section, select "Specific Dimensions"

» Click box near bottom of dialog box for "Add Secondary Calculation"

» In Secondary Calculation Type section, click caret to right of default selection "Difference From"

» Select "Percent of Total"

» In Compute Using section, select "Specific Dimensions"

» To close dialog box, click "X" in top right corner

» In Marks card, click caret to right of "Automatic" mark type

» Select "Line"

4 Create Dual Axis chart

» Drag and drop "Count" from Measures window onto Rows shelf to right of "SUM(Count)Δ" pill already on shelf

» Click "SUM(Count)" pill just added to Rows shelf highlighting it to interact with corresponding label header in Marks card.

» Click caret to right of Line to display drop-down menu

» Change Line to "Bar"

» Drag first pill to right of second pill so bar chart is on top in view

» Right-click "SUM(Count)Δ" pill on Rows shelf

» Select "Dual Axis" from context menu

» Click "SUM(Count)Δ" pill on Rows shelf to highlight Line view on Marks card

» While holding down Control key, drag and drop "SUM(Count)Δ" pill from Rows shelf onto Label on Marks card

» Right-click "SUM(Count)Δ" pill on Marks card

» Select "Format" from drop-down menu

» With Pane tab selected, click caret to right of "Numbers" in Default section

» Select "Percentage" and change Decimal places to "0"

» Click caret to right of "Alignment" in Default section of Format pane

» In Vertical alignment section, click icon farthest to right to position percentages above line

5 **Highlight 80% contribution with color**

» Click "SUM(Count)" pill on Rows shelf to highlight label header on Marks card

» While holding down Control key, drag and drop "SUM(Count) Δ" from Rows shelf to Color on Marks card

» Right-click "SUM(Count)Δ" on Color on Marks card

» Select "Edit in Shelf" from menu that appears

» Add to end of formula: "<=.8"

» Press "Enter"

6 **Format chart**

» Click caret to right of "Measure Names" color legend

» Select "Edit Colors"

» Change color palette to "Color Blind"

» Click Data item "% of Total Running Sum of Count" to highlight

» Select gray square in Color Palette

» Click "OK"

» From Fit selection box on Toolbar, click "Fit Width"

» Right-click column header "Root Cause of Repeat Laboratory Samples"

» Select "Hide Field Labels for Columns"

7 **Add title**

» Double-click Title Row to open Edit Title dialog box

» Enter title, "Root Causes of Repeat Laboratory Samples," then click "OK."

8 **Rename worksheet tab and save worksheet**

» Right-click worksheet tab at bottom of workspace, then select "Rename"

» Enter descriptive title, then click "Save" icon on Toolbar

CHAPTER 22

Gantt Chart (Modified)

The Gantt Chart is named after the American engineer Henry Gantt, who developed a bar chart showing the steps in a project over time. The length of the bar denotes units of time—i.e., the beginning and ending of a project task—as well as contingencies and dependencies that hinder or allow the beginning or end of another task. The Gantt Chart has become a standard way of visualizing different parts in order to plan, coordinate, and track a whole project.

For the Gantt Chart in this example, the time displayed is for each procedure performed in a hospital operating room. Modifying the way this chart is used allows the viewer to quickly understand the utilization of a single operating room, and to identify potential opportunities to improve utilization of all operating rooms.

How To: Build a modified Gantt chart displaying daily operating room use of elective & add-on cases by OR.

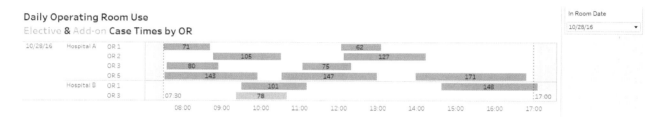

Data Source: *De-identified OR data*

About the Data: *Operating room data for elective and add-on (urgent/emergent) surgical procedures in-room time durations by operating room and by hospital.*

1 Create a new worksheet and connect to the data

》 At the bottom of the Tableau workspace, click the icon for a new worksheet.

》 In the Data pane select the "16 - Operating Room Data" dataset.

2 Create the chart

》 Right-click, drag, and drop "In Room Date" from the Dimensions window onto the Rows shelf.

》 Select "In Room Date (Discrete)" from the menu that appears.

》 Drag and drop "Hospital" from the Dimensions window onto the Rows shelf.

》 Drag and drop "Operating Room" from the Dimensions window onto the Rows shelf.

» Drag and drop "Room Minutes Actual" from the Measures window onto Label on the Marks card.

» At the top of the Marks card, change the chart from Automatic to "Gantt Bar."

Gantt Chart Creation ▶

The core concept for Gantt Chart creation in Tableau is that the chart does not plot a start and end timestamp.

Instead, the chart begins with a starting time of day; the Size shelf then encodes the bars to create lengths representing varying durations (in this case, minutes).

The chart initially looks like this:

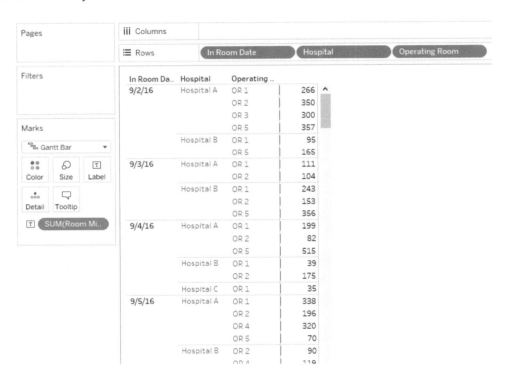

3 Create calculated fields

Create a Calculated Field named "Room In Time of Day."

> » Right-click "In Room Date/Time" in the Dimensions window.

> » Select "Create," then "Calculated Field" from the sub-menus.

> » For the Calculated Field Name, enter "Room In Time of Day."

> » For the formula, enter:
>
>   [In Room Date/Time] - [In Room Date]

> » Click "OK."

[In Room Date/Time] - [In Room Date]

◀ Time of Day Calculation

For this particular Gantt Chart, In-Room-Date/Time is plotted independently of In-Room-Date. The calculation to the left subtracts Date from Date + Time so that only Time remains as a number between 0 and 1. This number represents the minutes in a day as a part-to-whole relationship, with an entire day equal to 1. On the X axis below, the figures between 0 and 1 represent an entire day. A time of 12:00 will return a value of 0.5; 18:00 will return 0.75; and so on.

> » Drag and drop the new field "Room In Time of Day" from the Measures window onto the Dimensions window. (Even though this field is a numeric value, Room In Time of Day is to be treated here as a special kind of Date field—representing a period of time in a day—and Date fields are Dimensions.)

> » Drag and drop "Room In Time of Day" from the Dimensions window onto the Columns shelf.

> » Right-click the "Room In Time of Day" pill on the Columns shelf; from the context menu, select "Continuous."

> » While holding down the Control key, drag and drop "In Room Date" from the Rows shelf onto the Filters shelf.

> » In the Filter Field box, select "Individual Dates."

> » Click "Next."

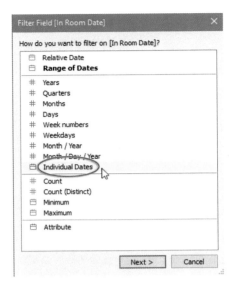

» Click "None" to remove all checkmarks, then select the individual date "10/28/2016" to have a manageable amount of data to create this example chart.

» Click "OK."

The chart now looks like this:

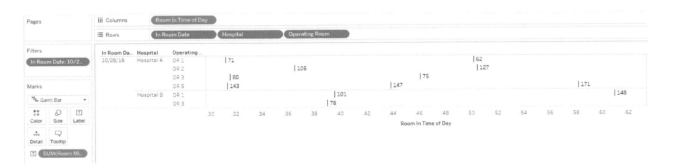

Create another Calculated Field to compute the size of the Gantt bars.

» Right-click "Room Minutes Actual" in the Measures window.

» Select "Create," then "Calculated Field" from the sub-menus.

» For the Calculated Field name, enter: "Room In Duration (for Gantt)."

» For the formula, enter:

```
[Room Minutes Actual]/1440
```

» Click "OK."

» Drag and drop "Room In Duration (for Gantt)" to Size on the Marks card.

The chart now looks like this:

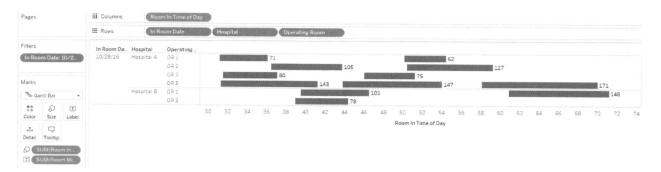

▲ Calculating the Size of the Gantt Bars

The Room In Duration (for Gantt) field is used to encode the horizontal length of the bars. This calculation converts the existing Room Minutes Actual (which is measured in minutes) to a new field that shows these minutes as a fraction of an entire day. There are 1440 minutes in a day, so a case that takes 12 hours will return a Room in Duration (for Gantt) of 0.5; 6 hours will be 0.25; and so on.

4 Format the chart

» Drag and drop "Add-on vs Scheduled Flag" from the Dimensions window to Color on the Marks card. If needed, edit color for "Elective" to blue and for "Add-on" to orange.

» Right-click the "SUM(Room Minutes Actual)" pill on the Marks card.

» Select "Format."

» With the Pane tab selected, change the Default Alignment to "Horizontal Center."

To lighten the colors of the bars:

» Click Color on the Marks card.

» Adjust Opacity to "50%."

To hide the Field Labels:

» Right-click either the "Hospital" or the "Operating Room" header.

» Select "Hide Field Labels for Rows."

5 Format the X axis

The marks on the X axis should display time in hours and minutes.

» Right-click the "Room In Time of Day" pill on the Columns shelf.

» Select "Format."

» Select the "Axis" tab at the top of the Format section.

» In the Scales section, select "Numbers."

» Select "Custom."

» In the Custom format field, enter "HH:MM"

» Right-click the X axis.

» Select "Edit Axis."

» Select the "Tick Marks" tab.

» Under Major tick marks, select "Fixed"; in the field "Every," enter "0.04167" units.

Refresher ▶

In this Gantt Chart, tick marks will be set at a custom interval, with each tick mark representing one hour. Because the X axis displays decimal values from 0 to 1, spanning a day, dividing 1 by 24 hours results in the constant interval of 0.04167.

Remove the X axis title:

» Right-click the X axis again.

» Select "Edit Axis."

» Delete the title contents. Since the times are listed on the X axis, the title is unnecessary.

The chart now looks like this:

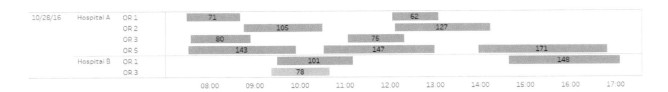

6 Add Reference Lines

To make the chart easier to read, add Reference Lines for two specific time points: 07:30 and 17:00. The hours in between these times represent Prime Time; the hours outside of these times are After Hours.

To add Reference Lines:

» Click the Analytics tab at the top of the Side Bar.

» Drag "Reference Line" to the worksheet and drop onto the "Table" option on the menu that appears.

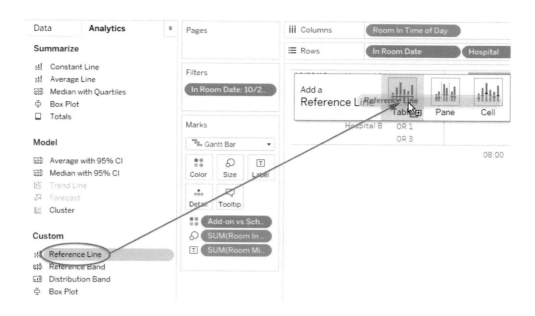

In the Edit Reference Line, Band, or Box dialog box that appears, enter the following to set up the reference line for 07:30 (refer to image below):

>> Line (refer to image below):

   • Value: Click the caret next to "Average" in the field at the right of the dialog box. Select "Constant" from the drop-down menu. Return to the "Value" field at the left and enter "0.3125."

   • Label: Click the caret to the right of "Label" and select "Custom" from the drop-down menu. Enter "07:30" in the field to the right of "Custom."

>> Formatting:

   • Line: Click the caret and select "Dotted" from the drop-down menu.

   • Fill Below: Click the caret and select light blue from the color palette.

   • Click "OK."

273

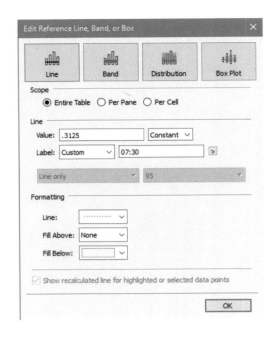

Refresher ▶

Static Reference Lines can be added to a report by changing the Line calculation to Constant, and entering a number. It is important to recall that the X axis still displays a range of numbers from 0 to 1, representing the length of one entire day.

To calculate a specific time, add up the minutes after midnight and divide by the number of minutes in a day (1440):

07:30 = *7 hours, 30 minutes or 450 minutes*

450 divided by 1440 = 0.3125

17:00 = *17 hours or 1020 minutes*

1020 / 1440 = 0.7083

» Follow the same steps to set up a Reference Line for 17:00 except:
- Line Value: "0.7083"
- Label: "Custom" from the drop-down menu; type "17:00"
- Fill Above: light blue

7 Add a Filter

» Right-click the "In Room Date" pill on the Filters shelf.

» Select "Show Filter." The Filter will appear to the right of the worksheet.

» Click the caret to the right of the Filter title "In Room Date" to open a drop-down menu.

» Select "Multiple Values Dropdown" to allow for the selection of one or more dates.

» Click the caret on the Add-on vs Scheduled color legend.

» Select "Hide Card." These colors will be encoded in the chart title.

8 Add a title

» Double-click the Title Row to open the Edit Title dialog box.

» Enter the title, "Daily Operating Room Use, Elective & Add-on Case Times by OR"

» Change the color of "Elective" to blue and of "Add-on" to orange to match the corresponding bars.

9 Rename the worksheet tab and save the worksheet

» Right-click the worksheet tab at the bottom of the workspace, then select "Rename."

» Enter an intuitive title, then click the "Save" icon on the Toolbar.

The final chart looks like this:

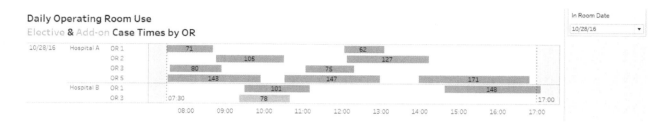

Insight: This Gantt chart allows us to see that Hospital A has four operating rooms open on this day; Hospital B has two. With better scheduling, Hospital A's staff could have performed the same number of cases in just three ORs; Hospital B's staff, in only one.

▐▖ *HDVizoom*™ ...to the Gantt Chart

1 Create new worksheet and connect to data

» At bottom of Tableau workspace, click icon for new worksheet

» In Data pane, select "16 - Operating Room Data" dataset

2 Create chart

» Right-click, drag, and drop "In Room Date" from Dimensions window onto Rows shelf

» Select "In Room Date (Discrete)" from menu that appears

» Drag and drop "Hospital" from Dimensions window onto Rows shelf

» Drag and drop "Operating Room" from Dimensions window onto Rows shelf

» Drag and drop "Room Minutes Actual" from Measures window onto Label on Marks card

» At top of Marks card, change chart from Automatic to "Gantt Bar"

3 Create calculated fields

» Right-click "In Room Date/Time" in Dimensions window

» Select "Create," then "Calculated Field" from sub-menus

» For Calculated Field Name, enter "Room In Time of Day"

» For formula, enter:

`[In Room Date/Time] — [In Room Date]`

» Click "OK"

» Drag and drop new field "Room In Time of Day" from Measures window to Dimensions window.

» Drag and drop "Room In Time of Day" from Dimensions window onto Columns shelf

» Right-click "Room In Time of Day" pill on Columns shelf; from context menu, select "Continuous"

» While holding down Control key, drag and drop "In Room Date" from Rows shelf to Filters shelf

» In Filter Field box, select "Individual dates"

» Click "Next"

» Click "None" to remove all checkmarks, then select individual date "10/28/2016"

» Click "OK"

» Right-click "Room Minutes Actual" in Measures window

» Select "Create," then Calculated Field" from sub-menus

» For Calculated Field name, enter: "Room In Duration (for Gantt)"

» For formula, enter:

`[Room Minutes Actual]/1440`

» Click "OK"

» Drag and drop "Room In Duration (for Gantt)" onto Size on Marks card

4 Format chart

» Drag and drop "Add-on vs Scheduled Flag" from Dimensions window to Color on Marks card. If needed, edit color for "Elective" to blue and for "Add-on" to orange

» Right-click "SUM(Room Minutes Actual)" pill on Marks card

» Select "Format"

» With Pane tab selected, change Default Alignment to "Horizontal Center"

» Click Color on Marks card

» Adjust Opacity to "50%"

» Right-click either "Hospital" or "Operating Room" header

» Select "Hide Field Labels for Rows"

5   Format X axis

» Right-click "Room In Time of Day" pill on Columns shelf

» Select "Format"

» Select "Axis" tab at top of Format section

» In Scales section, select "Numbers"

» Select "Custom"

» In Custom format field, enter "HH:MM"

» Right-click X axis

» Select "Edit Axis"

» Select "Tick Marks" tab

» Under Major tick marks, select "Fixed"; in field "Every," enter "0.04167" units

» Right-click X axis

» Click "Edit Axis"

» Delete title contents

6   Add Reference Lines

» Click Analytics tab at top of Side Bar

» Drag "Reference Line" to worksheet and drop onto "Table" option on menu that appears

» In Edit Reference Line dialog box:

   • Value: Click caret next to "Average" in field at right of dialog box. Select "Constant" from drop-down menu. Return to "Value" field at left and enter "0.3125"

   • Label: Click caret to right of "Label" and select "Custom" from drop-down menu. Enter "07:30" in field to right of "Custom"

» Formatting:

   • Line: click caret and select "Dotted" from drop-down menu

   • Fill Below: click caret and select light blue from color palette

   • Click "OK"

» Perform same steps to set Reference Line for 17:00 except:

   • Line Value: "0.7083"

   • Label: "Custom" "17:00"

   • Fill Above: light blue

7   Add Filter

» Right-click "In Room Date" pill on Filters shelf

» Select "Show Filter"

» Click caret to right of Filter title "In Room Date" to open drop-down menu

» Select "Multiple Values Dropdown" to allow for selection of one or more dates

» Click caret on Add-on vs Scheduled color legend

» Select "Hide card"

8   Add title

» Double-click Title Row to open Edit Title dialog box

» Enter title, "Daily Operating Room Use, Elective & Add-on Case Times by OR"

» Change color of "Elective" to blue and of "Add-on" to orange to match corresponding bars

9   Rename worksheet tab and save worksheet

» Right-click worksheet tab at bottom of workspace, then select "Rename"

» Enter intuitive title, then click "Save" icon on Toolbar

CHAPTER 23

Forecasting

Tableau uses built-in algorithms to forecast time-series data. This feature identifies any patterns that can be used to make predictions based on historical data.

The forecasting feature relies on a statistical concept called *Exponential Smoothing*. The details of this statistical technique will not be covered in this book; in general, the overall effect is an adjustment technique that produces a smoothed time series, where recent observations are given relatively more weight in forecasting than are older ones. Exponential smoothing is effective when the measure to be forecast exhibits trends or seasonality over the period of time on which the forecast is based.

Any time-series chart containing a minimum of five data points can be used to create a forecast. The Analytics pane contains a Forecast option that can be dragged and dropped onto the workspace to add a Forecast to the time-series chart. Alternatively, a forecast can be added by right-clicking a mark or the white space within the work area and selecting Forecast -> Show Forecast.

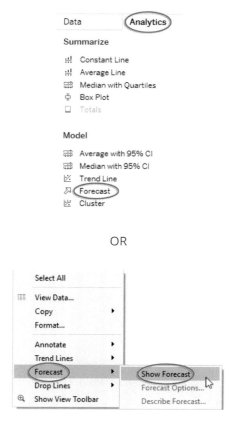

Tableau displays the forecast of estimated future values in a line of lighter color coupled with a shaded band representing the prediction interval. This interval represents the likelihood that the values will be within the shaded band.

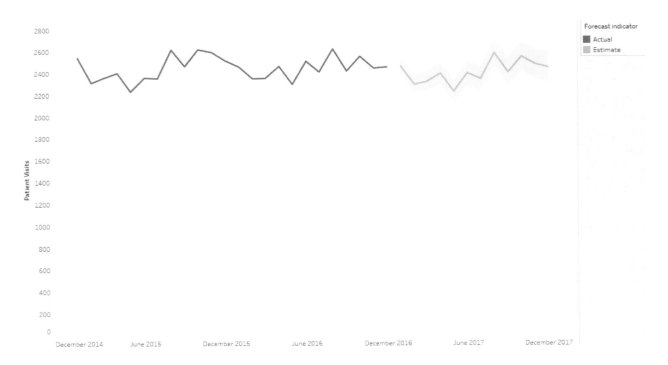

The default Forecast can be edited by right-clicking in the workspace, hovering the cursor over "Forecast" in the menu that appears, and selecting "Forecast Options…"

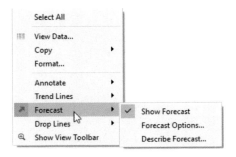

Forecast Options

The Forecast Options dialog box offers several ways to customize a forecast, including adjusting both the length of the forecast and the data's aggregation. The Forecast Model can be edited to exclude seasonality or create a custom model, using additive or multiplicative model types for both Trend and Season.

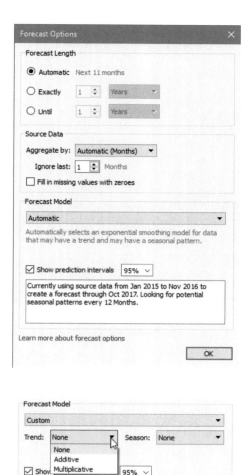

Describe Forecast

In the "Describe Forecast" dialog box, two tabs contain information for this description: Summary and Model.

- The Summary tab lists options for creating the forecast and summary data.

- The Model tab describes the Model used to create the forecast and displays statistical data for Quality Metrics and Smoothing Coefficients.

Requirements and Considerations for Forecasting

1) **Data Types:** Forecasts can be created with a minimum one date dimension and one measure present in the view. If no date dimension is available, a dimension field with integers can be used.

2) **Sufficient Data:** A trend forecast requires at least 5 data points; a seasonal forecast, at least 2 seasons or one season plus 5 periods.

3) **Granularity:** Selection of a level of granularity in the form of a date unit (Year, Month, Quarter, etc.) is required.

4) **Trimming:** If the data cuts off in the middle of the specified date unit (for example, the most recent month is incomplete for a monthly forecast), Tableau can trim the data. Select the option Ignore Last to ensure that the partial period does not decrease the accuracy of the forecast.

5) **Granularity Adjustments:** If there is not enough data to forecast at a particular granularity (for example, only six quarters of data are available), Tableau will instead base the forecast on a monthly algorithm, then aggregate the results by quarter. This happens by default and requires no special configuration.

6) **Improved Accuracy:** The more data points in the forecast model, the more accurate the prediction is likely to be.

Dashboards & Story Points

CHAPTER 24

Dashboards

A Dashboard, when properly designed, enables at-a-glance display and monitoring of crucial information. A well-designed Dashboard includes only what is necessary; condenses information without compromising its meaning; and employs display mechanisms that, even when small, can be easily read and understood. Tableau further defines a Dashboard as a combined display of worksheets in a single screen.

This section and the two that follow demonstrate how to construct a Surgical Volume Dashboard. The process emphasizes the best design practices and uses many of Tableau's interactive features to create an engaging user experience.

Section 1 builds and formats a simple Tableau Dashboard from three worksheets. Section 2 adds basic interactivity to the Dashboard using quick filters and action filters. Section 3 adds interactivity between two separate Dashboards with links, a back button, an information button, and dynamic titles.

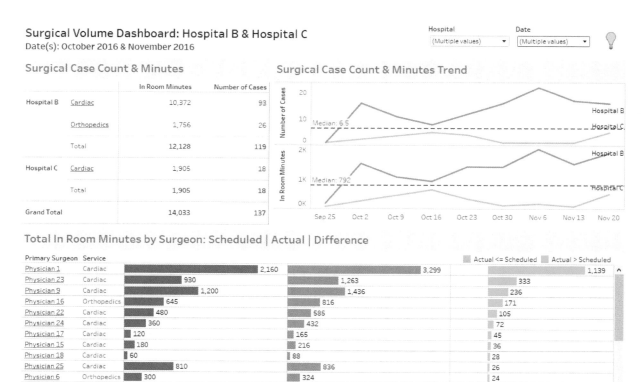

Special note for building the Dashboard example in this chapter: The data file entitled "Tableau 10 Training Workbook – Dashboard New" contains four pre-built worksheets. Three of these will be assembled in the primary Dashboard; the fourth will be part of a second Dashboard to illustrate interactivity between dashboards.

24.1 Dashboards: Basic Building and Formatting

How To: Build and format a simple Dashboard showing surgical case counts, case minutes, and comparison of actual versus scheduled case times.

Surgical Volume Dashboard
Dates of Operation: 9/2016 - 11/2016

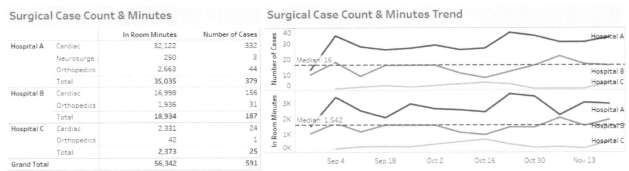

Surgical Case Count & Minutes

		In Room Minutes	Number of Cases
Hospital A	Cardiac	32,122	332
	Neurosurge.	250	3
	Orthopedics	2,663	44
	Total	35,035	379
Hospital B	Cardiac	16,998	156
	Orthopedics	1,936	31
	Total	18,934	187
Hospital C	Cardiac	2,331	24
	Orthopedics	42	1
	Total	2,373	25
Grand Total		56,342	591

Surgical Case Count & Minutes Trend

Total In Room Minutes by Surgeon: Scheduled | Actual | Difference

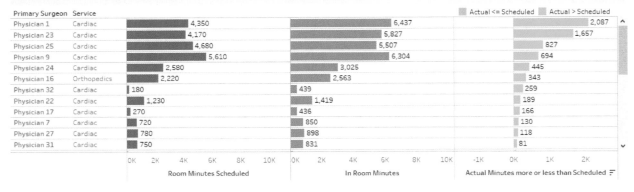

Data Source: *De-identified hospital surgical data*

About the Data: *The three worksheets created for this dashboard exercise display surgical case data that includes the number of surgical procedures performed and the time (in minutes) the procedures (a) were scheduled for and (b) actually took. The date range is September to November 2016. Data is displayed by hospital, service, and surgeon.*

1 Open a new dashboard

» There are two ways to open a new Dashboard:

Option 1: Click "Dashboard" on the File row, then select "New Dashboard."

Option 2: At the far right of the bottom row of tabs, click the Dashboard icon.

Tableau Dashboard Workspace

When a new Dashboard is opened, the multipurpose pane on the left side of the screen changes to show features and controls needed to create a dashboard.

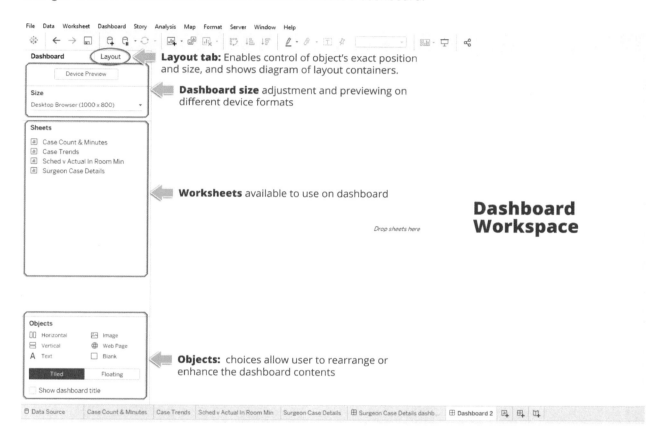

2 Create the dashboard

Worksheets are the building blocks of the Dashboard. The Surgical Volume Dashboard will be created from three of the four worksheets pre-built for this exercise.

» In the left column, "Sheets" section, click "Case Count & Minutes," then drag and drop it onto the Dashboard workspace.

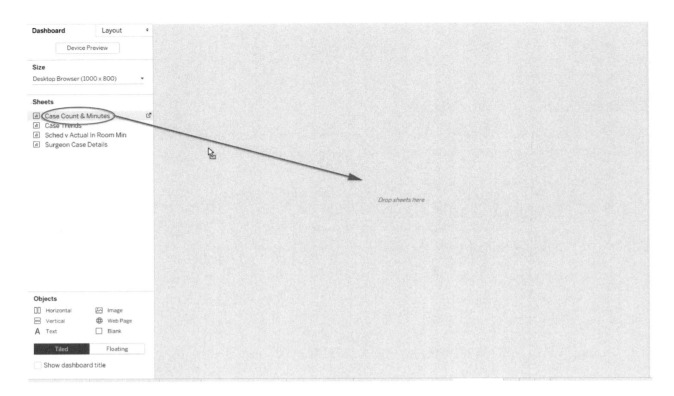

▲ **Worksheet Preview**

Hover over a selected Dashboard Worksheet to view a thumbnail image of the corresponding chart.

Notice that when a worksheet is dragged onto the Dashboard workspace, the color of the workspace changes to gray. This color change highlights active areas for worksheet placement.

» Drag the worksheet "Case Trends" to the Dashboard workspace.

» Drop the worksheet to the right of the "Case Count & Minutes" worksheet.

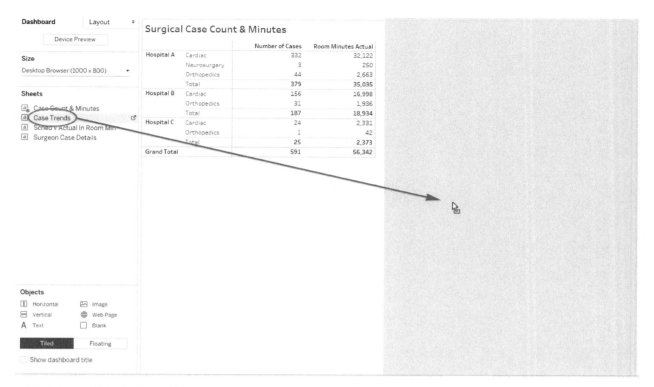

▲ Dashboard Worksheet Placement

*As worksheets are moved onto the Dashboard workspace, it is useful to experiment with placement to make location options clear. Try dragging one to the workspace and moving it around from place to place **before dropping it,** observing the movement of the active gray areas. The worksheet may be dropped in any active gray space.*

◀ Active Worksheets on Dashboard

Checkmarks in the Dashboard section highlight worksheets currently displayed in the workspace.

The third worksheet should now be located below the first two. However, unless the bottom of the display is visible, it is virtually impossible to place a worksheet there.

» Using the right scroll bar, move all the way to the bottom of the Dashboard.

» Drag and drop the "Sched v Actual In Room Min" worksheet onto the Dashboard in the gray highlighted section below the two worksheets already present.

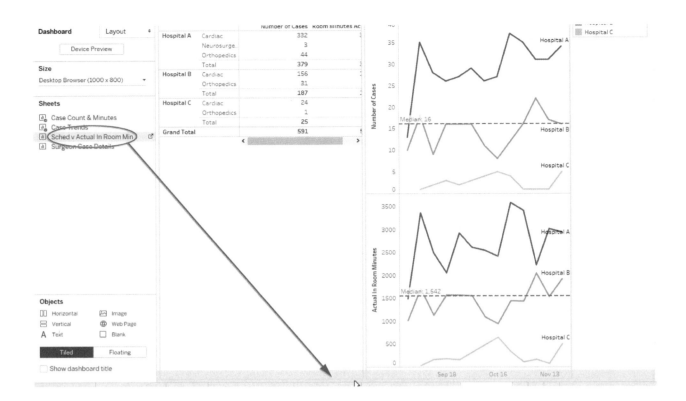

The dashboard now looks like this:

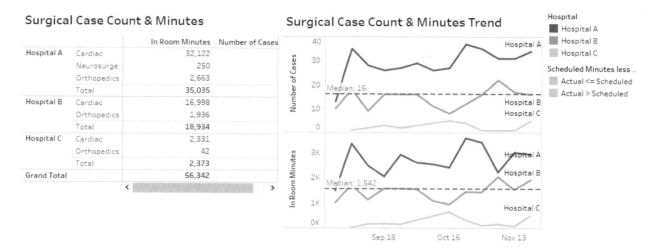

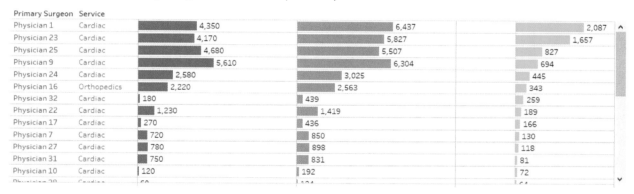

3 Adjust the dashboard display size

» Near the top of the Dashboard pane, find the "Size" section.

» Click the caret to the right of "Desktop Browser (1000 x 800)" to view display-size options. (Tableau defaults the Dashboard size to Desktop.)

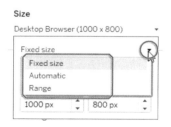

◄ **Dashboard Size Options**

There are three high-level overall size options:

Fixed size: contains a menu of many common resolutions to help inform choices

Automatic: dynamically adjusts the size of the dashboard based on the user's screen size

Range: permits setting minimum and/or maximum resolution to provide flexibility

» For this example dashboard, select "Fixed size."

The default "Desktop Browser (1000 x 800) appears below it.

» Click the caret to the right to view the many fixed size options.

» Select "Letter Landscape (1100 x 850).

Best Practice

Dashboard resolution can vary widely depending on the device used to display reports. If the end-user's device is known, Tableau makes it easy to optimize dashboards with a "Device Preview" tool. A gray box reveals how the dashboard will look on the selected device.

Consider the range of devices used by the target audience and build compatibility with the smallest resolution for that range. If reports are customarily printed, Letter Portrait and Letter Landscape are generally successful.

4 Format the dashboard

Dashboard real estate is very high value; it is therefore crucial to format with the goal of re-ducing white space and highlighting content. The example Dashboard below contains scroll-bars and some white space that need adjustment to ensure that the visualizations have as much room as possible. Scroll bars can be off-putting and impede at-a-glance comprehen-sion, so eliminating them where possible is desirable. Excess white space is often generated when a worksheet is moved to the workspace: any quick filters and legends associated with it are by default displayed at the right edge; the resulting white space needs to be eliminated.

Surgical Case Count & Minutes

Hospital	Service	In Room Minutes	Number of Cases
Hospital A	Cardiac	32,122	332
	Neurosurge.	250	3
	Orthopedics	2,663	44
	Total	35,035	379
Hospital B	Cardiac	16,998	156
	Orthopedics	1,936	31
	Total	18,934	187
Hospital C	Cardiac	2,331	24
	Orthopedics	42	1
	Total	2,373	25
Grand Total		56,342	591

Surgical Case Count & Minutes Trend

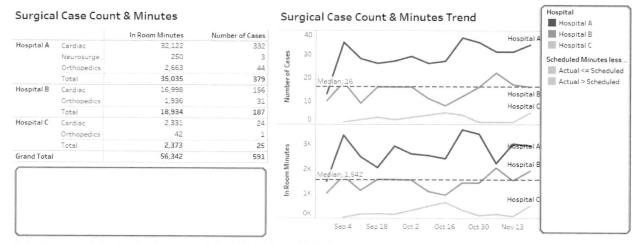

Total In Room Minutes by Surgeon: Scheduled | Actual | Difference

Primary Surgeon	Service			
Physician 1	Cardiac	4,350	6,437	2,087
Physician 23	Cardiac	4,170	5,827	1,657
Physician 25	Cardiac	4,680	5,507	827
Physician 9	Cardiac	5,610	6,304	694
Physician 24	Cardiac	2,580	3,025	445
Physician 16	Orthopedics	2,220	2,563	343
Physician 32	Cardiac	180	439	259
Physician 22	Cardiac	1,230	1,419	189
Physician 17	Cardiac	270	436	166
Physician 7	Cardiac	720	850	130
Physician 27	Cardiac	780	898	118
Physician 31	Cardiac	750	831	81

» Click the "Surgical Case Count & Minutes" worksheet on the Dashboard to highlight. A gray border appears around the worksheet indicating that it is active. In the right corner, a caret will appear.

» Click the caret to display a drop-down menu.

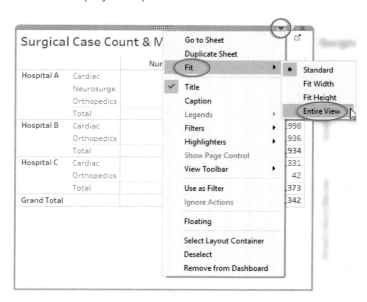

◄ Dashboard Adjustments

Nearly every object on a dashboard has this drop-down caret, providing many options to fine-tune appearance and control the object's behavior.

» Select "Fit."

» Select "Entire View."

» Follow the same steps for the "Surgical Case & Minutes Trend" worksheet.

» Follow the same steps for the "Total In Room Minutes by Surgeon..." worksheet, but choose "Fit Width."

▲ Refresher

When selecting a Fit option, keep in mind that a worksheet may grow if data is increased in the future. If for example many hospitals or services are added, displaying the worksheet in Entire View could make it cramped and illegible. Consider Fit Width instead: a scrollbar will enable the user to see additional data.

The top color legend corresponds to the Surgical Case Count & Minutes Trend worksheet. Each trend line is labeled with a hospital name, so the "Hospital" color legend is unnecessary.

» Click the "Hospital" color legend to highlight.

» Click the "X" in the top right corner to delete the legend.

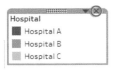

Relocate and format the "Scheduled less Actual" color legend to reduce excess white space.

» Click the "Scheduled less Actual" color legend to highlight.

» Click the caret.

» From the menu, select "Floating."

Tiled vs. Floating Layout ▶

Tiled worksheets are displayed side-by-side, with no overlaps, in the Dashboard workspace. The active gray space previously described provides a grid-like area for placement of worksheets. Tiled is Tableau's default layout, and is recommended practice for worksheets and filters. Floating worksheets, in contrast, can be placed anywhere on the Dashboard, and can overlap others; this ability is useful in the display of legends.

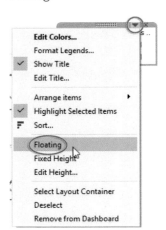

The "Scheduled less Actual" color legend is now highlighted and separated from the Dashboard.

» Click the dotted bar at the top of the floated color legend. The cursor changes to a bi-directional arrow, and the color legend can be moved.

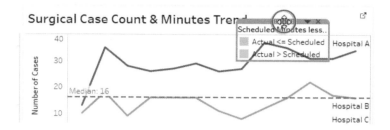

» Drag and drop the color legend to just above the orange and blue bars of the Scheduled less Actual (min) portion of the bottom worksheet.

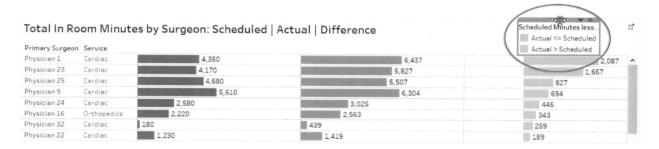

» Click the caret on the floated color legend.

» Click the "Show Title" option on the menu to remove the current checkmark.

» Click the caret on the floated color legend again.

» Select "Arrange Items."

» Select "Single Row."

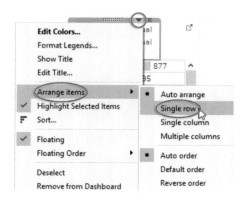

» Hover on the right border of the floated color legend until a bi-directional arrow appears.

» Click and drag to the appropriate width.

» Adjust the width, height, and location of the color legend to desired proportions.

» If the two color labels are not completely visible, hover between them to display a vertical dotted border. Click and drag the border to the right to display the labels.

» Click anywhere outside of the Dashboard workspace to de-select the floated color legend.

To adjust the size of individual worksheets:

» Hover the cursor over the right border of the "Surgical Case Count & Minutes" worksheet until it changes to a bi-directional arrow.

» Click and drag the border to the desired width. Note that when the border is dragged, it changes to a black line.

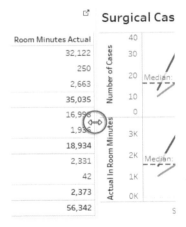

The height of the worksheets needs slight adjustment for visual balance.

» Hover the cursor over the bottom border of the same worksheet.

» Click and drag the border to the desired height.

» Adjust the placement of the floating "Sched v Actual" color legend as needed.

The dashboard now looks like this:

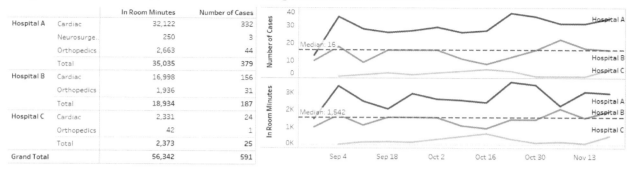

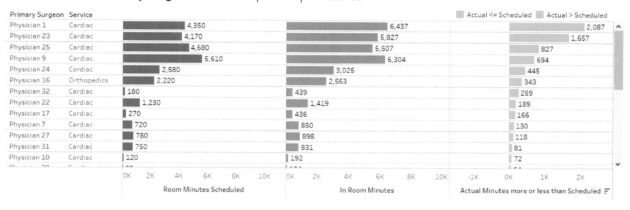

5 Format the worksheet titles

Formatting titles makes it easier to distinguish among similar worksheets, and enhances general readability.

» Click the "Surgical Case Count & Minutes" worksheet to highlight.

» Right-click the Title Row.

» Select "Edit Title" from the menu.

» Highlight the complete title.

» Click the caret for the color palette and select the dark blue square.

» Click "OK."

» Right-click the Title Row again.

» Select "Format Title..."

» Under "Shading," select a light blue square from the color palette.

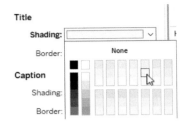

» Perform the same steps for the remaining worksheets on the Dashboard.

» To close the Format window, click the "X" in its upper right corner.

Best Practice

Using titles to frame individual dashboard sections as described above is one approach to layout and design. It is sensible to take audience, data, and potential use into consideration when selecting design elements such as color, arrangement, and labeling.

6 **Add a dashboard title**

» Drag and drop a Text box from the Dashboard pane to the top of the Dashboard sheet. (The active gray space will appear at the very top.)

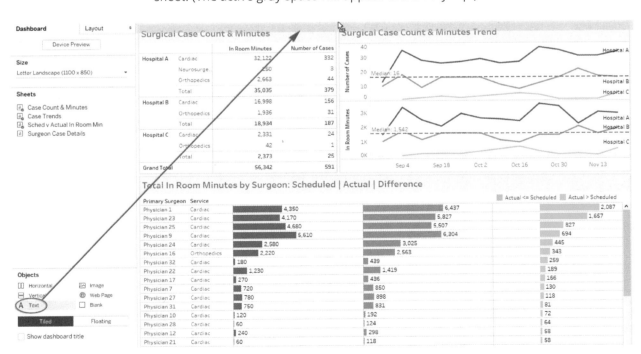

Layout containers are a formatting feature used to organize worksheets in a dashboard. They can sometimes cause confusion for new Tableau users because the alignment of objects is restricted to either horizontal or vertical. Checking the Show Dashboard Title button adds the title within a vertical layout container and prevents additional objects from being added to the right of the title. For this reason, a title using the Text Box object, which does not create a new layout container, is being added here.

» In the Edit Text dialog box, enter the title: "Surgical Volume Dashboard, Dates of Operation: 9/2016 – 11/2016"

» Choose font type and size. (This example uses Tableau Book, Bold, 18-point for the title, and 12-point for the subtitle. The font color has been changed to a dark gray.)

» Click "OK."

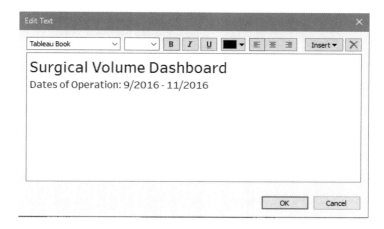

» Hover the cursor over the bottom border of the title text box on the Dashboard until it changes to a bi-directional arrow.

» Click and drag the title text box border to desired height.

7 Rename the dashboard tab and save the dashboard

» Right-click the "Dashboard 2" tab at the bottom of the workspace.

» Select "Rename Sheet."

» Enter title, "Surgical Volume Dashboard."

» Press the Enter key to save.

The dashboard now looks like this (below). It is simply formatted and contains no interactivity. A great deal more work will be required to transform it into a powerful tool that fully informs its viewers. *It is crucial to follow all remaining instructions in this chapter to create a production-ready dashboard.*

Surgical Volume Dashboard
Dates of Operation: 9/2016 - 11/2016

Surgical Case Count & Minutes

		In Room Minutes	Number of Cases
Hospital A	Cardiac	32,122	332
	Neurosurge...	250	3
	Orthopedics	2,663	44
	Total	35,035	379
Hospital B	Cardiac	16,998	156
	Orthopedics	1,936	31
	Total	18,934	187
Hospital C	Cardiac	2,331	24
	Orthopedics	42	1
	Total	2,373	25
Grand Total		56,342	591

Surgical Case Count & Minutes Trend

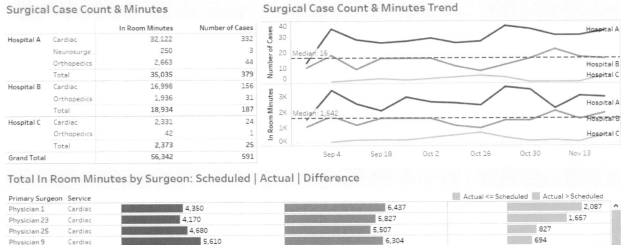

Total In Room Minutes by Surgeon: Scheduled | Actual | Difference

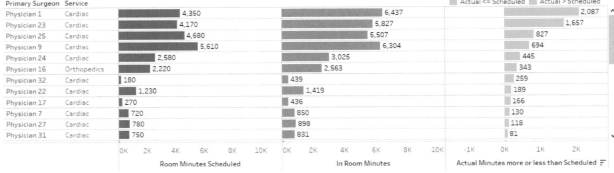

Insight: Organization of this Surgical Volume Dashboard allows the report viewer to see the data first, aggregated for all three months by Hospital and Service; then trended over time; then in a comparison of scheduled versus actual In Room times in minutes by Surgeon, per Service.

◨ *HDVizoom*™ ...to Dashboard Basics

1   Open new dashboard

» To open new dashboard, either:
  - Click "Dashboard" on File row, then select "New Dashboard" or
  - Click "Dashboard" icon at far right of bottom row of tabs

2   Create dashboard

» In left column, "Sheets" section, click "Case Count & Minutes" and drag and drop onto dashboard workspace

» Drag worksheet "Case Trends" onto Dashboard workspace and drop to right of "Case Count & Minutes" worksheet

» Using right scroll bar, move to bottom of Dashboard

» Drag and drop "Sched v Actual In Room Min" worksheet onto Dashboard in gray highlighted section below two worksheets already present

3   Adjust dashboard display size

» Near top of Dashboard pane, find "Size" section

» Click caret to right of "Desktop Browser (1000 x 800)" to view display-size options

» Select "Fixed Size"

» Click caret to right of lower "Desktop browser"

» Select "Letter Landscape (1100 x 850)"

4   Format dashboard

» Click "Surgical Case Count & Minutes" worksheet to highlight

» Click caret to display drop-down menu

» Select "Fit"

» Select "Entire View"

» Perform same steps for "Surgical Case & Minutes Trend" worksheet

» Perform same steps for "Total In Room Minutes by Surgeon..." worksheet; choose "Fit Width"

» Click "Hospital" color legend to highlight

» Click "X" in top right corner to delete legend

» Click "Scheduled less Actual" color legend to highlight

» Click caret

» From menu, select "Floating"

» Click dotted bar at top of floated color legend

» Drag and drop color legend to a spot just above orange and blue bars of Scheduled less Actual (min) portion of bottom worksheet

» Click caret on floated color legend

» Click "Show Title" option on menu to remove current checkmark

» Click caret on floated color legend again

» Select "Arrange Items"

» Select "Single Row"

» Hover on right border of floated color legend until bi-directional arrow appears

» Click and drag border to appropriate width

» Adjust width, height, and location of color legend to desired proportions

» If color labels are not completely visible, hover between labels to display vertical dotted border. Click and drag border to right to display labels

» Click anywhere outside of Dashboard workspace to de-select floated color legend

» Click "Surgical Case Count & Minutes" worksheet to highlight

» Hover cursor on right border until it changes to bi-directional arrow

» Click and drag border to desired width

» Hover cursor over bottom border of same worksheet

» Click and drag border to desired height

» Adjust placement of floating "Sched v Actual" color legend as needed

5 **Format worksheet titles**

» Click "Surgical Case Count & Minutes" worksheet to highlight

» Right-click Title Row

» Select "Edit Title" from menu

» Highlight complete title

» Click caret for color palette and select dark blue square

» Click "OK"

» Right-click Title Row again

» Select "Format Title..."

» Under Shading, select light blue square from color palette

» Perform same steps for remaining worksheets on Dashboard

» To close Format window, click "X" in its upper right corner

6 **Add Dashboard Title**

» Drag and drop Text box from Dashboard pane to top of Dashboard sheet

» In Edit Text dialog box, enter title: "Surgical Volume Dashboard, Dates of Operation: 9/2016 – 11/2016"

» Choose font type and size (example uses Tableau Book, Bold, 18-point for title, 12-point for subtitle)

» Click "OK"

» Hover cursor over bottom border of title text box on Dashboard until it changes to bi-directional arrow

» Click and drag title text box to desired height

7 **Rename dashboard tab and save dashboard**

» Right-click "Dashboard 2" tab at bottom of workspace

» Select "Rename Sheet"

» Enter title, "Surgical Volume Dashboard"

» Press Enter key to save

24.2 Dashboard: Basic Interactivity

nteractivity makes Tableau dashboards more powerful. Continuing with the dashboard developed in the previous section, Dashboards: Basic Interactivity shows how to implement different types of filters—specifically multi-worksheet Filters and Actions—that give the user more flexibility in viewing both *particular* data and *more* data within the same dashboard layout.

Filters for Multiple Worksheets

Filters applied to multiple worksheets enable the user to filter for a specific category of data and have that category apply to all the worksheets within the Dashboard. In the example Dashboard below, the Surgical Case Count & Minutes worksheet contains three Hospitals (A, B, and C). By adding a Filter for Hospital to the Dashboard, the user can select a specific hospital and view that hospital's data in each worksheet on the Dashboard.

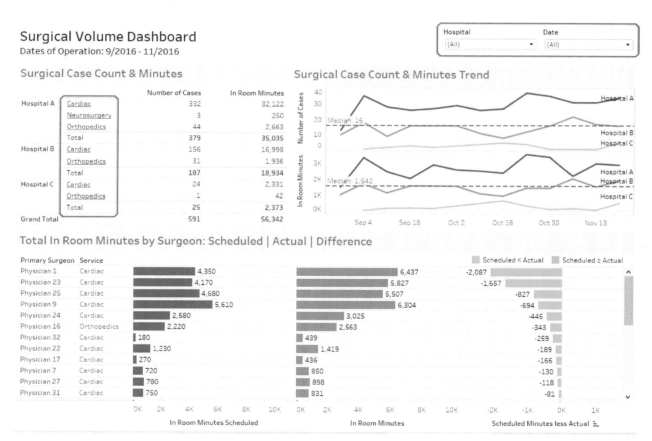

303

1 Insert and format a Hospital Filter

Begin by applying a Hospital Filter to the Dashboard.

» Click the "Surgical Case Count & Minutes" worksheet on the Dashboard to highlight.

» Click the caret that appears at the top right.

» Select "Filters."

» Select "Hospital."

The Filter appears at the top right of the Dashboard.

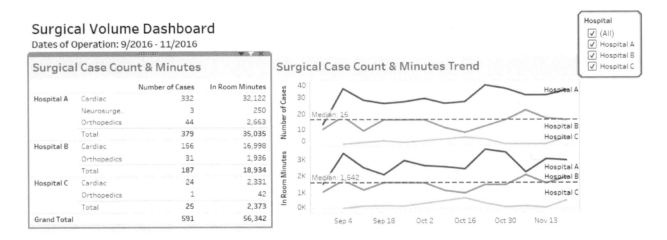

▲ **Refresher**

Just as with worksheets, Dashboard Filters can be customized to display values as check boxes, drop-downs, custom lists, or even sliders. Filter size and placement can be adjusted just like any other Dashboard object.

» Click the Filter to highlight.

» Click the caret that appears at the top right.

» Click "Apply to Worksheets."

» Select "Selected Worksheets..."

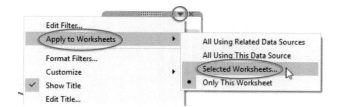

*A Filter can be applied to one or more worksheet(s) that use the same data source or a related data source with at least one common linking field. Remember that a Filter can control filters on other worksheets not present on the Dashboard, so be careful to include **only** the worksheets that really are to be filtered.*

» Click the boxes next to each worksheet (or, more efficiently, click the "All on dashboard" button at the bottom of the dialog box).

» Click "OK."

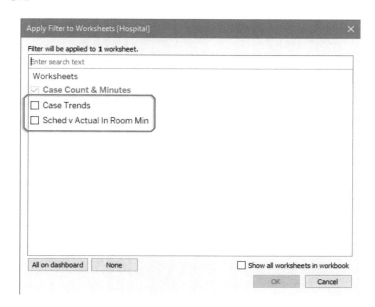

Now, test the filter.

» Select one hospital (e.g., Hospital A) and observe how the filter displays the data on all worksheets for the selected hospital.

2 Insert and format a Date Filter

Another type of filter that can be added to a Dashboard is a Date Filter, which allows the user to focus on a specific day, week, or month of data. Adding a Date Filter requires a different procedure from the one previously discussed; it cannot be added the same way the Hospital Filter was. There is no date option on the Filter menu, because a date field is not present on the worksheet. To add a Date Filter, therefore, start with an addition to the worksheet—a Date field.

» Hover over the top right corner of the "Surgical Case Count & Minutes" worksheet.

» Click it to navigate to the worksheet.

In the Case Count & Minutes worksheet:

> » Drag and drop "In Room Date" from the Dimensions window onto the Filters shelf.

> » Select "Month/Year" from the dialog box that appears.

> » Click "Next."

> » Click the "All" button, then click "OK."

Notice two of the pills on the Filters shelf: "Hospital" and "MY(In Room Date)." The "Hospital" pill has a small icon to its left. Hovering over the icon reveals that it represents the filter being applied to selected worksheets on the Dashboard. The "MY(In Room Date)" pill, with no icon, currently applies only to the active worksheet.

Filter Icons ▶

An icon next to a pill on the Filters shelf will indicate whether the filter applies only to the active worksheet (no icon); to multiple worksheets (stacked chart icon); to all worksheets using this data source (database cylinder icon); or to worksheets using related data sources (two cylinders with a connecting arrow).

> » Navigate back to the Dashboard by selecting the "Surgical Volume Dashboard" tab at the bottom of the worksheet.

> » Click the caret that appears on the highlighted "Surgical Case Count & Minutes" worksheet.

> » Click "Filters." Now the "Month, Year of In Room Date" is listed as a Filter selection.

> » Select "Month, Year of In Room Date."

Making Filters Available on a Dashboard ▶

As demonstrated in the example to the left, a Filter will be available for use on a Dashboard only if the field is currently present on the selected worksheet. Here, for example, the option to add a Date Filter was not visible until it was manually added to the Filters shelf of the worksheet.

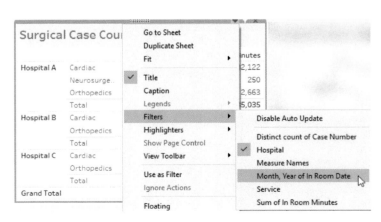

"Month, Year of In Room Date" appears as a Filter beneath the Hospital Filter on the Dashboard. The Date Filter now needs to be applied to the selected worksheets.

> » Click the "Month, Year of In Room Date" Filter to highlight.
> » Click the caret that appears at the top right.
> » Click "Apply to Worksheets."
> » Select "Selected Worksheets..."
> » Click the "All on Dashboard" button.
> » Click "OK."

Test the Date filter.

> » Select one date and observe how the data displays on all worksheets for the selected date.

3 Format the dashboard

The new Filters create unnecessary, wasteful white space on the right side of the Dashboard. Eliminate this space with additional formatting.

> » Click the "Hospital" Filter to highlight.
> » Hover the cursor over the top center border until it changes to a cross shape.

> » Click and drag the Filter box to the right of the Dashboard title. A gray rectangle appears to show where the Filter can be dropped.
> » Release the Filter to the right of the title.

The Hospital Filter requires a different selection option to work better in this space.

>> Click the "Hospital" Filter caret to display a menu.

>> Select "Multiple Values (dropdown)"

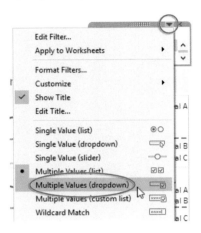

>> Follow the same steps for the Date Filter.

>> Adjust the width of the Filters and, if necessary, the height of the Dashboard title text box to fit all three components legibly into the allotted space.

The title of the "Month, Year of In Room Date" Filter can be shortened to "Date."

>> Double-click the "Month, Year of In Room Date" Quick Filter title.

>> Shorten the title to "Date."

>> Test the Filters by selecting different hospitals and different dates to ensure that all sheets change as the filters change.

The Dashboard now looks like this:

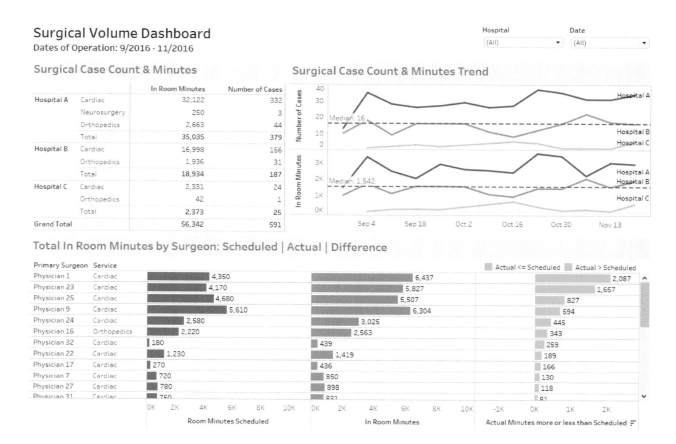

4 Add and format an Action (Intra-dashboard)

While Quick Filters reside on the periphery of the Dashboard in a menu section, Action Filters reside within the dashboard itself. These allow the user to select data in one worksheet to filter results in another one. Action Filters are useful for minimizing the clutter of multiple Quick Filters while still enabling the user to control what data is displayed. For this example, an Action Filter will be set up using the Service field.

> » Click the "Surgical Case Count & Minutes" worksheet to highlight.

> » Click the caret that appears at the top right.

> » Select "Use as Filter."

Use as Filter Feature ▶

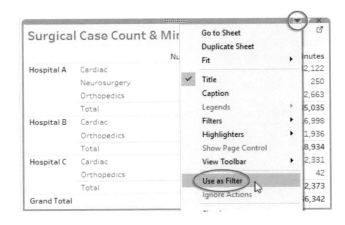

This feature designates a particular worksheet as the source of an Action Filter that will affect every other worksheet in the Dashboard. Tableau automatically applies every single dimension as a filter to the other worksheets, assuming they share a data source. In this example, choosing Use as Filter creates an Action Filter that applies Hospital and Service to the other worksheets in the Dashboard. If the user clicks on Hospital A, the other worksheets filter only for Hospital A. If the user clicks the bar for Cardiac at Hospital A, the other worksheets filter for both Cardiac and Hospital A.

Rather than searching for Use as Filter on the drop-down menu, save time by clicking the funnel icon in the right corner of the worksheet.

To set Service as an exclusive filter (regardless of what Hospital the Service is under), edit the Action as follows:

>> Click "Dashboard" on the Menu row.

>> Select "Actions…"

Edit Actions ▶

*In the Actions context box in the screenshot below, notice **Filter 1 (generated)**. When the **Use as Filter** option was selected, it caused Tableau to generate an Action Filter applying all possible fields of the original worksheet to the target worksheets. For additional options, the Action Filter can be edited or even removed.*

Highlight Actions and URL Actions can also be created via this menu. Highlight Actions intensify the colors of all marks of interest while fading those of others; URL Actions navigate to a website or web-hosted file via a new browser tab.

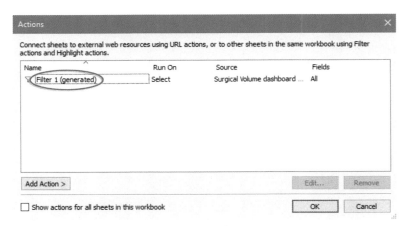

» Click the "Filter 1 (generated)" title to highlight.

» Click the "Edit..." button.

Follow these steps in the Edit Filter Action dialog box:

» Change Name to "Service Filter."

» Under Source Sheets, ensure that only the "Case Count & Minutes" box is checked.

» Under Run action on, click the "Select" button.

» Under Target Sheets, leave all boxes checked.

» Under Clearing the selection will: make sure that "Show all values" is selected.

» Under Target Filters, choose "Selected Fields."

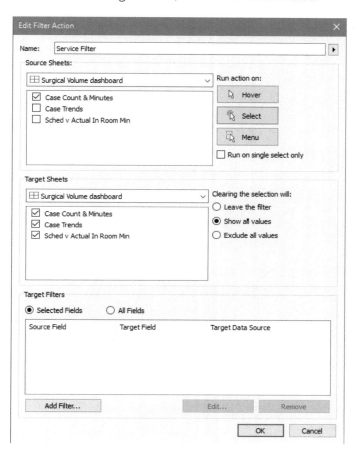

◀ Elements of an Action

1) Name: *Provide a descriptive name so that each Action on a list can be easily identified by other developers.*

2) Source Sheets: *Start here to select the worksheet that will initiate the Action.*

3) Run action on: *This option specifies what user prompt (Hover, Select, or Menu) starts the action. Select is the most frequently chosen trigger.*

4) Target Sheets: *Designates the worksheets to be filtered when the Source Sheet is activated. The dropdown menu permits selecting worksheets on the same dashboard as the Source Sheet's; on a different dashboard from the Source Sheet's; or on individual worksheets not present on a dashboard.*

5) Clearing the selection will: *When the Action on the source sheet is deselected, this option allows the user to leave the filter displayed on the target sheets; show all data on the target sheets; or remove all data until a new Action is initiated.*

6) Target Filters: *This section enables transmitting either all possible fields to the target sheets or only specific ones. (Actions can pass only Dimensions that are present somewhere on the source sheet.)*

311

» Click the "Add Filter..." button at the bottom of the dialog box.

» Under each of the two "Field" options, choose "Service" from the drop-down menu.

» Click "OK" to close all three open dialog boxes.

Selected Fields ▶

When working with multiple data sources, and to ensure precision, use the Selected Fields option (under Target Filters in the Edit Filter Action dialog box) to focus exclusively on one or more fields. Applying only Selected Fields gives more control over exactly what will be sent from Source to Target worksheets. Using this menu, Tableau can pass an Action across different data sources. The fields for Source and Target must be defined in the Add Filter dialog box.

After the addition of the Service Action, click any one of the Services in the Surgical Case Count & Minutes worksheet to test that all worksheets filter for the selected Service. Click the same Service again to undo the Action.

It will not, however, be immediately evident that this Action is present; to make it more obvious, format each Service name as a hyperlink. Clicking on any Service hyperlink redisplays the Dashboard viewed through the Service Action.

   » Right-click any Service name.

   » Select "Format" from the menu.

   » In the Format window, select the "Header" tab.

   » Click the caret to the right of "Font."

   » Click the underline option, "U."

   » Select a bright blue square from the color palette. (Select the "More Colors" option to reveal all choices.)

   » In the "Totals" and "Grand Totals" section of the Format window, reverse the above steps to remove the underline and return the font color to gray.

Now each Service name looks like a hyperlink, inviting the user to click it and thus engage the Action.

The third and final part of the Dashboards section, Advanced Interactivity, covers maneuvering to a second dashboard and creating navigation and information buttons. This section guides the user in completingpreparation of this example Dashboard for production.

▐▙ *HDVizoom*™...to Dashboard Basic Interactivity

1 Insert and format Hospital Filter

» Click "Surgical Case Count & Minutes" worksheet on Dashboard to highlight

» Click caret that appears top right

» Select "Filters"

» Select "Hospital"

» Click Filter to highlight

» Click caret that appears at top right

» Click "Apply to Worksheets"

» Select "Selected Worksheets..."

» Click boxes next to each worksheet (or Click "All on Dashboard" button)

» Click "OK"

» Select one hospital (e.g., Hospital A) and observe how filter displays data on all worksheets for selected hospital

2 Insert and format Date Filter

» Hover over top right corner of "Surgical Case Count & Minutes" worksheet. Click small box with arrow to navigate to corresponding worksheet

» Drag and drop "In Room Date" from Dimensions window onto Filters shelf

» Select "Month/Year" from dialog box that appears

» Click "Next"

» Click "All" button, then click "OK"

» Navigate back to Dashboard by selecting "Surgical Volume Dashboard" tab at bottom of worksheet

» Click caret of highlighted "Surgical Case Count & Minutes" worksheet

» Click "Filters"

» Select "Month, Year of In Room Date" from list

» Click "Month, Year of In Room Date" Filter to highlight

» Click caret that appears at top right

» Click "Apply to Worksheets"

» Select "Selected Worksheets..."

» Click "All on Dashboard" button

» Click "OK"

» Select one date in Filter and observe how data displays on all worksheets for selected date

3 Format dashboard

» Click "Hospital" Filter to highlight

» Hover cursor over top center border until cursor changes to cross shape

» Click and drag Filter box to right of Dashboard title

» Release Filter to right of title

» Click "Hospital" Filter caret to display menu

» Select "Multiple Values (dropdown)"

» Follow same steps for Date Filter

» Adjust width of Filters and, if necessary, height of Dashboard title text box to fit all three components legibly into allotted space

» Double-click "Month, Year of In Room" Filter title

» Shorten title to "Date"

» Test Filters by selecting different hospitals and different date selections to ensure that all sheets change as filters change

4 **Add and format Action (intra-dashboard)**

» Click "Surgical Case Count & Minutes" worksheet to highlight

» Click caret that appears at top right

» Select "Use as Filter"

» Click "Dashboard" on Menu row

» Select "Actions..."

» Click "Filter 1 (generated)" title to highlight

» Click "Edit..." button

» Follow these steps in Edit Filter Action dialog box:

   • Change Name to "Service filter"

   • Under Source Sheets, ensure that only "Case Count & Minutes" box is checked

   • Under Run action on, click "Select" button

   • Under Target Sheets, leave all boxes checked

   • Under Clearing selection will: make sure "Show all values" is selected

   • Under Target Filters, choose "Selected Fields"

   • Click "Add Filter..." button at bottom of dialog box

   • Under each of two "Field" options, choose "Service" from dropdown menu

   • Click "OK" to close all three open dialog boxes

» Right-click any Service name

» Select "Format" from menu

» In Format window, select "Header" tab

» Click caret to right of "Font"

» Click underline option, "U"

» Select bright blue square from color palette (select "More Colors" option to reveal all choices)

» In "Totals" and "Grand Totals" sections of Format window, reverse above steps to remove underline and return font color to gray

24.3 Dashboards: Advanced Interactivity

n addition to their other functions, Tableau Dashboards convey the ability to interact with and navigate between dashboards or between a dashboard and a worksheet. This section details how to create a[n]:

- Action to navigate to another dashboard

- Back Button to return to a previous dashboard

- Information Button to reveal or hide additional text

- Dynamic Title that changes based on the filters selected

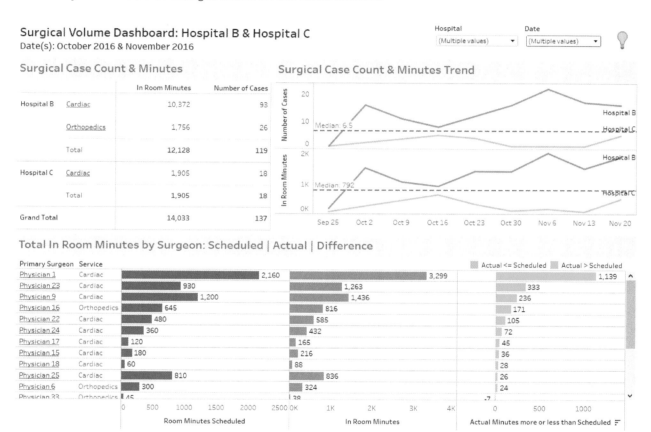

315

Best Practice

In addition to design and layout, report interactivity is a crucial element in creating a high-impact dashboard suite. This interactivity includes filtering within a dashboard; drilling down to more detailed dashboards, then returning to the starting point; and hovering to obtain additional information. This section will help designers turn individual reports into a unified user experience.

Continuing with the construction of the Surgical Volume Dashboard, this section creates an Action allowing the user to navigate from the existing Surgical Volume Dashboard to a more granular dashboard ("Surgeon Case Details") provided in the current example workbook. The Action is engaged by clicking a primary surgeon's name in the source Dashboard to drill down to surgical case details.

1 **Add and format an Action (Inter-dashboard)**

» Open the "Surgical Volume Dashboard."

» Click "Dashboards" on the Menu bar.

» Click "Actions..." (the "Service filter" that appears under "Name" was created in the previous section)

» Click the "Add Action" button.

» Select "Filter..."

Types of Actions ▶

From the Actions menu, a Filter, Highlight, or URL Action can be added.

Filter: *Passes data from the Source to the Target worksheet(s) in order to navigate to and filter results on the latter.*

Highlight: *Passes data from the Source to the Target worksheet(s) in order to highlight the selected results without filtering the data.*

URL: *Sends the user to a website defined in the URL Action dialog box. This web address can encode data from a field in the data source if configured to do so.*

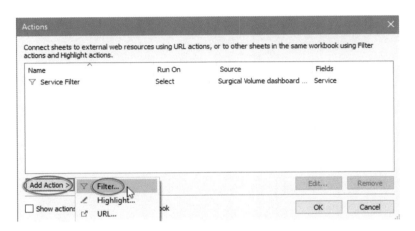

» Name the filter "Surgeon drill-down."

» Under Source Sheets / Surgical Volume Dashboard, uncheck all boxes except for "Scheduled v Actual In Room Min."

» Under Run action on, click the "Select" box.

» Under Target Sheets, click the caret and select "Surgeon Case Details Dashboard." This will display the only target worksheet, "Surgeon Case Details," which will be checked. The Action will be directed to the worksheet(s) checked that reside within the target dashboard. In this case, the single worksheet within this dashboard will be checked by default.

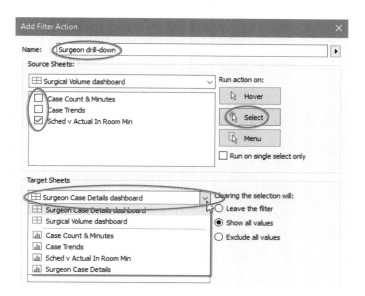

◀ **Refresher**

Remember that applying an Action sends a set of criteria to the Target worksheet. In this exercise, slightly more complexity is added because the Target is a worksheet in another Dashboard. The second Dashboard must be selected before the filter can be applied.

» Under Target Filters, click "Selected Fields."

» Click the "Add Filter..." button.

» Under Source, click the caret beneath "Field."

» Select "Primary Surgeon" on the drop-down menu.

317

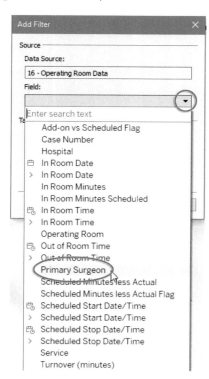

Ensure that the Target Field is also "Primary Surgeon."

 » Click "OK."

Action Field Mapping ▷

Tableau matches the field name in the Target Field if that name precisely replicates the selection in the Source Field. Here, it matches Primary Surgeon. If, however, this is not the right choice because the Target Field is different, another Field name can be substituted. Similarly, if the Source and Target Data Sources are different, the Target Field can be manually mapped.

The Filter Action box should now look like this:

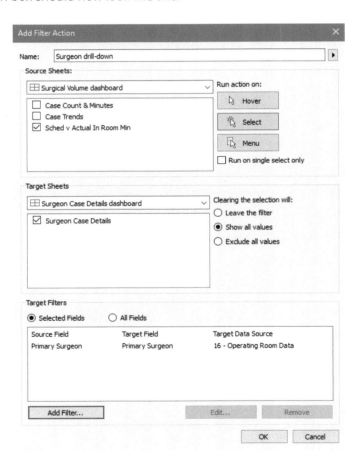

 » Click "OK."

The Action for "Surgeon drill-down" is now present on the Actions list in addition to the Service filter.

»   Click "OK" again.

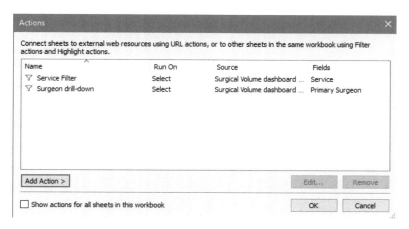

»   Test the Action by clicking on a Primary Surgeon name on the Surgical Volume dashboard. This should navigate to the Surgeon Case Details dashboard and filter for only the selected Primary Surgeon. From the tabs at the bottom of the screen, choose the Surgical Volume dashboard tab to return to the primary dashboard.

To signal the link, format the Primary Surgeon column in a blue, underlined font (signaling "hyperlink").

»   Click the "Total In Room Minutes by Surgeon" worksheet on the Surgical Volume dashboard to highlight.

»   Select "Format" from the Menu bar.

»   Select "Font..."

»   Click the "Fields" caret.

»   Select "Primary Surgeon."

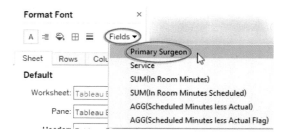

»   Select the "Header" tab.

»   Click the "Default Font" caret.

»   Select a blue square on the color palette. (Click "More Colors..." to view the full color palette.)

» Click the "Underline" icon.

» Click the "Bold" icon to remove the font bolding.

» Click the "X" to the right of the Format window title to close this window.

The Total In Room Minutes by Surgeon worksheet on the Dashboard now looks like this:

Creating Specialized Worksheets to Improve Dashboard Interactivity

Up to this point, worksheets have been created to visualize data. In the following sections, they will be built for other purposes. Instructions follow for three separate worksheets designed to add additional information and interactivity to the Dashboard: Back Buttons, Information Buttons, and Dynamic Titles.

2 Create and format a Back Button

A Back Button helps the user navigate from the Surgeon Case Details dashboard back to the primary Surgical Volume dashboard.

Surgeon Case Details

Primary Surgeon	Hospital	Operating Room	Case Number	In Room Date	In Room Time	Out of Room Time	In Room Minutes Scheduled	In Room Minutes	Actual Minutes more or less than ...
Physician 1	Hospital A	OR 5	1002	10/01/16	15:45	19:13	120	208	88
			1008	09/24/16	14:50	16:58	150	128	-22
			1015	09/29/16	16:20	19:17	120	177	57

Best Practice

Incorporating Back Buttons into dashboards provides a seamless experience for report users by allowing them to quickly drill into and out of their data.

A Back Button will now be created using these three main processes:

1) Build a separate worksheet with a Back Button shape, but no data.

2) Add this worksheet to the Dashboard, and format the sheet to look like a stand-alone button.

3) Set up an Action that returns the user to the Surgical Volume dashboard via a click of the Back Button (which does not filter any data).

To begin:

» Open a new worksheet.

» Right-click the white space of either the Dimensions or Measures window.

» Select "Create Calculated Field…"

» Enter the following in the Calculated Field dialog box:
    • Name: "Blank"
    • Formula: "" (a set of double quotation marks)

◄ **Blank Calculated Field**

The "Blank" calculated field, a string field where all values are set to "", is handy for performing formatting tricks in Tableau. In this example, the field helps create a worksheet with a single shape (a Back Button) and no data. This field can also be used as a placeholder Dimension to manipulate header spacing.

» Drag "Blank" from the Dimensions window to Detail on the Marks card.

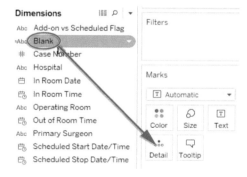

Tableau automatically formats this field as a square. Change the square to the desired shape.

» Click the Marks Types caret.

» Select "Shape."

» Click the "Shape" square that now appears on the Marks card.

» Select "More Shapes..."

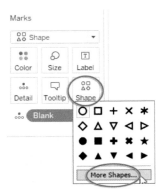

» Under Select Shape Palette, click the caret.

» Select "Arrows."

Adding Custom Shapes ▷

Tableau offers a selection of shapes that can be incorporated into worksheets. If none of the included shapes suits the designer's needs, custom shapes can be added by importing image files to the My Tableau Repository\Shapes folder. (Make sure to restart Tableau after new shapes have been added.) One of Tableau's default arrow shapes will be used in this exercise.

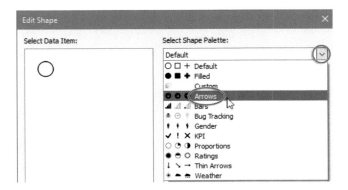

» Select any left-pointing back arrow.

» Click "OK."

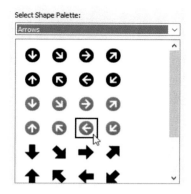

Select Shape Palette:
Arrows

» To increase the size of the left-pointing arrow, click Size on the Marks card and adjust the slider as desired (here, about a 50% size works best).

» Drag and drop the "Blank" pill on the Marks card to Color. This changes the Back Button's background to blue.

» Rename the worksheet tab "Back Button."

3 Add and format the Back Button onto the dashboard

» Click the "Surgeon Case Details" dashboard tab to open it.

» Drag and drop the "Back Button" worksheet to the right of the title "Surgeon Case Details."

Primary Surgeon	Hospital	Operating Room	Case Number	In Room Date	In Room Time	Out of Room Time	In Room Minutes Scheduled	In Room Minutes	Scheduled Minutes less Actual
Physician 1	Hospital A	OR 5	1002	10/01/16	15:45	19:13	120	208	-88
			1008	09/24/16	14:50	16:58	150	128	22
			1015	09/29/16	16:20	19:17	120	177	-57
			1018	09/29/16	11:27	14:14	120	167	-47

Hide the Color Legend:

» Click the Color Legend for "Blank" to highlight.

» Click the "X" in its top right corner to remove the Legend from the Dashboard.

Format the new Back Button:

- » Right-click the "Back Button" title.
- » Click "Title" to remove the checkmark and hide the title.

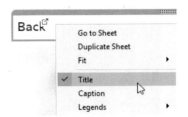

The Back Button is now visible, but very small.

Surgeon Case Details

- » Click the caret in the upper right corner of Back Button worksheet.
- » Click "Fit."
- » Select "Entire View."

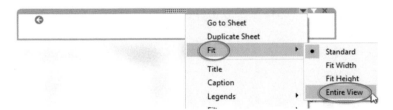

- » Click the left border of the Back Button worksheet and drag it to the right to reduce the size of the worksheet on the dashboard title space.

If a larger Back Button is preferred,

- » Navigate to the Back Button worksheet.
- » Click Size on the Marks card and adjust the slider as desired.

Edit the Tooltip. Hovering over or clicking on the Back Button make a Tooltip appear. This Tooltip requires some editing.

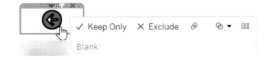

» Navigate back to the Back Button worksheet.

» Click "Tooltip" on the Marks card.

» Change the text to "Click to return to Surgical Volume Dashboard."

» Uncheck the box next to "Include command buttons."

4 Add an Action filter to the Back Button

If the Back Button is clicked now, nothing happens. An Action needs to be added to the Button.

» On the open Surgeon Case Details Dashboard, click "Dashboard" on the Menu row.

» Select "Actions..." A dialog box appears.

» Click the "Add Action" button in the lower left corner.

» Select "Filter" from the menu.

In the resulting Add Filter Action dialog box,

» To the right of Name: enter "Back Button."

» Under Source Sheets: "Surgeon Case Details Dashboard," check only the "Back button" box.

» Under Run action on: click the "Select" box.

» Under Target Sheets, click the caret and select "Surgical Volume Dashboard" from the drop-down menu. Ensure that the checkboxes for the three worksheets are checked.

» Under Target Filters, click the "Selected Fields" radio button.

» Click "OK."

Since the Back Button worksheet uses a blank field, there is no need to specify target fields. The goal here is to navigate back to the Surgical Volume dashboard.

**Actions for Navigation |
Passing No Data ▷**

An Action is most useful here thanks to its navigational abilities. Using "Selected Fields" with no fields chosen ensures that Target worksheets are not filtered in any way. There is no data to pass from the "Back Button" source sheet to the "Surgical Volume Dashboard" target sheets; the Back Button's only purpose is to take the user to the "Surgical Volume Dashboard."

>> Click the Back Button to test its functionality. The button should navigate back to the Surgical Volume dashboard. **Note:** If Back Button is highlighted, click once to un-highlight, then click again to engage the Action and navigate back.

5 Create and format an Information Button

Information buttons are useful for including a detailed written description of dashboards. Information buttons take up minimal real estate; pop-up messages provide the necessary space to relay information.

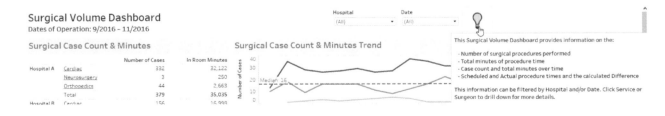

Best Practice

Most dashboards do not have the space to display full written descriptions or lengthy instructional text. Further, once it is read, this type of text often distracts from the dashboard's message. Using an information button to hide the text is a great way to save space and enhance focus.

The Information Button is built the same way as the Back Button, except that it requires a different shape. The steps that parallel those in Back-Button development will be arranged in the style of an HDVizoom; steps specific to the Information Button will display screenshots necessary to assist development.

» Open a new, blank worksheet.

» Drag the previously created calculated field "Blank" to Details on the Marks card.

» Click the Marks Type caret.

» Select "Shape."

» Click the "Shape" box.

» Select "More Shapes..."

» Under "Select Shape Palette," click the caret to the right of "Default."

» Select "Bug Tracking."

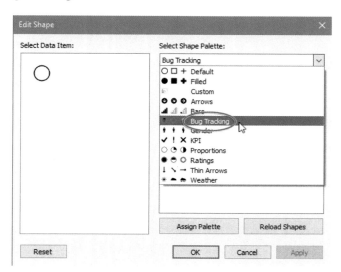

» Select the light bulb image.

» Click "OK."

» Click Size on the Marks card.

» Move the slider about halfway to the right.

» Rename the worksheet "Information Button."

6 **Add and format the Information Button onto the dashboard**

» Open the Surgical Volume Dashboard.

» Drag and drop the "Information Button" worksheet to the right of the Dashboard title and of Hospital and Date quick filters.

» Right-click the "Information Button" title.

» Select "Hide Title."

» Click the "Information Button" worksheet caret.

» Click "Fit."

» Select "Entire View."

If the dimensions of the Information Button icon need re-sizing:

» Highlight the Information Button worksheet.

» Click the caret to display the sub-menu.

» Click "Go to Sheet."

» Click Size on the Marks card.

» Adjust the size as desired.

To re-size the Information Button border on the Dashboard:

» Click the Information Button worksheet to highlight.

» Click the left edge and drag it to re-size as desired.

7 **Edit the Tooltip for the Information Button**

» Navigate back to the Information Button worksheet.

» Click Tooltip on the Marks card.

» Uncheck the box next to "Include command buttons."

» Change the text to read:

"This Surgical Volume Dashboard provides information on the
- Number of surgical procedures performed
- Total minutes of procedure time
- Case count and total minutes over time
- Scheduled and actual procedure times as well as the difference between the two

The information can be filtered by Hospital and/or Date. Click Service or Surgeon to drill down for more details."

» Click the "Preview" button to view how the Tooltip will look.

» Click "OK."

» Hover the cursor over the Information Button on the dashboard to display the Tooltip.

This Surgical Volume Dashboard provides information on the:

- Number of surgical procedures performed
- Total minutes of procedure time
- Case count and total minutes over time
- Scheduled and actual procedure times as well as the difference between the two.

The information can be filtered by Hospital and/or Date. Click Service or Surgeon to drill down for more details.

8 Create and format a Dynamic Title

A worksheet title can be filtered according to data in that worksheet. Dynamic Titles enable the user to see and confirm what is being filtered in the Dashboard.

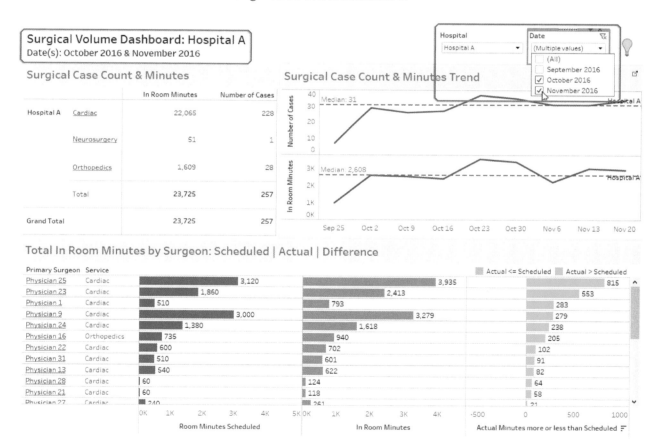

▲ Dynamic Titles

These Titles are created by using a worksheet that appears to have no data on it. All the data to be displayed is hidden in Details on the Marks card. Adjusting the transparency of Color on the Marks card to zero ensures that no data is showing. This will make sense once the worksheet is added to the dashboard, because only the Title is displayed there.

This section creates a separate worksheet designed to display a Dynamic Title for the Dashboard.

> » Open a new worksheet and rename it "Dynamic Title."

> » Drag "Hospital" to Details on the Marks card.

> » Click Color on the Marks card.

> » Change Opacity to "0."

> » Double-click the Title Row to open the Edit Title dialog box.

> » Change the title to "Surgical Volume Dashboard:".

> » Click the "Insert" button.

> » Select "Hospital" from the drop-down menu.

Refresher ▶

In this example, the Hospital field is inserted into the worksheet title so that the latter changes dynamically as the dataset is filtered for different hospitals. The Insert menu can also enable the addition of parameters, last-updated timestamps, or the report-developer's name.

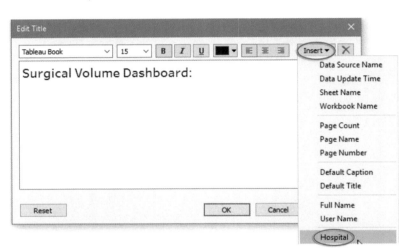

> » Highlight title and increase font to "16."

> » Click "OK."

9 **Add and format the Dynamic Title onto the dashboard**

> » Open the Surgical Volume Dashboard.

> » Drag the new "Dynamic Title" worksheet to the right of the current Text title box.

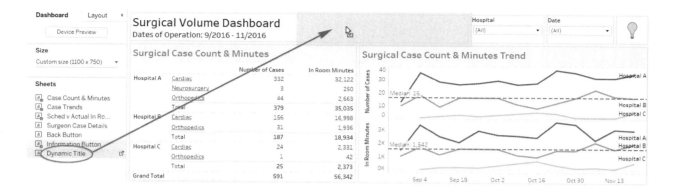

» Click the original Dashboard Title to highlight.

» Click the "X" in the top right corner to delete the text box.

» Click the new "Dynamic Title" worksheet to highlight.

» Click the worksheet caret.

» Click "Fit."

» Select "Entire View."

10 Link the Filters to the Dynamic Title

» Click the "Hospital" filter to highlight.

» Click the caret in the upper right corner.

» Click "Apply to Worksheets."

» Click "Selected Worksheets."

» Click the "Dynamic Title" box to apply the Filter to the Dynamic Title worksheet.

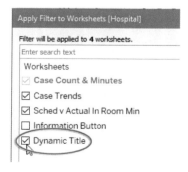

» Select a Hospital in the filter to check that the Dynamic Title is working correctly.

Dynamic Dates also can be added to the title. To add:

>> Click the "Date" filter to highlight.

>> Click the caret in the upper right corner.

>> Click "Apply to Worksheets."

>> Click "Selected Worksheets."

>> Click the checkbox next to "Dynamic Title."

>> Click "OK."

To navigate to the Dynamic Title worksheet:

>> Click the "Dynamic Title" worksheet on the Dashboard to highlight.

>> Hover the cursor over the right corner and click the "Go to Sheet" box that appears.

>> Double-click the title.

>> Type "Date(s):" below "Surgical Volume Dashboard:"

>> Click the "Insert" button.

>> Select "MY(In Room Date)."

>> Change Date title font to "12."

>> Click "OK."

>> Test the Dynamic Title by selecting a date (or two) from the Date filter. The Dynamic Title will reflect the filter selections.

>> Test all Filters and Actions to ensure correct performance.

11 Final dashboard formatting tips

When the report viewer first opens a dashboard, consider the initial view. It may be helpful to pre-select filters or sort pertinent charts to draw attention to important findings.

Hide worksheet tabs so that the report viewer sees only dashboard tabs. To hide all worksheets:

>> Right-click one of the worksheet dashboard tabs, and select "Hide All Sheets" from the menu.

>> Repeat for the second dashboard tab.

The order of the dashboard tabs can be changed to reflect the order in which they should be reviewed.

» Click the "Surgical Volume Dashboard" tab and drag it to the left of the "Surgeon Case Details Dashboard" tab.

The final Dashboard looks like this:

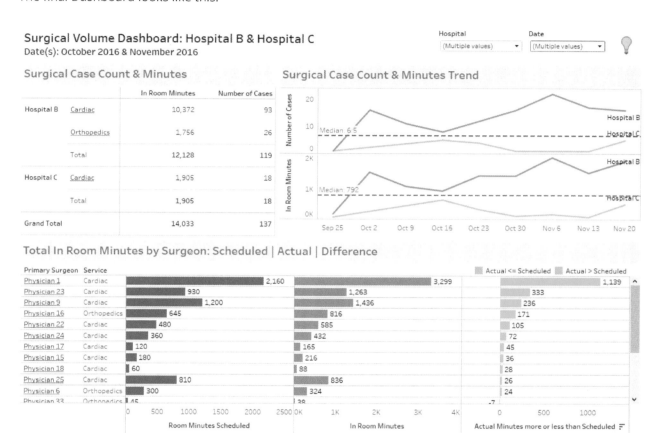

Insight: For October and November 2016, Surgical Volume for Hospital B was higher than Hospital C. Surgical Volume and Case-Minute Trends followed a similar pattern within each hospital. Several of the cardiac surgeons performed cases that ran longer than the scheduled time; Physician 1 used considerably more minutes than the scheduled time allotment.

▌▋▐ *HDVizoom*™...to Dashboard Advanced Interactivity

1 **Add and format Action filter (inter-dashboard)**

» Open "Surgical Volume Dashboard"

» Click "Dashboards" on Menu row

» Click "Actions..."

» Click "Add Action" button

» Select "Filter..."

» Name filter: "Surgeon drill-down"

» Under "Source Sheets|Surgical Volume Dashboard," uncheck all boxes except for "Scheduled v Actual In Room Min"

» Under "Run action on," click "Select" box

» Under "Target Sheets," click caret and select "Surgeon Case Details Dashboard"

» Under Target Filters, click "Selected Fields"

» Click "Add Filter..." button

» Click caret beneath "Field"

» Select "Primary Surgeon" on drop-down menu

» Click "OK" to close Action menus

» Test action filter by clicking on primary surgeon name on Surgical Volume dashboard

» From tabs at bottom of screen, choose Surgical Volume Dashboard tab to return to Dashboard

» Click "Scheduled v Actual In Room Min" worksheet in Surgical Volume dashboard to highlight

» Select "Format" from File menu

» Select "Font..."

» Click "Fields" caret

» Select "Primary Surgeon"

» Select "Header" tab.

» Click "Default Font" caret

» Select a blue square on color palette and click "Underline" icon

2 **Create and format Back Button**

» Open new, blank worksheet

» Right-click in blank section of either Dimensions or Measures window

» Select "Create Calculated Field..."

» Enter following in Calculated Field dialog box:

• Name: "Blank"

• Formula: " " (set of double quotation marks)

» Drag "Blank" from Dimensions window to Details on Marks card

» Click Marks caret

» Select "Shape"

» Click "Shape" box

» Select "More Shapes..."

» Click caret to right of word "Default"

» Select "Arrows"

» Select a left-pointing back arrow

» Drag and drop "Blank" pill to Color on Marks card

» Rename worksheet "Back Button"

3 **Add and format Back Button onto dashboard**

» Open "Surgeon Case Details" Dashboard

» Drag and drop "Back Button" worksheet to right of title "Surgeon Case Details"

» Click Color Key to highlight

» Click "X" to remove it from Dashboard

» Right-click "Back Button" title

» Select "Hide Title"

» Click caret in upper right corner of Back Button worksheet

» Click "Fit"

» Select "Entire View"

» Highlight "Back Button" worksheet

» Click worksheet caret to display submenu

» Click "Go to Sheet"

» Click Size on Marks card

» Adjust size as desired

» Click Back Button worksheet on Dashboard to highlight

» Click left border and drag to size as desired

» Navigate back to Back Button worksheet

» Click Tooltip on Marks card

» Uncheck box next to "Include command buttons"

» Change text to "Back"

4   **Add Action to Back Button**

» With Surgeon Case Details Dashboard open, click "Dashboard" on Menu row

» Select "Actions..."

» Click "Add Action" button in lower left corner

» Select "Filter" from menu

» To right of Name: enter "Back Button"

» Under Source Sheets: "Surgeon Case Details Dashboard," check only "Back Button" box

» Under Run action on: click "Select" box

» Under Target Sheets, click caret and select "Surgical Volume Dashboard" from drop-down menu

» Under Target Filters, click "Selected Fields" radio button

» Click Back Button to test functionality

5   **Create and format Information Button**

» Open new, blank worksheet

» Drag previously created calculated field "Blank" to Details on Marks card

» Click caret to right of "Marks"

» Select "Shape"

» Click "Shape" box

» Select "More Shapes..."

» Select "Bug Tracking"

» Select light bulb image

» Click Size on Marks card

» Move slider about halfway to right

» Rename worksheet "Information Button"

6   **Add and format Information Button onto dashboard**

» Open "Surgical Volume" Dashboard

» Drag and drop "Information Button" worksheet to right of Dashboard title

» Right-click "Information Button" title

» Select "Hide Title"

» Click "Information Button" worksheet caret

» Click "Fit"

» Select "Entire View"

» Highlight Information Button worksheet

» Click caret to display sub-menu

» Click "Go to Sheet"

» Click Size on Marks card

» Adjust size as desired

» Click Information Button worksheet on Dashboard to highlight

335

» Click left edge and drag to re-size as desired

7 Edit Tooltip for Information Button

» Navigate back to Information Button worksheet

» Click Tooltip on Marks card

» Uncheck box next to "Include command buttons"

» Change text to read:

"This Surgical Volume dashboard provides information on the

• Number of surgical procedures performed

• Total minutes of procedure time

• Case Count and Total Minutes over time

• Scheduled versus Actual procedure times and differences between the two

The information can be filtered by Hospital and/or Date. Click Service or Surgeon to drill down for more details."

» Click the Information Button to display the Tooltip

8 Create and format Dynamic Title

» Open new worksheet and rename as "Dynamic Title"

» Drag "Hospital" to Details on Marks card

» Click Color on Marks card

» Change Opacity to "0"

» Double-click Title Row to open Edit Title dialog box

» Change title to "Surgical Volume Dashboard:"

» Click "Insert" button

» Select "Hospital," increase font to "16"

» Click "OK"

9 Add and format Dynamic Title onto dashboard

» Open Surgical Volume Dashboard

» Drag new "Dynamic Title" worksheet to title location

» Click Text Title to highlight

» Click "X" in top right corner to delete

» Click new "Dynamic Title" worksheet to highlight

» Click worksheet caret

» Click "Fit"

» Select "Entire View"

» Double-click title

» Highlight text

» Adjust font size as desired

10 Link filters to Dynamic Title

» Click "Hospital" filter to highlight

» Click caret in upper right corner

» Click "Apply to Worksheets"

» Click "Selected Worksheets"

» Click "Dynamic Title" box to apply filter to Dynamic Title worksheet

» Click caret to right of "Date" filter title

» Click "Apply to Worksheets"

» Click "Selected Worksheets"

» Click checkbox next to "Dynamic Title"

» Click "OK"

» Click "Dynamic Title" worksheet to highlight

» Hover cursor over right corner; click "Go to Sheet" box that appears

» Double-click title

» Type in "Date(s):" below "Surgical Volume Dashboard:"

» Click "Insert" button

» Select "MY(In Room Date)"

» Change date title font to "12"

» Click "OK"

11 Final dashboard formatting tips

» Right-click one of dashboard tabs, and select "Hide All Sheets" from menu

» Repeat for second dashboard tab

» Click the "Surgical Volume Dashboard" tab and drag it to left of "Surgeon Case Details Dashboard" tab

CHAPTER 25

Story

Tableau's Story tool enables digital storytelling formatted directly in a visualization. A Story is a type of sheet, like a worksheet or dashboard. The tool puts context in sequential progression to narrate the story of the data. Each Story Point captures a particular view or insight, guiding the audience through the analysis. As with any good story, these points create the smooth flow of a compelling visual narrative.

Stories can be put to good use in various ways. In addition to simply creating a presentation to emphasize a specific trend or element in reports, a Story can also be used to walk an audience through the functionality of a new suite of reports or dashboards.

How To: Create a Story to describe the current opioid addiction crisis.

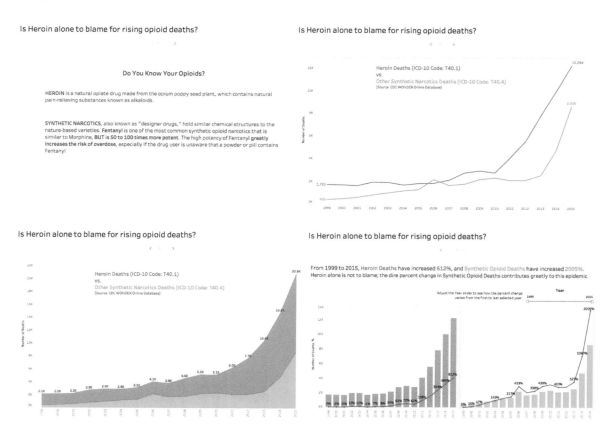

Data Source: CDC WONDER online databases provide data and analysis to support evidence-based assessment of public health programs and population health trends.

About the Data: Centers for Disease Control and Prevention, National Center for Health Statistics. Multiple Cause of Death 1999-2015 on CDC WONDER Online Database, released December 2016. Data are from the Multiple Cause of Death Files, 1999-2015, as compiled from data provided by the 57 vital statistics jurisdictions through the Vital Statistics Cooperative Program.

The Story Workspace (version 10.2 +)

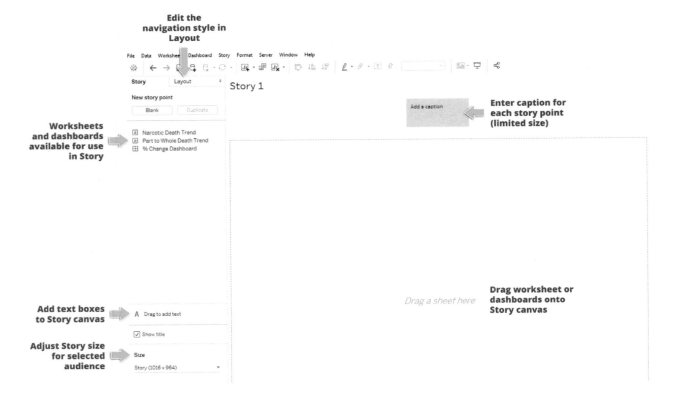

Edit the navigation style in Layout

Worksheets and dashboards available for use in Story

Enter caption for each story point (limited size)

Add text boxes to Story canvas

Adjust Story size for selected audience

Drag worksheet or dashboards onto Story canvas

1 Create a new Story

This Story example describes the current national opioid crisis, comparing heroin deaths to synthetic opioid deaths. Two worksheets and one dashboard have been created to display heroin and synthetic opioid trends. This Story contains a considerable amount of explanation via text; therefore, Text Boxes instead of Captions are used to create it.

 » Open the "Tableau 10 Training Workbook – Story New" workbook already created.

To open a new Story:

Option 1:
- On the Menu bar, click "Story."
- Click "New Story."

Option 2:

- On bottom row of Worksheet/Dashboard tabs, click far-right icon to add new Story.

2 Set the Navigation Style and rename the story tab

The navigation style can be edited to find the best fit for each Story. The large amount of text in this Story makes the "Dots" style the best choice for a cleaner, less distracting appearance.

» Click the "Layout" tab at the top of the left pane.

» Click the "Dots" radio button.

» Click the "Story" tab at the top of the left pane.

» Right-click the "Story 1" tab at the bottom of the workbook and select "Rename Sheet."

» Change name to "Opioid Deaths."

» Click the "Save" icon on the Toolbar to save the workbook.

3 Create the first Story Point

The first page of the Story is an introduction, describing the current opioid crisis. Three text boxes will be created.

» Drag and drop a Text box from the Story window onto the workspace.

» Enter the text, "Do You Know Your Opioids?"

» Highlight and bold the text, then change the font size to "18."

» Click "OK."

» Drag and drop the second Text box onto the workspace.

» Enter the text, "HEROIN is an opiate drug made from the opium poppy; it contains naturally-occurring pain-relieving substances known as alkaloids."

» Left-align the text, bold the word "HEROIN," and click "OK."

» Drag and drop a third Text box onto the workspace.

» Enter the text, "SYNTHETIC OPIOIDS, also known as "designer drugs," have chemical structures similar to the nature-based varieties. Fentanyl is one of the most common synthetic opioids; it is similar to morphine, BUT 50 to 100 times more potent. The high potency of Fentanyl greatly increases the risk of overdose, especially if the drug user is unaware that a powder or pill contains Fentanyl."

» Left-align the text. Bold the following text: "SYNTHETIC OPIOIDS," "Fentanyl," "BUT is 50 to 100 times more potent," and "greatly increases the risk of overdose."

» Click "OK."

4 Format the text boxes and add a Story title

» Right-click the first text box and select "Format description" from the menu.

» In the Format window, click the "Shading" caret, then change the color as desired (the example uses light blue).

» Click the "Borders" caret, then change the line to "None."

» Follow the same steps to edit the other two text boxes.

To adjust the width of the Text boxes:

» Click a Text box to highlight.

» Click and drag the borders to a desired width. Adjust the height in the same way.

To add a Story title:

» Double-click the Title row to open the Edit Title dialog box.

» Change the title to "Is heroin alone to blame for the increase in opioid deaths?"

» Highlight the text and change the font size to "20."

Is heroin alone to blame for the increase in opioid deaths?

Do You Know Your Opioids?

HEROIN is an opiate drug made from the opium poppy; it contains naturally-occurring pain-relieving substances known as alkaloids.

SYNTHETIC OPIOIDS, also known as "designer drugs," have chemical structures similar to the nature-based varieties. Fentanyl is one of the most common synthetic opioid narcotics; it is similar to morphine, BUT 50 to 100 times more potent. The high potency of Fentanyl greatly increases the risk of overdose, especially if the drug user is unaware that a powder or pill contains Fentanyl.

5 **Add a new Story Point**

» In the Story pane, under "New story point," click the "Blank" button.

» Drag and drop the "Opioid Deaths Trend" worksheet from the Story pane onto the canvas.

» Drag and drop a Text box onto the canvas.

» Enter the following description:

Heroin Deaths (ICD-10 Code: T40.1)
vs.
Other Synthetic Opioid Deaths (ICD-10 Code: T40.4)
(Source: CDC WONDER Online Database)

» Color-code the corresponding text to match the line colors.

» Format the text box to match previous text boxes.

6 **Set the Story Size**

The size of the Story with the Opioid Deaths Trend chart may be too large for the screen to accommodate. This is a good time to set the size of the Story. Evaluate the smallest resolution readers will use, then select a Story size. As with Dashboards, there are many size choices. The default setting is "Story (1016 x 964)."

» In the Size section at the bottom of the Story pane, click the caret to the right of the default size setting and select the desired size (in this example, Letter Landscape).

Refresher ▶

As with dashboards, a small blue checkmark indicates that the worksheet (or dashboard) is active—in this case, on the Story canvas.

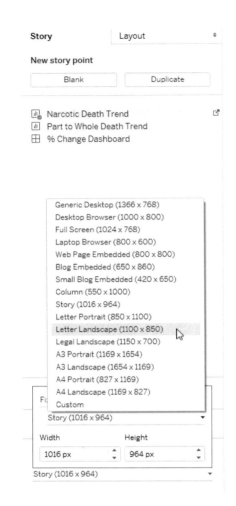

The Story Point now looks like this:

Is heroin alone to blame for the increase in opioid deaths?

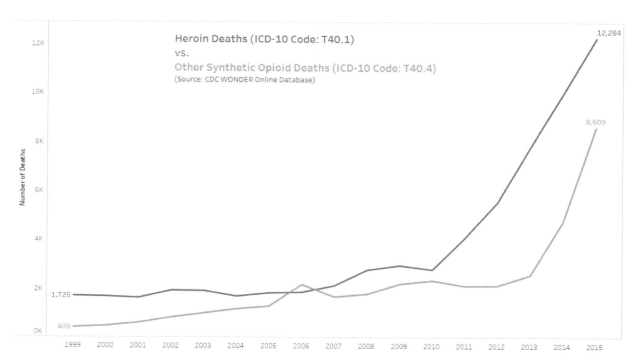

7 Add a new Story Point

A second option for adding a new Story Point is to drag and drop a worksheet or dashboard onto the navigation bar.

» Drag "Part-to-Whole Deaths Trend" from the Story window to the navigation bar. Arrows will appear on the navigation bar indicating where the sheet can be placed. Drop the worksheet when the arrows appear at the far right.

» Drag and drop a Text box onto the canvas.

» Enter the following description:

"The number of combined heroin and other synthetic opioid deaths is rising. Is something changing?"

» Italicize "Is something changing?"

» Color-code the corresponding text to match the Area chart colors.

» Format the text box to match previous text boxes.

Is heroin alone to blame for the increase in opioid deaths?

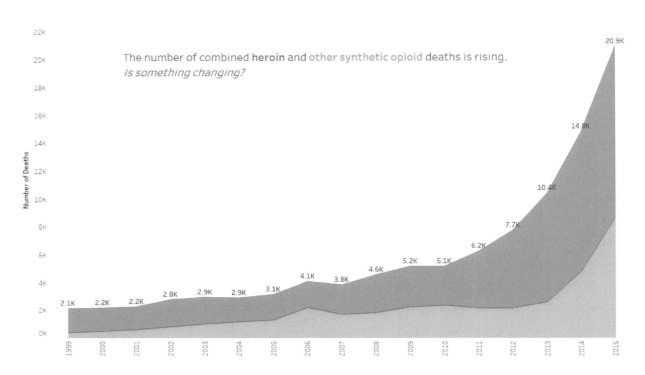

8 Add a final Story Point

» Add a new Story Point, then drag and drop "% Change Dashboard" onto the workspace.

This dashboard's size is different from the Story's; a horizontal and a vertical slide bar appear.

To set the dashboard to the correct size:

» Click the "% Change Dashboard" tab at the bottom of the workbook to navigate to the dashboard.

» In the Dashboard pane on the left, in the Size section, click the carets to the right of the dashboard's set size to display the drop-down menu.

» Select the "Fit to Opioid Deaths" size option.

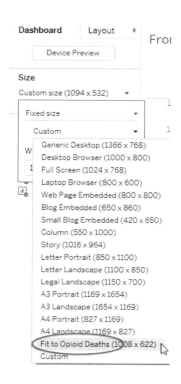

» At the bottom of the workbook, click the "Opioid Deaths" tab to return to the Story. The dashboard now fits the size of the Story.

Adjusting the Year slider changes the displays and the dynamic title. When the slider has been moved, a pop-up icon box appears above the navigation dots, offering options to :

- **Delete:** deletes the active Story Point
- **Revert:** changes the view back to the prior view
- **Update:** saves the edited view
- **Save as a New Story Point:** saves the view as a new Story Point

If the slider has been adjusted, click the "Revert" icon to return the slider to the previous setting.

» Click the "Save" icon on the Toolbar.

The final Story Point now looks like this:

Is heroin alone to blame for the increase in opioid deaths?

‹   • ›

From 1999 to 2015, heroin deaths increased 612%; synthetic opioid deaths, 2005%.
As these staggering numbers make clear, heroin was not chiefly responsible for the sharp increase in deaths; the dire percent change in mortality due to synthetic opioids was a majority contributor to this epidemic.

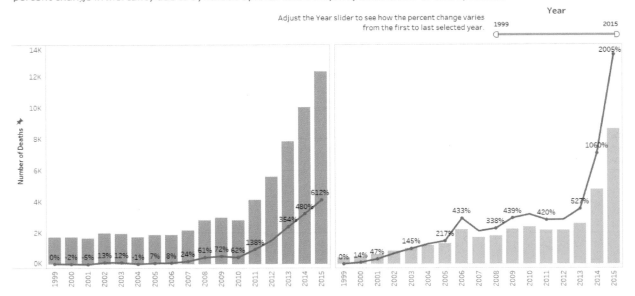

▲ Presentation Mode

Full-screen Presentation Mode is perfect for displaying reports in front of any audience in Tableau Desktop or Reader. This mode hides the shelves, menus, and Sidebar to cleanly showcase the visualization. To activate Presentation Mode, either select the Presentation Mode icon from the Toolbar or press F7.

HDVizoom™...to Story

1 Create new Story

» Open "Tableau 10 Training Workbook – Story - new" workbook already created

To open new Story:

Option 1:

- On Menu bar, click "Story"
- Click "New Story"

Option 2:

- On bottom row of Worksheet/ Dashboard tabs, click far-right icon to add new Story

2 Set Navigation Style and rename Story tab

» Click "Layout" tab at top of left pane

» Click "Dots" radio button

» Click "Story" tab at top of left pane

» Right-click "Story 1" tab at bottom of workbook and select "Rename Sheet"

» Change name to "Opioid Deaths"

» Click "Save" icon on Toolbar to save workbook

3 Create first Storypoint

» Drag and drop Text box from Story window onto workspace

» Enter text "Do You Know Your Opioids?"

» Highlight and bold text, then change font size to "18"

» Click "OK"

» Drag and drop second Text box onto workspace

» Enter text "HEROIN is an opiate drug made from the opium poppy; it contains naturally-occurring pain-relieving substances known as alkaloids."

» Left-align text, bold word "HEROIN," and click "OK"

» Drag and drop third Text box onto workspace

» Enter text "SYNTHETIC OPIOIDS, also known as "designer drugs," have chemical structures similar to the nature-based varieties. Fentanyl is one of the most common synthetic opioids; it is similar to morphine, BUT 50 to 100 times more potent. The high potency of Fentanyl greatly increases the risk of overdose, especially if the drug user is unaware that a powder or pill contains Fentanyl."

» Left-align text. Bold following text: "SYNTHETIC OPIOIDS," "Fentanyl," "BUT is 50 to 100 times more potent," and "greatly increases the risk of overdose."

» Click "OK."

4 Format text boxes and add Story title

» Right-click first text box and select "Format description" from menu

» In Format window, click "Shading" caret, then change color as desired (example uses light blue)

» Click "Borders" caret, then change line to "None"

» Follow same steps to edit other two text boxes

To adjust width of Text boxes:

» Click Text box to highlight

» Click and drag borders to desired width and height

To add Story title:

» Double-click Title row to open Edit Title dialog box

349

» Change title to "Is heroin alone to blame for the increase in opioid deaths?"

» Highlight text and change font size to "20"

5 **Add new Story Point**

» In Story pane, under "New story point," click "Blank" button

» Drag and drop "Opioid Deaths Trend" worksheet from Story pane onto canvas

» Drag and drop Text box onto canvas

» Enter following description: "Heroin Deaths (ICD-10 Code: T40.1) vs.Other Synthetic Opioid Deaths (ICD-10 Code: T40.4 (Source: CDC WONDER Online Database)"

» Color-code corresponding text to match line colors

» Format text box to match previous text boxes

6 **Set Story Size**

» In Size section at bottom of Story pane, click caret to right of default size setting and select desired size (in this example, Letter Landscape)

7 **Add new Story Point**

» Drag "Part-to-Whole Deaths Trend" from Story window to navigation bar. Arrows will appear

on navigation bar indicating where sheet can be placed. Drop worksheet when arrows appear at far right.

» Drag and drop Text box onto canvas

» Enter following description: "The number of combined heroin and other synthetic opioid deaths is rising. Is something changing?"

» Italicize "Is something changing?"

» Color-code corresponding text to match Area chart colors

» Format text box to match previous text boxes

8 **Add final Story Point**

» Add new Story Point, then drag and drop "% Change Dashboard" onto workspace

» Click "% Change Dashboard" tab at bottom of workbook to navigate to dashboard

» In Dashboard pane on left, in Size section, click carets to right of dashboard's set size to display drop-down menu

» Select "Fit to Opioid Deaths" size option

» At bottom of workbook, click "Opioid Deaths" tab to return to Story

» Click "Save" on Toolbar to save Story

Advanced Skills

351

CHAPTER 26

Calculated Fields and Advanced Calculations

26.1 Calculated Fields

Tableau's Calculated Fields are an effective way to quickly add data and information unavailable in the original data source(s) to reports and dashboards. If a dataset is missing a key piece of information, Tableau offers several ways to manipulate existing data fields to create new calculated ones. Think of this new field as an additional dataset column that supplies the missing information. As with other data fields, the new calculated field [identified by an equal sign (=) preceding its icon] will reside in the Dimensions or Measures window, and can be placed on any shelf to build the visualization.

Be certain to consider dashboard and report performance when creating Calculated Fields in Tableau. If the calculations will be used in numerous views, or by a large number of report-builders, it may be prudent to create a new field in the source database. Doing so could also ease maintenance woes: adjusting a calculation once in a database is far easier than doing so in every workbook.

The following section details how to create Calculated Fields of the String, Number, Date, Type Conversion, Logical, User, Aggregate, Level of Detail Expression, and Table Calculation types. Special attention will be given to the latter three advanced calculation topics.

How To: Create a Calculated Field.

» Right-click any Dimension or Measure to be used in a calculation or in the blank space in the Data pane.

- If a Dimension or Measure is right-clicked, select "Create," then "Calculated Field..." from the sub-menus.
- If a blank space is right-clicked, select "Create Calculated Field" from the sub-menu.

Calculated Field dialog box overview:

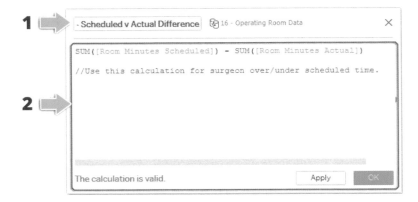

1) **Name:** Replace the default name "Calculation 1" with a descriptive one. Since the newly created Calculated Field will be listed among all the other fields in the Data Window, a descriptive name will make it easier to find.

2) **Formula:** The Formula Editor box includes validation to help avoid syntax errors and a color-coding system to help users recognize specific parts of the formula. The Formula parts consist of:

   a. **Fields:** Display in orange. All data source fields and calculated fields are available for calculations. To add a field to the Formula Editor, *either*:

   » Begin typing the field name in the Formula Editor box and select the name from the menu that appears. Note: the menu will list field names as well as function names corresponding to the entered letter(s).

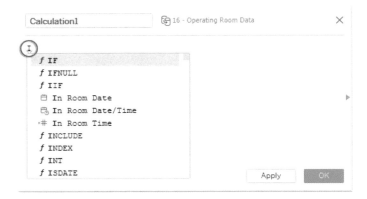

   » Drag and drop the field from the Dimension or Measure window into the Formula Editor box.

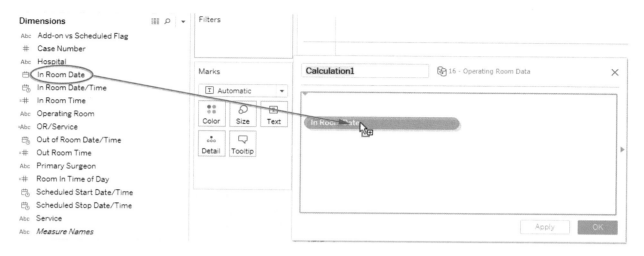

b. **Operators:** Display in **black**. Operators are entered into the Formula Editor when the calculation calls for addition (+), subtraction (-), multiplication (*), and division (/). Operators used in logical calculations also include IF, THEN, CASE, WHEN, AND, OR, >, >=, =, <=, <, and <>. Operators are not case-sensitive.

c. **Parameters:** Display in **purple**. Parameters are placeholders for variables that can be inserted into the Formula Editor to replace constant values. Parameters are discussed in chapter 27.

d. **Functions:** Display in blue. To view the list of available functions, click the caret on the right border of the Formula Editor box. If "All" is selected, an alphabetical list displays every Function available for creating a formula. Click the caret to the right of "All" and select a Function category to narrow the list of corresponding Functions. Click on a Function to view its definition and formatting requirements. Double-click on a Function name to add it to the Formula Editor box, or type the Function name directly.

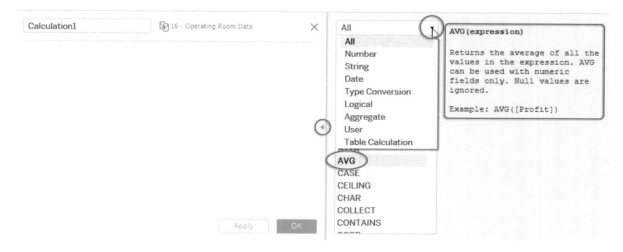

e. **Comments:** Display in gray. Comments are optional. To annotate the formula with comments, start the Comment text in the Formula Editor with two

355

forward-slash characters. As an example: "//Use this calculation for surgeon over/under scheduled time."

Help and Validation

Directly beneath the Formula, the Formula Editor displays a message confirming that the calculation syntax has been entered correctly and is valid, or that it contains errors. In the latter case, click the red caret for hints on solving the problem. As a further help, some syntax errors are underscored with a red wavy line.

Calculation Categories

This section introduces the broad categories of calculations that Tableau offers, with specific healthcare-related examples.

 » Click the caret beneath and to the right of the Functions section of the Calculated Field dialog box to see the Functions list:

- String
- Number
- Date
- Type Conversion
- Logical
- User
- Aggregate (including Level of Detail Expression)
- Table Calculation

A brief review of functions and examples corresponding to each category follows. The final three categories require additional explanation and are discussed in section 26.2, below.

STRING

Calculations performed on one or more string (text) fields.

STARTSWITH: Returns true if the string starts with the substring.

Example: If the calculation is **STARTSWITH([Staff Name],"Dr."),** then on a row where Staff Name is "Dr. Williams," the calculation will return TRUE.

Starting Field	Calculation	Result
Staff Name		
Dr. Williams	STARTSWITH([Staff Name],"Dr.")	TRUE

REPLACE: Returns a string in which every occurrence of the substring is replaced with the replacement string. If the substring is not found, the string is unchanged.

Example: If the calculation is **REPLACE([Staff Name],"Dr.","Doctor"),** then on a row where Staff Name is "Dr. Williams," the calculation will return "Doctor Williams."

Starting Field	Calculation	Result
Staff Name		
Dr. Williams	REPLACE([Staff Name],"Dr.","Doctor")	Doctor Williams

Additional String Manipulation: Strings can also be connected using the "+" operator.

Example: If there is a field called [First Name] with a record of "James" and a field called [Last Name] with a record of "Williams" on the same row, then the calculation **[Last Name]+", "+[First Name]** will return "Williams, James."

	Starting Field	Calculation	Result
First Name	Last Name		
James	Williams	`[Last Name]+", "+[First Name]`	Williams, James

NUMBER

Mathematical calculations performed on a number field.

ABS: Returns the absolute value of the given number. Use this function to find the difference between values, whether positive or negative.

Example: A field called [ALOS Variance] represents the difference between the average lengths of stay for each month. If the calculation is **ABS([ALOS Variance])**, then on a row where ALOS Variance is -4, the calculation will return 4.

Starting Field		Calculation	Result
ALOS Variance			
-4		`ABS([ALOS Variance])`	4

SIGN: Returns the sign of a number: 1 if the number is positive, zero if the number is zero, or -1 if the number is negative.

Example: If the calculation is **SIGN([Surgery Cost])**, then on a row where Surgery Cost is -$500, the calculation will return -1.

Starting Field		Calculation	Result
Surgery Cost			
-500		`SIGN([Surgery Cost])`	-1

DATE

Calculations that manipulate dates or transform dates into integers.

DATEADD: Adds an increment to the specified date and returns the new date. The increment is defined by the interval and the date_part.

Example: If the calculation is **DATEADD("month",1,[Surgery Date])**, then on a row where Surgery Date is 04-15-2014, the calculation will return 05-15-2014.

Starting Field	Calculation	Result
Surgery Date		
04-15-2014	DATEADD("month",1,[Surgery Date])	05-15-2014

DATETRUNC: Truncates the specified date to the accuracy specified by the date_part and returns the new date.

Example: If the calculation is **DATETRUNC("year",[Surgery Date])**, then on a row where Surgery Date is 04-15-2014, the calculation will return 01-01-2014.

Starting Field	Calculation	Result
Surgery Date		
04-15-2014	DATETRUNC("year",[Surgery Date])	01-01-2014

TODAY: Returns the current date. Useful for computing rolling dates and other time-related calculations relative to the current view date.

Starting Field	Calculation	Result
N/A	TODAY()	<Current Date>

TYPE CONVERSION

Calculations that change the data type of a field.

STR: Returns a String given an expression. (That is, converts an expression to a String.)

Example: **STR(4)** would convert the integer 4 to a string value of 4 that can then be linked with other strings.

Starting Field	Calculation	Result
Integer		String
4	STR(4)	4

INT: Returns an Integer given an expression. This function truncates results to the closest integer toward zero.

Example: **INT (4.7)** would convert the value 4.7 to the integer 4.

Starting Field	Calculation	Result
Value		Integer
4.7	INT(4.7)	4

LOGICAL

These calculations test for specific scenarios in order to organize data in a manner other than the way it is already displayed in the database. Common uses for logical expressions include grouping dimensions, excluding values, creating custom bins, and comparing values.

IF/THEN: Tests a series of expressions returning the <then> value for the first true <expr>.

Example: The calculation **IF [Surgery Start] > [Scheduled Surgery Start] THEN "Late Case" ELSE "On Time Case" END** will return a value of "Late Case" if the Surgery Start date/time field occurred after the Scheduled Surgery Start date/time field.

Starting Field		Calculation	Result
Surgery Start	Scheduled Surgery Start		
4-14-2014 8:15 AM	4-14-2014 8:00 AM	IF[Surgery Start] > [Scheduled Surgery Start] THEN "Late Case" ELSE "On Time Case" END	Late Case
4-14-2014 10:00 AM	4-14-2014 10:05 AM		On Time Case

CASE / WHEN: Finds the first <value> that matches <expr> and returns the corresponding <return>.

Example: The calculation **CASE [Continent] WHEN "North America" THEN "Americas" WHEN "South America" THEN "Americas" WHEN "Africa" THEN "Africa" END** will return a value of "Americas" for a continent of either "North America" or "South America."

Starting Field	Calculation	Result
Continent		
North America	CASE [Continent] WHEN "North America" THEN "Americas" WHEN "South America" THEN "Americas" WHEN "Africa" THEN "Africa" END	Americas
South America		Americas
Africa		Africa

USER

These calculations are performed when a user is logged in to Tableau Server and viewing a report. User functions most often manage row-level security.

USERNAME: Returns the username for the current user. This is the Tableau Server or Tableau Online username when the user is signed in; otherwise, it is the local or network username for the Tableau Desktop user. When logged into Tableau Server through Tableau Desktop and incorporating a user function into the report, a Filter as User menu appears at the bottom right of the screen, allowing a report builder to impersonate other server users.

This calculation is used in conjunction with a field in the dataset that associates user names with specific rows of data. It requires that the username of the person logged on precisely matches a [Tableau Username] field contained in the data source to return TRUE. If this is the case, the user will be able to see all data associated with the "TRUE" user name. Row-level security built in to the calculation prevents this user from seeing any other [Tableau Username] data.

Example: When Doctor A is logged into the Tableau Server, if **USERNAME()=[Tableau Username]** is filtered for TRUE, then s/he will see only the two "ADoctor" rows of data, and not the "BDoctor" row.

Starting Field		Calculation	Result
Tableau Username	Doctor Name	When ADoctor is logged in to Tableau Server	
ADoctor	Doctor A		TRUE
ADoctor	Doctor A	USERNAME()=[Tableau Username]	TRUE
BDoctor	Doctor B		FALSE

26.2 Advanced Calculations

Comprehensive coverage of advanced calculations could fill a book. This chapter is a concise and manageable introduction to some of Tableau's most powerful analytical capabilities, particularly, Basic Calculations and Aggregation; Level of Detail Expressions; and Table Calculations.

Basic Calculations and Aggregation

Basics of Granularity | Level of Detail | Aggregation

Instead of building calculations into a data source, Tableau returns results by aggregating data in real time based on the Dimensions present in a worksheet. Every time a new Dimension is incorporated into a visualization, Tableau recalculates this aggregation. The most common aggregations are Sum Average, Minimum, Maximum, Count, and Count Distinct.

The aggregation results change based on the level of detail (LOD) of the visualization. The first image below shows a count of Patient IDs by Gender from a sample patient data source with 167 records. The second image adds another Dimension, Race, increasing the granularity of the visualization.

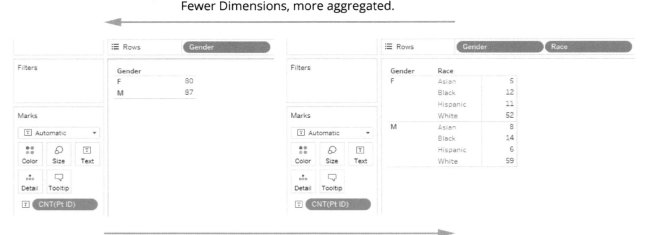

Fewer Dimensions, more aggregated.

More Dimensions, more granular.

Aggregate vs. Row-Level Calculations

On every worksheet, calculations and aggregations are generated as part of Tableau's query of the underlying data source. Row-level calculations are performed on each record in a dataset. Aggregate calculations are computed across the set of records based on the level of detail of the visualization. Understanding when to use row-level or aggregate calculations improves the accuracy of results. Three examples follow.

Example 1 - Row-Level Calculations: Calculating Excess Days

Excess Days is a metric tracked in hospitals to determine if patients stay longer than expected. For example, a seven-day stay when five was the expected number yields two excess days. A three-day stay in this instance yields zero excess days.

Patient ID	Expected LOS	Actual LOS	Excess Days
1	14.7	31	16.3
2	9.2	15	5.8
3	6.4	9	2.6
4	3.4	2	0.0
5	12.0	10	0.0
6	5.1	8	2.9
7	5.2	10	4.8
8	2.6	5	2.4
9	10.2	8	0.0
10	6.7	5	0.0

An aggregate calculation cannot be used in the table above to calculate total Excess Days. Performing a Sum on all Actual LOS values and subtracting them from the Sum of all Expected LOS values would not yield an accurate result because it would inaccurately account for patients who left earlier than expected. Instead, a row-level calculation is used in a logic statement, like this:

```
Excess Days

IF [Actual LOS] - [Expected LOS] > 0 THEN [Actual LOS] - [Expected LOS] ELSE 0 END
```

With a row-level calculation (in this case, combined with an IF/THEN logic statement), each patient's Excess Days are computed individually. Results can then be aggregated (with SUM or AVG, for example).

Example 2 - Aggregate Calculations: Computing the Rate of Falls per 1,000 Patient Days

Calculating Rate of Patient Falls per 1,000 Patient Days is an example of a calculation wherein aggregation must precede algebraic functions. The rate is calculated by dividing the Sum of Patient Falls by the Sum of Patient Days.

```
Rate of Patient Falls (per 1,000

SUM([Total Patient Falls (count)]) / SUM([Total Patient Days])*1000
```

The Sum aggregation function in front of each field name tells the source database to return the aggregate of each column prior to dividing the results.

Type of Care	Total Patient Falls	Total Patient Days			
Critical Care	18	26811			
Med-Surg Combined	97	28937			
Medical	276	79953			
Step Down	34	17079			
Surgical	115	58199			
	↓	↓			
	540 /	210979 x	1000 →	2.56 (Correct)	

Only an aggregate calculation works here; a row-level one returns an incorrect result. As the image below shows, a row-level calculation evaluates each row of data in the data source, then sums those results, generating an incorrect rate.

Type of Care	Total Patient Falls		Total Patient Days					
Critical Care	18	/	26811	x	1000	→	0.67	
Med-Surg Combined	97	/	28937	x	1000	→	3.35	
Medical	276	/	79953	x	1000	→	3.45	
Step Down	34	/	17079	x	1000	→	1.99	
Surgical	115	/	58199	x	1000	→	1.98	
							↓	
							11.44	(Incorrect)

Example 3 - NULL values: Calculating Total Surgery and Turnover Minutes

The choice between an aggregate or a row-level calculation for computing total Operating Room Surgery Minutes and Turnover Minutes (the amount of time it takes to "turn over" an OR for the next case) may seem inconsequential, but if the dataset contains NULL values, then the two return different results.

An aggregate calculation sums each field individually (ignoring NULL values), then adds the results of the two sums.

Aggregate Calculation

SUM([Surgery Minutes]) + SUM([Turnover Minutes])

Case Number	Surgery Minutes		Turnover Minutes			
1	10		5			
2	20		15			
3	50		NULL			
	↓		↓			
	80	+	20	→	100	(Correct)

This aggregate calculation returns a correct value of 100 minutes.

A row-level calculation attempts to add the two fields on each row in the dataset first, then sums the results. For a row-level calculation, a value plus a NULL returns a NULL result, so not all minutes would be counted.

Row-Level Calculation

[Surgery Minutes] + [Turnover Minutes]

Case Number	Surgery Minutes		Turnover Minutes			
1	10	+	5	→	15	
2	20	+	15	→	35	
3	50	+	NULL	→	NULL	
					↓	
					50	(Incorrect)

This row-level calculation evaluates the row for Case Number 3 as "50 + NULL = NULL." Only the first two rows return non-NULL values, totaling 50 minutes—and thus an incorrect result.

Level of Detail (LOD) Expressions

It is often necessary to calculate data at a granularity different from the level of detail resulting from the Dimensions present in the worksheet. Level of Detail Expressions can be performed at a more granular level (via INCLUDE), a less granular level (via EXCLUDE) or an entirely independent level (via FIXED) by "scoping" Dimensions directly into a calculated field.

The **Scoping Keyword** defines the LOD Expression as either **FIXED, INCLUDE,** or **EXCLUDE**.

The **Aggregate Expression** defines the incorporated measure and how it will be aggregated.

`{EXCLUDE [Summary Payor]: SUM([Total Direct Cost])}`

The **Dimension Declaration(s)** indicate which dimensions are included, excluded, or fixed. Multiple dimensions are separated by a comma.

The entire LOD Expression is contained in **Curly Brackets: {}**

▲ Scoping Keywords

- *FIXED defines exactly the Dimension(s) to be incorporated in the LOD Expression. The Dimensions in the View do not affect the aggregation. FIXED LOD Expressions are calculated before Dimension filters, but after Context filters.*

- *INCLUDE defines any Dimension(s) included in the LOD Expression in addition to the Dimensions present in the View. INCLUDE LOD Expressions are calculated after Dimension filters.*

- *EXCLUDE defines any Dimension(s) excluded from the LOD Expression, regardless of whether those Dimensions are present in the View. EXCLUDE LOD Expressions are calculated after Dimension filters.*

- *Table-Scoped Level of Detail performs the expressed aggregation on the entire data source, independent of all Dimensions. This is the equivalent of performing a FIXED LOD Expression without specifying any Dimensions. A Table-Scoping LOD Expression is accomplished by framing an aggregation in curly brackets without including a scoping keyword.*

Example 1 - Manipulating Level of Detail

The table below shows Cost ($) created using a sample subset of the US Healthcare Expenditures data with a LOD Expression showing the result of each calculation.

The first column is a basic SUM aggregation of Cost ($) broken out by Year, Type of Service, and Categories. These three Dimensions define the default Level of Detail for the worksheet. Compare each calculation to the results in the table to see how the various LOD Expressions work.

The second column: {EXCLUDE [Categories]: SUM([Cost ($)])}

This LOD calculates the sum of Cost for each year and each Type of Service. Note that the same value displays for all categories nested within each Type of Service and Year.

The third column: {EXCLUDE [Type of Service/Source of Funds],[Categories]: SUM([Cost ($)])}

This LOD calculates the sum of Cost for each Year. The same value displays for Type of Service and Categories, changing only for each Year.

The fourth column: {FIXED[Type of Service/Source of Funds]:SUM([Cost ($)])}

This LOD calculates the sum of Cost only for Type of Service. The values change for Type of Service, but remain the same for Categories and Year.

The fifth column: `{FIXED: SUM([Cost ($)])}`   - same as -   `{SUM([Cost ($)])}`

This LOD calculates the total sum of Cost for the entire table, ignoring Year, Type of Service, and Categories.

Table Calculations

Table Calculations leverage the results of an initial query and perform an additional calculation on the data to render a visualization. Although other calculated fields allow the comparison of two or more separate measures in a dataset, Table Calculations can compare a single measure to itself to generate Running Totals, Year-over-Year Growth, Percent of Totals, and Rank, among many others. Table Calculations always return aggregated measures; they depend on the amount, type, and orientation of data present.

Table Calculations can be added to the View using either a Quick Table Calculation or a custom one. Quick Table Calculations are one-click short cuts that eliminate the need to create common formulas manually.

Right-clicking the Measure pill on a shelf or the Marks card brings up the Quick Table Calculation menu.

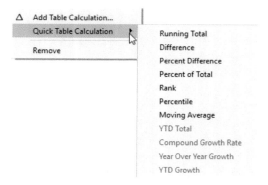

More complex table calculations can be made via the "Add Table Calculation..." option.

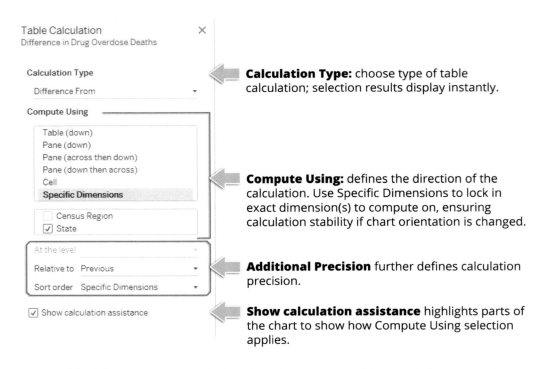

Calculation Type: choose type of table calculation; selection results display instantly.

Compute Using: defines the direction of the calculation. Use Specific Dimensions to lock in exact dimension(s) to compute on, ensuring calculation stability if chart orientation is changed.

Additional Precision further defines calculation precision.

Show calculation assistance highlights parts of the chart to show how Compute Using selection applies.

Because Table Calculations are applied to the values computed in a worksheet, they depend on the structure and layout of the worksheet itself. Dimensions that control the operation of a Table Calculation are not part of calculation syntax (as they are with LOD Expressions, which embed the Dimension control in that syntax). Instead, they are specified in the "Compute Using" menu, which tells Tableau on what Dimension(s) it needs to perform the calculation and in what direction the calculation should be performed.

Example 1 - Quick Table Calculation: % of Total

In this example, a Quick Table Calculation is used to calculate the Percent of Total Patients by Gender and Race. The default calculation is set to compute along "Table Down," which results in the data's being grouped or "partitioned" by the two Dimensions oriented down the table, Gender and Race.

▲ Table Calculation Tip

Double-click the Measures pill with the delta symbol to see the underlying calculation formula. It may be easier to copy this code into a calculated field window to take a closer look at how Tableau is calculating behind the view.

For this table calculation:

The background calculation uses the TOTAL() Tableau Calculation function.

```
COUNT([Pt ID]) / TOTAL(COUNT([Pt ID]))
```

Example 2 - Table Calculation Menu: Running Total

In the example below, a bar chart displays the running total of costs along each Type of Service/Source of Funds, starting and stopping with each Category. The calculation is computing along "Type of Service/Source of Funds" field under Specific Dimensions; and is grouped ("partitioned) to stop and start with each "Categories" field. (Note: checking the box in front of any Specific Dimension tells Tableau to compute along that Dimension; leaving the box blank tells Tableau to group|partition by that Dimension.)

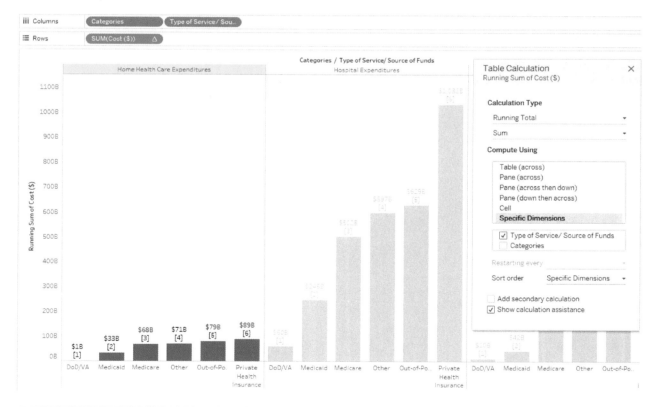

Best Practice

*Set **Compute Using** to specific fields instead of to table orientation [i.e., Table (Down) or Table (Across)] whenever possible. This setting ensures that the calculation is less likely to break if the table orientation changes.*

CHAPTER 27

Parameters

arameters are dynamic values that can replace constant ones in multiple functionalities (filters, calculations) and display elements (reference lines, titles). A Parameter Control placed on a dashboard or worksheet allows the report viewer to manage the display for ad-hoc exploration. Parameters enable the addition of flexible interactivity to a report, or experimentation with what-if scenarios by creating values or options not available in the dataset—without making it necessary to alter the design of the view.

This section covers two common Parameter types : Field Swap and Top N. A Field Swap Parameter allows the user to switch between two Dimensions without having to re-create the chart. The Field Swap Parameter illustrated below, for example, permits toggling between Service and Operating Room for exploring inefficiencies of surgical case scheduling and performance. The second type is a Top N (Number) Parameter, which affords control of the number of top items displayed in the view. The example report (in section 27.2, below) displays the Top N states for cancer death rates.

27.1 Field Swap Parameter

How To: Build a Field Swap Parameter control on service and operating room for use in comparing hospitals by projected and actual surgical case times.

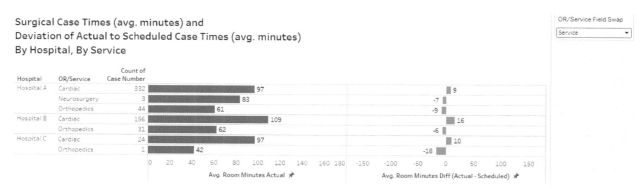

Data Source: *De-identified OR data*

About the Data: *Operating room data for elective procedures, length of time of surgical procedures, and comparison of scheduled vs. actual in-room minutes by operating room, service, and hospital.*

1 **Create a new worksheet and connect to the data**

》 At the bottom of the Tableau workspace, click the icon for a new worksheet.

》 In the Data pane, select the "16 – Operating Room Data" dataset.

2 **Create the chart**

》 Drag and drop "Hospital" from the Dimensions window onto the Rows shelf.

》 Drag "Operating Room" from the Dimensions window and drop it to the right of "Hospital" on the Rows shelf.

》 Drag and drop "Case Number" from the Dimensions to the Measures window.

》 Drag and drop "Case Number" from the Measures window onto the Columns shelf.

Case Number has the data type "Number (whole)"; as a result, the default aggregation (when Case Number is placed on the Columns shelf) is SUM. This aggregation needs to be changed to COUNT.

》 Right-click the "SUM(Case Number)" pill.

》 From the menu that appears, select "Measures (Sum)"; then from the submenu, "Count."

》 Drag "Room Minutes Actual" from the Measures window and drop it to the right of "CNT (Case Number)" on the Columns shelf.

》 Right-click the "SUM(Room Minutes Actual)" pill and repeat the above steps to change the aggregation from "Sum" to "Average."

》 Drag "Room Minutes Diff (Actual – Scheduled)" from the Measures window and drop it to the right of "AVG (Room Minutes Actual)" on the Columns shelf.

》 Right-click the SUM(Room Minutes Diff (Actual – Scheduled))" pill and again change the aggregation to "Average."

The chart now looks like this:

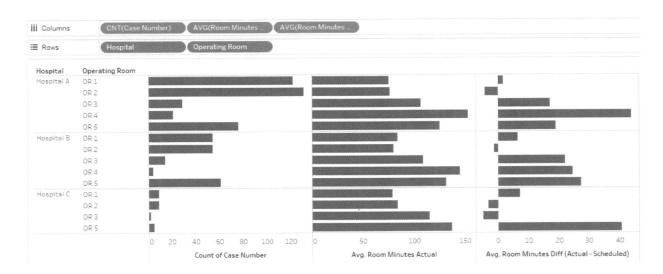

3 Create a Parameter

» Click the caret to the right of the Dimensions window header.

» Select "Create Parameter."

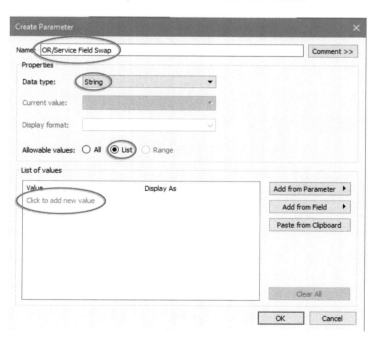

◀ **Creating and Using Parameters**

Create Parameters by following the four steps below:

1. Create the Parameter.
2. Use the Parameter in a Calculation.
3. Show the Parameter Control.
4. Use the Calculated Field in the visualization.

In the Create Parameter dialog box:

» To the right of Name, enter "OR/Service Field Swap."

» To the right of Data Type, select "String."

» To the right of Allowable values, click "List."

» In the List of values section, select "Click to add new value."

>> Enter the following values:

- "Operating Room" [Press the "Tab" key to move to the next cell; click "Add" to add the next value.]

- "Service"

>> Click "OK."

Parameters ▶

Each newly created Parameter appears on a list in the Parameters window, below the Measures window. The former window is generated by the creation of the first Parameter; if none has been created, no window will be displayed.

Parameters can be found on the Top tab of the Filter dialog box, and in the Reference Line dialog box, as well as in the Data window.

Parameters are global across the workbook and can be used in any worksheet.

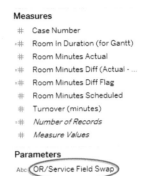

Measures

- \# Case Number
- \# Room In Duration (for Gantt)
- \# Room Minutes Actual
- \# Room Minutes Diff (Actual - ...
- \# Room Minutes Diff Flag
- \# Room Minutes Scheduled
- \# Turnover (minutes)
- \# *Number of Records*
- \# *Measure Values*

Parameters

Abc OR/Service Field Swap

>> Right-click the new "OR/Service Field Swap" field in the Parameters window.

>> Select "Show Parameter Control."

The Parameter Control is now displayed to the right of the chart.

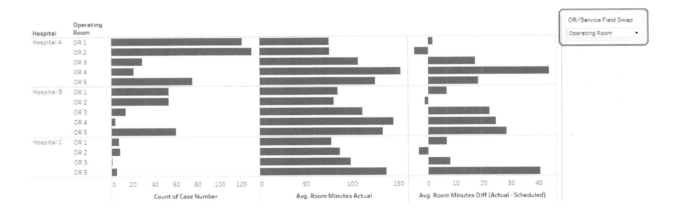

▲ Parameter Control

The menu for Parameter Controls opens by way of a caret in the upper right corner of the parameter display, and allows the user to customize its appearance.

The list of values on the menu can be displayed as a series of radio buttons, a compact list, a slider, or a type-in field. The options shown on the menu depend on the data type of the parameter.

374

▲ Show Parameter Control

*Parameter Controls are very similar to quick filters in that they contain controls that modify the view; however, each performs different functions. Quick filters enable the user to filter the report data; Parameter Controls permit replacing a static value with a **dynamic** one for calculated fields, reference lines, bins, and filters.*

Before it can do the latter task, however, the Parameter Control must be visible in the workspace. To display it, right-click the parameter field, then select Show Parameter Control from the menu that appears.

Currently this Parameter Control displays the drop-down selection, but the Control is not linked to the target data. The next step is to link it.

- » Click the caret to the right of the Dimensions window header.

- » Select "Create Calculated Field."

- » Change the field name to "OR/Service."

- » Enter the following formula:

      CASE [OR/Service Field Swap]

      WHEN "Operating Room" THEN [Operating Room]

      WHEN "Service" THEN [Service]

      ELSE NULL

      END

◀ Linking the Parameter Control to the Target Data

A formula must be created to link the string values defined in the Parameter to the field names in the Data Source.

The formula to the left associates the selected parameter with the related field names. In the Formula Editor, the color purple designates parameters; orange designates field names.

In the Calculated Field shown, the quoted text after the WHEN statements is case-sensitive and must be identical to the text previously defined in creating the Field Swap Parameter.

- » Review the calculation message below the Formula area to verify that the calculation is valid.

- » Click "OK."

This new "OR/Service" field is now displayed in the Dimensions window.

- » Drag the "OR/Service" field to the Rows shelf and drop it *on top of* the "Operating Room" pill to replace that pill.

Test that the OR/Service Field Swap Parameter is working correctly:

- » Click the caret on the "OR/Service Field Swap" Parameter Control.

- » Select "Service."

The chart should adjust to display the data by Service.

4 Format the chart

> » Click the framed "T" icon on the Toolbar to add labels to the bars

To reduce decimal places to zero:

> » Right-click the "AVG (Room Minutes Actual)" pill and select "Format."
>
> » With the Pane tab selected, in the Default section, click the caret to the right of "Numbers."
>
> » Select "Numbers (custom)"; change the decimals to "0."
>
> » Click the "AVG (Room Minutes Diff (Actual – Scheduled))" pill to highlight (confirm that the Format pane header now displays this field name).
>
> » Click the "Numbers" caret, select "Numbers (Custom)," and change the decimals to "0."

The count of Case Numbers can remain useful while taking less space if displayed as a column of numbers instead of as bars. Adjusting the display requires changing the pill from continuous to discrete, then moving it to the Rows shelf.

> » Right-click the "CNT (Case Number)" pill on the Columns shelf.
>
> » Select "Discrete" in the menu.

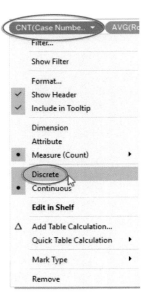

This changes the view for this pill from an axis to headers, with one column header per Case Number.

To correct this unwanted result:

» Drag the blue "CNT(Case Number)" pill from the Columns shelf onto the Rows shelf, and drop it to the right of the "OR/Service" pill.

To adjust the border to display the complete field label:

» Hover the cursor over the horizontal header border. When it changes to a bi-directional arrow, click and drag the border down until the header label is completely visible.

To right-align the Case Numbers:

» Right-click the "CNT(Case Number)" pill on the Rows shelf; select "Format."

» With the Header tab selected, in the Default section, click the caret to the right of "Alignment" and change to "right-aligned."

The two X axes display similar values (Minutes). For proper comparison, the axes need to contain the same range.

Determine the highest end value for the axes by evaluating the "Avg. Room Minutes Actual" axis for both "Operating Room" and "Service." The highest value is for Operating Room at 152. The axes will be fixed to a rounded value of 180 to allow for extra space to display the labels.

» Set the Parameter Control to "Operating Room."

» Right-click the X axis for "Avg. Room Minutes Actual" and select "Edit Axis..."

» In the Edit Axis dialog box, Range section, select the "Fixed" radio button.

» Change the Fixed end value to "180."

Best Practice

If two Measures have the same unit type (in this case, Minutes), the axes' ranges must be identical for accurate comparison. If one of the Measures is displayed as a deviation, the negative variance of the axis should also be fixed.

» Right-click the X axis for "Avg. Room Minutes Diff (Actual – Scheduled)."

» In the Edit Axis dialog box, Range section, select the "Fixed" radio button.

» Change the value for Fixed start to "-180."

» Change the value for Fixed end to "180."

To distinguish the Deviation Bar chart from the general Bar chart, edit its colors:

>> On the Marks card, click the header "AVG(Room Minutes Diff (Actual – Scheduled))" to select its Marks card.

>> Click "Color," select a light blue square.

5 Add a title

>> Double-click the Title Row to open the Edit Title dialog box.

>> Enter the title, "Surgical Case Times (avg. minutes) and Deviation of Actual to Scheduled Case Times (avg. minutes) By Hospital, By "

>> With the cursor in the second space after "By ," click the Insert button and select "Parameters.OR/Service Field Swap" to reflect the Parameter Control selection.

>> Click "OK."

6 Rename the worksheet tab and save the worksheet

>> Right-click the worksheet tab at the bottom of the workspace, then select "Rename."

>> Enter a descriptive title, then click the "Save" icon on the Toolbar.

The final chart looks like this.

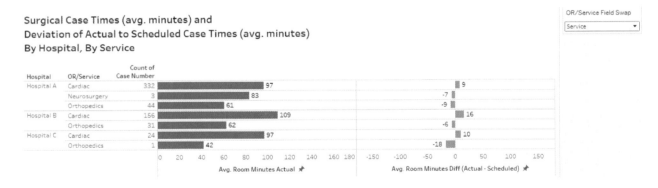

Insight: The Parameter Control allows the report viewer to compare each hospital's case count, average actual room minutes, and deviation of actual to scheduled room minutes (avg.) by either of the Dimensions (Operating Room or Service) via the drop-down menu, instead of by creating two separate charts.

⬛▏ *HDVizoom*™ ...to a Field Swap Parameter

1 Create new worksheet and connect to data

» At bottom of Tableau workspace, click icon for new worksheet

» In Data pane, select "16 – Operating Room Data" dataset

2 Create chart

» Drag and drop "Hospital" from Dimensions window onto Rows shelf

» Drag "Operating Room" from Dimensions window and drop it to right of "Hospital" on Rows shelf

» Drag and drop "Case Number" from Dimensions to Measures window

» Drag and drop "Case Number" from Measures window onto Columns shelf

» Right-click "SUM(Case Number)" pill

» From menu that appears, select "Measures (SUM)"; then from submenu, "Count"

» Drag "Room Minutes Actual" from Measures window and drop it to right of "CNT (Case Number)" on Columns shelf

» Right-click SUM(Room Minutes Actual) pill and repeat above steps to change aggregation from "Sum" to "Average"

» Drag "Room Minutes Diff (Actual – Scheduled)" from Measures window and drop it to right of "AVG (Room Minutes Actual)" on Columns shelf

» Right-click SUM(Room Minutes Diff (Actual – Scheduled))" pill and again change aggregation to "Average"

3 Create Parameter

» Click caret to right of Dimensions window header

» Select "Create Parameter"

In Create Parameter dialog box:

» To right of Name, enter "OR/Service Field Swap"

» To right of Data Type, select "String"

» To right of Allowable values, click "List"

» In List of values section, select "Click to add new value"

» Enter following values:

  • "Operating Room" [Press "Tab" key to move to next cell; click "Add" to add next value]

  • "Service"

» Click "OK"

» Right-click new "OR/Service Field Swap" field in Parameters window

» Select "Show Parameter Control"

» Click caret to right of Dimensions window header

» Select "Create Calculated Field"

» Change field name to "OR/Service"

» Enter following formula:

```
CASE [OR/Service Field Swap]
WHEN "Operating Room" THEN [Operating Room]
WHEN "Service" THEN [Service]
ELSE NULL
END
```

» Review calculation message below Formula area to verify that calculation is valid

» Click "OK"

» Drag "OR/Service" field to Rows shelf and drop it on top of

"Operating Room" pill to replace that pill

» Click caret on "OR/Service Field Swap" Parameter Control

» Select "Service"

4 Format chart

» Click framed "T" icon on Toolbar to add labels to bars

» Right-click "AVG (Room Minutes Actual)" pill and select "Format"

» With Pane tab selected, in Default section, click caret to right of "Numbers"

» Select "Numbers (custom)" and change decimals to "0"

» Click "AVG (Room Minutes Diff (Actual – Scheduled))" pill to highlight (confirm that Format pane header now displays this field name)

» Click "Numbers" caret, select "Numbers (Custom)," and change decimals to "0"

» Right-click "CNT (Case Number)" pill on Columns shelf

» Select "Discrete" in menu

» Drag blue "CNT(Case Number)" pill from Columns shelf onto Rows shelf and drop it to right of "OR/Service" pill

» Hover over horizontal header border. When it changes to bi-directional arrow, click and drag border down until header label is completely visible

» Right-click "CNT(Case Number)" pill on Rows shelf and select "Format"

» With Header tab selected, in Default section, click caret to right of "Alignment" and change to "right-aligned"

To set axes to same range:

» Set Parameter Control to "Operating Room"

» Right-click X axis for "Avg. Room Minutes Actual" and select "Edit Axis..."

» In Edit Axis dialog box, Range section, select "Fixed" radio button

» Change Fixed end value to "180"

» Right-click X axis for "Avg. Room Minutes Diff (Actual – Scheduled)"

» In Edit Axis dialog box, Range section, select "Fixed" radio button

» Change value for Fixed start to "-180"

» Change value for Fixed end to "180"

» On Marks card, click header "AVG(Room Minutes Diff (Actual – Scheduled))" to select its Marks card

» Click "Color," select light blue square

5 Add title

» Double-click Title Row to open Edit Title dialog box

» Enter title, "Surgical Case Times (avg. minutes) and Deviation of Actual to Scheduled Case Times (avg. minutes) By Hospital, By "

» With cursor in second space after "By" word, click Insert button and select "Parameters.OR/Service Field Swap" to reflect Parameter Control selection

» Click "OK"

6 Rename worksheet tab and save worksheet

» Right-click worksheet tab at bottom of workspace, then select "Rename"

» Enter descriptive title, then click "Save" icon on Toolbar

27.2 Top N Parameter

The second type of Parameter is a Top N (Number) Parameter, which allows control of the number of top items displayed in the view. This example report displays the top N states for cancer death rates.

How To: Build a Top N Parameter control for a bar chart display of states with the highest cancer death rates.

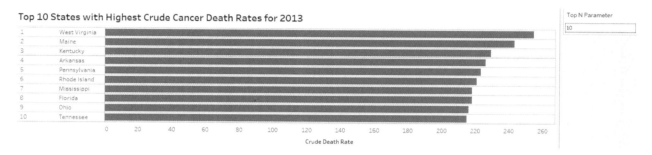

Data Source: *National Cancer Institute (www.cancer.gov)*

About the Data: *2013 cancer death rates by state (all types of cancer, per 100,000 people)*

1 Create a new worksheet and connect to the data

» At the bottom of the Tableau workspace, click the icon for a new worksheet.

» In the Data pane, select the "13 - Cancer Deaths by State" dataset.

2 Create the chart

» Drag and drop "State" from the Dimensions window onto the Rows shelf.

» Drag and drop "Crude Death Rate" from the Measures window onto the Columns shelf.

3 Sort the data by Rank

Rank the states from highest to lowest mortality rates.

» Right-click any blank area of the Dimensions or Measures window.

» Select "Create Calculated Field."

» Change the name to "Rank."

» For the formula, enter "Index()."

» Click "OK."

Refresher ▶

Signaled by the color blue, the INDEX() formula is a built-in function, a command that performs a specific task in a calculated field. In this case, the formula also acts as a table calculation, and requires definition of the "compute using" criteria.

» Drag and drop the newly created "Rank" field onto the Rows shelf.

As "Rank" is a Measure, it is currently a Continuous (green) field; it should be a Discrete (blue) one.

» Right-click the "Rank" pill and select "Discrete."

» Drag "Rank" to, and drop onto, the space before "State" on the Rows shelf.

The chart now looks like this:

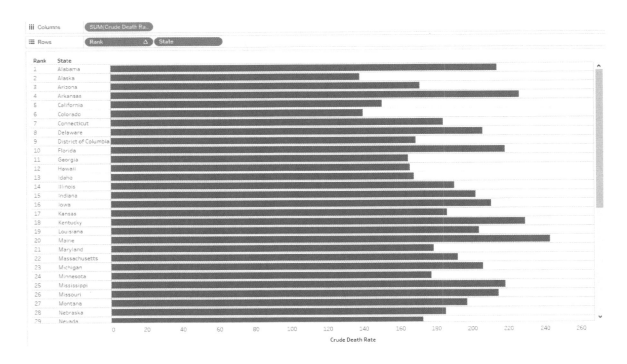

The ranking is currently alphabetical by State (the default order of the worksheet); it should be changed to one based on the Crude Death Rate.

» Right-click the "Rank" pill on the Rows shelf.

» Select "Edit Table Calculation."

» In the Compute Using section, select "Specific Dimensions."

» For Sort order, click the caret, then click the "Custom" radio button.

» Ensure "Crude Death Rate" is selected.

» Select "Descending."

» Click the "X" at the top right of the dialog box to close it.

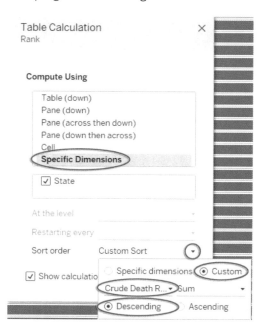

The chart now looks like this:

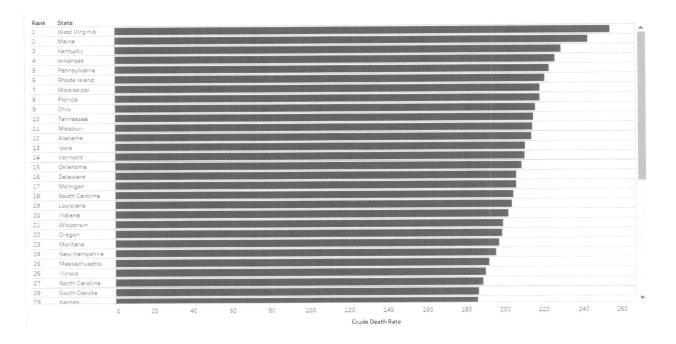

4 Create a Parameter

» Right-click any blank space in the Dimensions or Measures window.

» Select "Create Parameter."

» Name this parameter "Top N."

» Change Data Type to "Integer."

» Change Current value to "10."

» Click "OK."

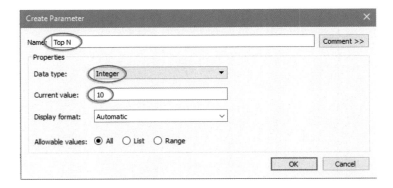

» Right-click on any blank space in the Dimensions or Measures window.

» Select "Create Calculated Field."

» For the title, enter "Top N Filter."

» In the Calculated Field Formula space below, enter this formula:

`[Rank]<=[Top N]`

» Click "OK."

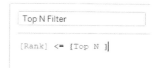

Top N Filter

[Rank] <= [Top N]

» Drag and drop the "Top N Filter" field from the Measures window to the Filters shelf.

» In the Filter dialog box, click to place a checkmark in the "True" box.

» Click "OK."

Filter [Top N Filter]

General

◉ Select from list ○ Custom valu

Enter search text

☐ False
☑ True

The chart now looks like this:

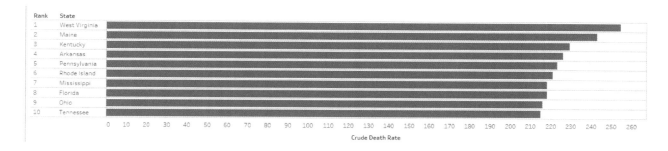

To change the Top N Parameter to see the Top 15, 20, or any other number of deaths displayed on this chart, a Parameter Control is needed.

» Right-click the Parameter field "Top N" in the Parameters window.

» Select "Show Parameter Control."

» Enter the desired number in the Parameter Control window to test the parameter function.

5 Format the chart

» Right-click "Rank" or "State" header on the chart and select "Hide Field Labels for Rows."

6 Create a dynamic title

» Double-click the Title Row to open the Edit Title dialog box.

» Enter the title "Top States with Highest Crude Cancer Death Rates for 2013."

» Click to place the cursor between "Top" and "States."

» Click the caret to open the "Insert" menu.

» Select "Parameters.Top N" from the menu.

» Click "OK."

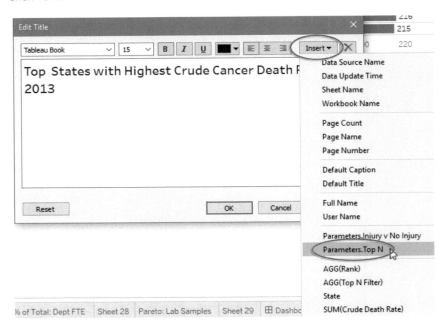

7 Rename the worksheet tab and save the worksheet

» Right-click the worksheet tab at the bottom of the workspace, then select "Rename."

» Enter a descriptive title, then click the "Save" icon on the Toolbar.

The final chart looks like this:

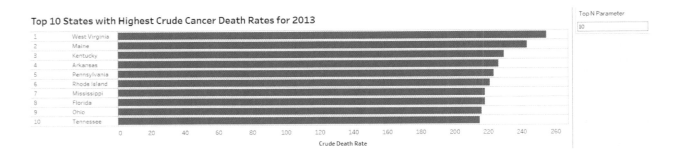

HDVizoom™...to a Top N Parameter

1 Create new worksheet and connect to data

» At bottom of Tableau workspace, click icon for new worksheet

» In the Data pane, select "13 - Cancer Deaths by State" dataset

2 Create chart

» Drag and drop "State" from Dimensions window onto Rows shelf

» Drag and drop "Crude Death Rate" from Measures window onto Columns shelf

3 Sort data by Rank

» Right-click any blank area of Dimensions or Measures window

» Select "Create Calculated Field"

» Change name to "Rank"

» For formula, enter "Index()"

» Click "OK"

» Drag and drop newly created "Rank" field onto Rows shelf

» Right-click Rank pill and select "Discrete"

» Drag "Rank" to, and drop onto, the space before "State" on Rows shelf

» Right-click "Rank" pill on Rows shelf

» Select "Edit Table Calculation"

» In Compute Using section, select "Specific Dimensions"

» For Sort order, click caret, then click "Custom" radio button

» Ensure "Crude Death Rate" is selected

» Select "Descending"

» Click "X" at top right of dialog box to close

4 Create Parameter

» Right-click any blank area in Dimensions or Measures window

» Select "Create Parameter"

» Name parameter "Top N"

» Change Data Type to "Integer"

» Change Current value to "10"

» Click "OK"

» Right-click any blank space in Dimensions or Measures window

» Select "Create Calculated Field"

» For Name, enter "Top N Filter"

» Enter formula:

`[Rank]<=[Top N]`

» Click "OK"

» Drag and drop "Top N Filter" from Measures window to Filters shelf

» In Filter pop-up box, click to place checkmark in "True" box

» Right-click Parameter field "Top N" in Parameters window

» Select "Show Parameter Control"

» Enter desired number in parameter control to test parameter function

5 Format chart

» Right-click "Rank" or "State" header on chart and select "Hide Field Labels for Rows"

6 Create dynamic title

» Double-click Title Row to open Edit Title dialog box

» Enter title "Top States with Highest Crude Cancer Death Rates for 2013"

» Click to place cursor between "Top" and "States"

» Click caret to open "Insert" menu

» Select "Parameters.Top N" from menu

» Click "OK"

7 **Rename worksheet tab and save worksheet**

» Right-click worksheet tab at bottom of workspace, then select "Rename"

» Enter descriptive title, then click "Save" icon on Toolbar

CHAPTER 28

Data Blending & Cross-Data Source Filtering

Data Blending defines a relationship between common fields in any *two separate Tableau data sources* as a way to combine data within a single worksheet. Table Joins produce a single Tableau data source; Data Blending combines two separate Tableau data sources.

How To: **Build a multiple-data source dashboard with Data Blending and Cross-Data Source Filtering.**

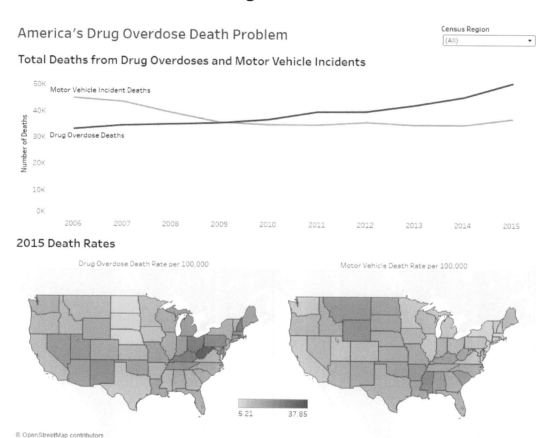

Data Source: *CDC WONDER online databases provide data and analysis to support evidence-based assessment of public health programs and population health trends.*

About the Data: *Centers for Disease Control and Prevention, National Center for Health Statistics. Multiple Cause of Death 1999-2015 in CDC WONDER Online Database, released December 2016. Data are from the Multiple Cause of Death Files, 1999-2015, as compiled from data provided by the 57 vital statistics jurisdictions through the Vital Statistics Cooperative Program. The data are representative of the continental USA.*

Before building out the activity, it is important to understand the mechanics of Data Blending.

28.1 Mechanics of Data Blending

With a single data source, using fields in a worksheet triggers requests for data from that source.

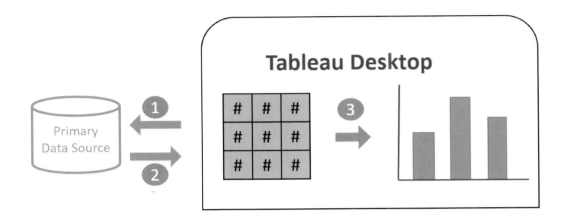

The three numbered arrows above represent the following processes:

1) As fields are dragged and dropped onto the worksheet, requests for data are sent to the primary data source. This process works via Tableau's proprietary VizQL (Visual Query Language). The first data source used in a worksheet is designated as the "primary data source."

2) The data source carries out the request, including aggregating/summarizing values based on fields present in the worksheet, and returns the results.

3) Tableau uses that results-set to build the visualization. As the visualization is manipulated further, fresh queries are made to the primary data source and the process continues.

During Data Blending, requests are made to 2 or more data sources simultaneously.

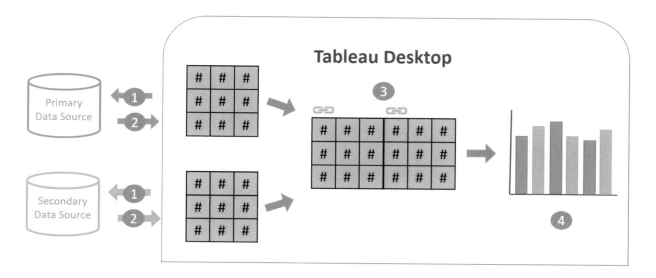

The four numbered arrows above represent the following processes:

1) During Data Blending, Tableau queries two or more data sources simultaneously.

2) All data sources queried return results-sets; all are then aggregated/summarized.

3) The level to which the results are aggregated is set according to the linking field(s). Each data source aggregates its data to that level, and the linking field(s) is/are used to "line up" the tables row by row and merge the data.

4) Tableau uses the resulting merged dataset to generate the visualization.

Important Notes on Data Blending

- All data values from the primary data source are kept in the final dataset. Data values from the secondary data source(s) make it to the final dataset only if they correspond to matching values in the primary source. Any rows in the secondary data source that do not have matches in the primary source are eliminated, while any values for which the secondary data source has no matches in the primary return Null (a result similar to that in a left table join).

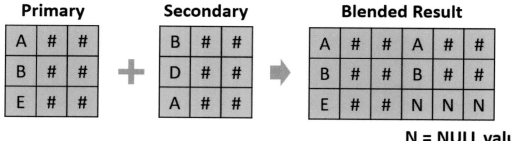

N = NULL values

- With each new worksheet, a new primary data source is selected. A primary data source in one worksheet may be used as a secondary source in another.

- There can be only one primary data source per worksheet; however, multiple secondary data sources may be present in the same worksheet. Similarly, there can be only one set of Measure Names and Measure Values fields for the worksheet; primary data source fields are active, while those in secondary data sources are grayed out.

- Data Blending merges data locally rather than in the underlying data source (this distinction differentiates a Data Blend from a Table Join). Tableau Desktop handles the processing necessary to merge the data during a blend. The level of aggregation for the linking field will determine how resource-intensive the blending process is. If the linking field contains millions of distinct values, hardware resources may run out during the blending process, causing the report to slow or even crash. If Blending results in slow downs and system crashes, another approach should be used.

Data Blending Activity

The following training/practice example describes how to define the relationship between two data connections. The datasets used have been taken from the Multiple Cause of Death dataset provided by CDC WONDER (cited above).

The first (17 – Drug Overdose Deaths) contains the count of deaths caused by drug overdoses summarized by Underlying Cause of Death Code, State, and Year. The second (18 – Motor Vehicle Incident Deaths) contains the count of deaths caused by motor vehicle incidents summarized by State and Year. While the level of aggregation for each dataset is different, the two share common fields (State and Year) that can be used to link the data.

Validation of Blending Results

1 **Establish the primary data source**

>>   Create a new worksheet and select the "17 - Drug Overdose Deaths" dataset.

>>   Drag and drop "Number of Records" from the Measures window onto Label on the Marks card.

Primary Data Source Indicator ▷

When a field is first placed on the canvas, a blue checkmark appears next to the data source in the Data pane, indicating that it is the primary data source for the worksheet.

2 **Determine the data granularity of the primary data source**

This dataset's total Number of Records is 7,840. The user needs to know the lowest level of aggregation present; in other words, *what does one row of data represent* here? Placing Dimensions in the view disaggregates the data to answer this question. To determine the level of granularity:

» Drag and drop "State" from the Dimensions window onto the Rows shelf.

The text table now shows that there are 160 rows of data per State.

» Drag "Report Date" from the Dimensions window; drop it to the right of "State" on the Rows shelf.

There are 10 years in the dataset; the Number of Records for each row now decreases to 16.

» Drag "Underlying Cause of Death" from the Dimensions window; drop it to the right of "YEAR(Report Date)" on the Rows shelf.

There are 16 underlying causes of death in the dataset; the Number of Records now drops to 1.

In summary: for the Drug Overdose Deaths dataset,

One Row = One Underlying Cause of Death for each Year for each State

State	Year of Report Date	Underlying Cause of Death	
Alabama	2006	Accidental poisoning by and exposure to antiepilepti..	1
		Accidental poisoning by and exposure to narcotics a..	1
		Accidental poisoning by and exposure to nonopioid a..	1
		Accidental poisoning by and exposure to other and u..	1
		Accidental poisoning by and exposure to other drugs..	1
		Assault by drugs, medicaments and biological subst..	1
		Intentional self-poisoning by and exposure to antiep..	1
		Intentional self-poisoning by and exposure to narcot..	1
		Intentional self-poisoning by and exposure to nonop..	1
		Intentional self-poisoning by and exposure to other ..	1
		Intentional self-poisoning by and exposure to other ..	1
		Poisoning by and exposure to antiepileptic, sedative..	1
		Poisoning by and exposure to narcotics and psychod..	1
		Poisoning by and exposure to nonopioid analgesics, ..	1
		Poisoning by and exposure to other and unspecified ..	1
		Poisoning by and exposure to other drugs acting on ..	1

» Remove both the "Report Date" and "Underlying Cause of Death" fields from the Rows shelf before continuing.

3 Establish the secondary data source and create a relationship on "State"

» Select the "18 - Motor Vehicle Deaths" dataset

There is now an orange vertical stripe along the left edge of the Data pane. This is a visual cue that it is **not** the primary data source. There is also a gray broken-link icon to the right of "Census Region" in the Dimensions window. Tableau has identified a matching field in the primary and the secondary data sources for a potential relationship.

» Drag "State Name" to the Rows shelf; drop it to the right of "State."

An error message appears, stating that a relationship needs to be created between the two datasets.

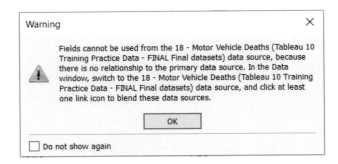

> » Click "OK" to close the Warning dialog box.

There is no established relationship between the two datasets yet. A relationship will now be created between State and State Name.

> » Click "Data" on the Menu bar; select "Edit Relationships..."
>
> » In the Relationships context dialog box:
> - Under Primary data source, ensure that "17 - Drug Overdose Deaths" is selected.
> - Under Secondary data source, select "18 - Motor Vehicle Incident Deaths."
> - Census Region, a field in both data sources, is automatically recognized for a relationship. Leave this as it is. Click the "Custom" radio button.
> - Click "Add."
> - Select "State" from the primary data source field and "State Name" from the secondary data source field.
> - Click "OK." The selections are now displayed on the list.
>
> » Click "OK." again.

Custom Relationships ▶

If the primary and secondary data sources have field names in common, these fields will be identified as potential linking fields and will show up automatically on the Relationships menu. A custom relationship can be defined between two fields with different names as long as they are the same data type.

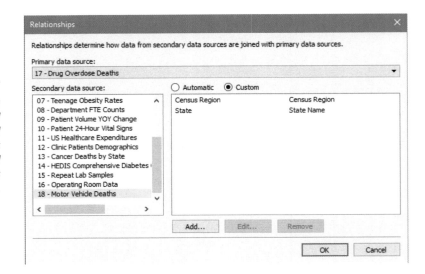

The State names are now displayed in the text table. In the Dimensions window of the secondary data source, an orange link icon now appears to the right of "State Name." (The Census Region link remains gray and "broken" because the field is not currently in use in the text table.)

» Ensure the accuracy of the Data Blend by checking that the State Name values align.

» From the secondary data source, "18 - Motor Vehicle Incident Deaths," double-click "Number of Records" to create a text table with Number of Records from both data sources used in the blend.

In the secondary data source, there are 10 rows of data per state name.

» Click the "View Data" icon in the Data pane. Notice that the secondary data source contains 10 years of vehicle-death data per state.

» Switch to the primary data source, "17 - Drug Overdose Deaths."

» Drag "Report Date" onto the Rows shelf; drop it to the right of "State Name."

The 160 records for the primary data source drop to 16 because it is now broken out by Year in addition to State. Only the 16 rows of various "Underlying Cause of Death" are being aggregated.

» Now switch to the secondary data source, "18 - Motor Vehicle Incident Deaths."

» Drag "Date" onto the Rows shelf; drop it to the right of YEAR(Report Date).

Asterisks appear in the cells for the YEAR(Date) column.

State	State Name	Year of Report Date	Year of Date	Number of Records	Number of Records
Alabama	Alabama	2006	*	16.000	10.000
		2007	*	16.000	10.000
		2008	*	16.000	10.000
		2009	*	16.000	10.000
		2010	*	16.000	10.000
		2011	*	16.000	10.000
		2012	*	16.000	10.000
		2013	*	16.000	10.000
		2014	*	16.000	10.000
		2015	*	16.000	10.000

◄ **Linking Field and Aggregation**

*The linking field indicates the level to which each data source aggregates its values **before** the resulting tables are merged in a blend.*

The asterisks here indicate there is more than one Year value for each row in the secondary data source. Because the data blend occurs *only* on "State Name," the numeric fields are aggregated to the State level, repeating the same value for all years.

To correct this situation, both "State" and "Year" should be used as linking fields.

4 Create relationship on "Year"

» Click "Data" on the Menu bar; select "Edit Relationships..."

» In the Relationships dialog box:

- Under Primary data source, ensure that "17 - Drug Overdose Deaths" is selected.
- Under Secondary data source, ensure that "18 - Motor Vehicle Incident Deaths" is selected.
- Click "Add."

There are now two Date fields in each column. The Date fields have carets because they can expand to display the possible date parts available for the data blend.

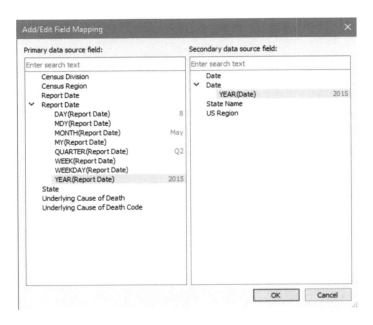

- Expand both fields, then map "YEAR(Report Date)" to "YEAR(Date)."
- Click "OK."

» Confirm that Year values now match up.

Asterisks (*) vs. Nulls ▶

During Data Blending, values from the secondary data source can appear with nulls or asterisks when the two data sources are not at the same level of aggregation or do not match.

Secondary data source "NULL" values occur when there is no match between the linking fields in the primary and secondary data sources.

Secondary data source "" values occur when there is more than one discrete secondary data source value on a single partition (column or row) in a worksheet.*

State	State Name	Year of Report Date	Year of Date	Number of Records	Number of Records
Alabama	Alabama	2006	2006	16.00	1.00
		2007	2007	16.00	1.00
		2008	2008	16.00	1.00
		2009	2009	16.00	1.00
		2010	2010	16.00	1.00
		2011	2011	16.00	1.00
		2012	2012	16.00	1.00
		2013	2013	16.00	1.00
		2014	2014	16.00	1.00
		2015	2015	16.00	1.00

» Label the worksheet "Blending Validation" and save.

Build the Analysis

5 **Use the Data Blend to create a line graph showing yearly deaths due to drug overdoses compared to motor vehicle incidents**

» Create a new worksheet.

» Select the "17 - Drug Overdose Deaths" data source.

» Drag and drop "Drug Overdose Deaths" onto the Rows shelf.

» Drag and drop "Report Date" onto the Columns shelf.

» Select the "18 - Motor Vehicle Related Deaths" data source.

Notice that "Date" has an orange link icon next to it, indicating that it is being used as the blending field. There is a gray broken-link icon next to "State Name" indicating that it is not an active blending field. The "Date" field link is orange because its corresponding linking field "YEAR(Report Date)" is in the worksheet. That is not the case for the "State Name."

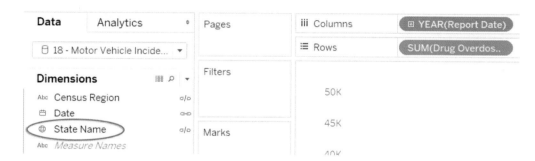

» Click the Link icon next to the "State Name" field to reestablish the link so the data are blended correctly.

» Drag and drop the "Motor Vehicle Incident Deaths" field onto the "Drug Overdose" axis (the parallel ruler icon will appear to indicate that a shared axis chart is about to be generated).

» Name the worksheet tab "Deaths Timeline."

6 **Format the view and edit the title**

» Assign the color dark gray to the "Drug Overdose Deaths" line, as it is the focus of the chart. Make the "Motor Vehicle Incident Deaths" line light gray as a reference for comparison.

» Right-click the "Report Date" header label; select "Hide Field Labels for Columns."

» Right-click the Y axis; select "Edit axis."

» Change the title to "Number of Deaths."

» Holding down the Control key (to create a copy), drag and drop the "Measure Names" pill currently on Color onto Label on the Marks card.

» Click Label to open its controls.

» Under "Marks to Label,"select "Line Ends," then uncheck "Label end of line."

» Double-click the worksheet title row; change the title to "Total Deaths from Drug Overdoses and Motor Vehicle Incidents."

» Click the "Save" icon on the Toolbar.

The chart now looks like this:

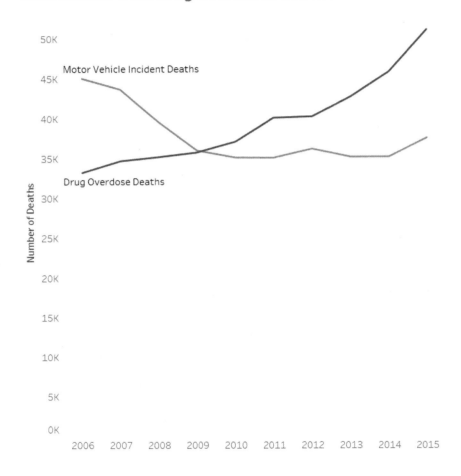

28.2 Blended Calculations & Cross-Data Source Filter

ata Blending can be used to perform complex analytics and achieve advanced interactivity within a workbook. The following exercise shows how to use Data Blending to create:

- Blended calculations that include fields from the primary and secondary data sources.

- A Cross Data Source Filter that affects two primary data sources connected by a relationship already established in the workbook.

Two calculated fields are needed to display the rate of deaths per 100,000 population for Drug Overdose Deaths and Motor Vehicle Incident Deaths. The basic calculation formula is:

```
Number of Deaths/Population*100,000
```

Each data source contains a field representing its number of deaths; however, only one data source (18 – Motor Vehicle Deaths) has a Population field. To calculate the rate for Drug Overdose Deaths, a blended calculation is required.

1 Create calculated fields for death rates per 100,000

» Create a new worksheet.

» Select the "18 – Motor Vehicle Incident Deaths" data source.

» Right-click in the white space of the Dimensions or Measures window; select "Create Calculated Field..."

The first calculated field is for the Death Rate for Motor Vehicle Incidents. This data source contains both fields required for the calculation.

» Name the field "Motor Vehicle Death Rate per 100,000."

» Enter the formula "**SUM([Motor Vehicle Incident Deaths]) /SUM([Population]) * 100000**" then click "OK."

```
SUM([Motor Vehicle Incident Deaths])/SUM([Population]) * 100000
```

The second calculated field is for the Death Rate for Drug Overdoses. Because the Drug Overdose Deaths data source does not contain a Population field, a blended calculation is needed.

» Ensure that the primary data source "18 – Motor Vehicle Incident Deaths " is selected.

» Right-click in the white space of the Dimensions or Measures window; select "Create Calculated Field..."

» Name the field "Drug Overdose Death Rate per 100,000."

» Enter the formula: "**SUM([17- Drug Overdose Deaths].[Drug Overdose Deaths])/SUM([Population]) * 100000**".

```
SUM([17 - Drug Overdose Deaths].[Drug Overdose Deaths])/SUM([Population]) * 100000
```

▲ Blended Calculation

A field drawn from another data source must be labeled with its full name arranged as follows: [Data Source Name].[Field Name]. The field must be aggregated: when the blend occurs, Tableau requests aggregated tables at the level of the linking field(s) from the applicable data sources. The calculation builds on the merged results set that has already been aggregated.

A quick way to add a field name from another data source into a calculation is to start typing its name, then select the full term desired from the display of field names that appears. Tableau automatically formats the correct name structure and incorporates an aggregate function into the calculation.

2 Build a Map view of 2015 Death Rates

» Ensure that the "18 – Motor Vehicle Incident Deaths " data source is selected.

» Double click "State Name" to create a map.

» Hold down the Control key to select the two Death Rate fields, then drag them to the map.

» Drop the field onto the middle of the map. This automatically generates the Measure Names and Measure Values pills, and creates a Symbol Map with Measure Values on Size on the Marks card.

» On the Marks card, drag and drop the "Measure Values" pill from Size to Color. This step converts the view to Filled Maps, showing the death rates as color gradients.

» Move the "Measure Names" pill from the Rows shelf to the Columns shelf to position the maps side by side.

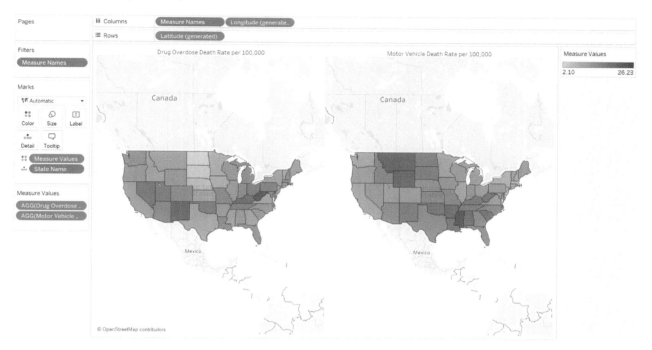

To filter data only for only 2015:

» Drag and drop "Date" onto the Filters Shelf; choose discrete Years; and select only "2015." This action causes the color gradients to change. The Motor Vehicle Death Rate map is now a solid color.

Evaluate the blending fields:

» Select the "17 – Drug Overdose Deaths" data source. The link for "State Name" is orange (active); the link for "Report Date" is gray (broken).

» Click the linking icon next to "Report Date" to reactivate the link. The colors now vary by death rate.

» Rename the worksheet title and tab "2015 Death Rates."

Adjust Formatting to simplify the background map:

» Click "Map" on the Menu bar, then select "Map Layers."

» In the left "Map Layers" pane, under the "Map Layers" section, deselect all but the "Base" option.

3 Create a Dashboard with a Cross-Data Source Filter

» Open a new dashboard; rename the tab "America's Drug Problem"

» Drag and drop the "Deaths Timeline" to the dashboard and position the "2015 Death Rates" worksheet so that it occupies the lower half of the space.

» Drag a Text box to the top of the dashboard; add the title "America's Drug Overdose Death Problem." Change the font to 18-point bold.

» Resize the text box to an appropriate title size.

▲ Cross-Data Source Filters

Even if no blending occurs, Cross-Data Source Filters can provide valuable interactivity to compare data from different data sources.

For example, if a dashboard contains several worksheets, each built on its own data source, as long as those sources are related (and those relationships established in the Data > Edit Relationships controls for the workbook), a Cross-Data Source Filter can be created to affect all desired worksheets in the dashboard, or even across an entire workbook.

4 Create a Cross Data Source Filter for the field Census Region

» Navigate to the "Deaths Timeline" worksheet.

» Ensure that the primary data source "17 – Drug Overdose Deaths" is selected.

» Drag and drop the "Census Region" field onto the Filters shelf.

» Select all Census Regions, then click OK.

» Navigate back to the "America's Drug Problem" Dashboard.

» Click the "Deaths Timeline" worksheet to highlight it.

» Click the caret at the top right, select "Filters," then "Census Region."

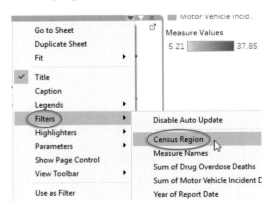

» Click the "Census Region" filter in the right column to highlight, then click the caret near the top right corner.

» Click "Apply to Worksheets" and select "All Using Related Data Sources."

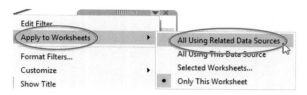

◄ Applying Filters to "All Using Related Data Sources"

When a workbook contains worksheets built from related primary data sources, this option is a quick way to add a filter to all worksheets across that entire workbook.

However, most often the filter should apply to all worksheets on a dashboard; but other worksheets using the same data sources exist outside the dashboard, and should not be affected by the filter. In these situations, choosing the Selected Worksheets option allows the user to pick precisely which worksheets the filter should affect.

» Change the filter display format to "Multiple Values (dropdown)."

» Move the "Census Region" filter to the top of the dashboard next to the title.

5 Format the dashboard

» Click the Measure Names color legend in the top right corner to highlight, then click the "X" to remove it. Since the lines are labeled, this color legend is not needed.

» Click the Measure Values color legend to highlight it, then click the caret.

» Select "Floating."

» Move the color legend to float between the two Death Rates maps.

» Click the color legend caret and uncheck "Show Title."

America's Drug Overdose Death Problem

Census Region
(All) ▾

Total Deaths from Drug Overdoses and Motor Vehicle Incidents

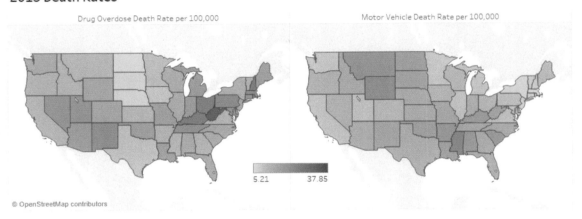

2015 Death Rates

Drug Overdose Death Rate per 100,000

Motor Vehicle Death Rate per 100,000

5.21   37.85

© OpenStreetMap contributors

404

Insight: Nationally, the drug overdose death count continues to rise; it surpassed the Motor Vehicle Incidents count in 2009. It should further be noted that death rates by state for the most recent year available (2015) reveal regional disparities.

▌▖ *HDVizoom*™...to Data Blending

Mechanics of Data Blending

1 Establish primary data source

» Create worksheet and select "17 - Drug Overdose Deaths" dataset

» Drag and drop "Number of Records" from Measures window onto Label on Marks card

2 Determine data granularity of primary data source

» Drag and drop "State" from Dimensions window onto Rows shelf

» Drag "Report Date" from Dimensions window; drop it to right of "State" on Rows shelf

» Drag "Underlying Cause of Death" from Dimensions window; drop it to right of "YEAR(Report Date)" on Rows shelf

   One Row = One Underlying Cause of Death for each Year for each State

» Remove "Report Date" and "Underlying Cause of Death" fields from Rows shelf

3 Establish secondary data source and create relationship on "State"

» Select "18 - Motor Vehicle Deaths" dataset

» Drag "State Name" to Rows shelf; drop it to right of "State"

» Click "Data" on Menu bar, then select "Edit Relationships..."

» In Relationships dialog box:

• Under Primary data source, ensure that "17 - Drug Overdose Deaths" is selected

• Under Secondary data source, select "18 - Motor Vehicle Incident Deaths"

• Click "Custom" radio button (leave automatic Census Region relationship as it is)

• Click "Add"

• Select "State" from primary data source field and "State Name" from secondary one

» Click "OK" again

» Ensure accuracy of Data Blend by checking that State Name values align

» From secondary data source, "18 - Motor Vehicle Incident Deaths," double-click "Number of Records" to create text table with Number of Records from both sources used in blend

» Switch to primary data source, "17 - Drug Overdose Deaths"

» Drag "Report Date" onto Rows shelf; drop it to right of "State Name"

» Now switch to secondary data source, "18 - Motor Vehicle Incident Deaths"

» Drag "Date" onto Rows shelf; drop it to right of YEAR(Report Date)

4 Create relationship on "Year"

» Click "Data" on Menu bar; select "Edit Relationships..."

» In Relationships dialog box,

405

- Under Primary data source, ensure that "17 - Drug Overdose Deaths" is selected
- Under Secondary data source, ensure that "18 - Motor Vehicle Incident Deaths" is selected
- Click "Add"

» Expand both fields, then map "YEAR(Report Date)" to "YEAR(Date)"

» Click "OK"

» Confirm that Year values now match up

» Label worksheet "Blending Validation" and save

5 **Use Data Blend to create line graph showing yearly deaths due to drug overdoses compared to motor vehicle incidents**

» Create new worksheet

» Select "17 - Drug Overdose Deaths" data source

» Drag and drop "Drug Overdose Deaths" onto Rows shelf

» Drag and drop "Report Date" onto Columns shelf

» Select "18 - Motor Vehicle Related Deaths" data source

» Click Link icon next to "State Name" field to re-establish link

» Drag and drop "Motor Vehicle Incident Deaths" field onto "Drug Overdose" axis

» Name worksheet tab "Deaths Timeline"

» Assign color dark gray to "Drug Overdose Deaths" line; make "Motor Vehicle Incident Deaths" line light gray as reference for comparison

» Right-click "Report Date" header label; select "Hide Field Labels for Columns"

» Right-click Y axis; select "Edit axis"

» Change title to "Number of Deaths"

» Holding down Control key, drag and drop "Measure Names" pill currently on Color onto Label on Marks card

» Click Label to open its controls

» Under "Marks to Label," select "Line Ends," then uncheck "Label end of line"

» Double-click worksheet title row; change title to "Total Deaths from Drug Overdoses and Motor Vehicle Incidents"

» Click "Save" icon on Toolbar

Blended Calculations & Cross-Data Source Filter

1 **Create calculated fields for death rates per 100,000**

» Create new worksheet

» Select "18 – Motor Vehicle Incident Deaths" data source

» Right-click in white space of Dimensions or Measures window; select "Create Calculated Field..."

» Name field "Motor Vehicle Death Rate per 100,000"

» Enter formula: "**SUM([Motor Vehicle Incident Deaths])/ SUM([Population]) * 100000**" then click "OK"

» Ensure that primary data source "18 – Motor Vehicle Incident Deaths " is selected

» Right-click in white space in Dimensions or Measures window; select "Create Calculated Field..."

» Name field "Drug Overdose Death Rate per 100,000"

» Enter formula: "**SUM([17– Drug Overdose Deaths]. [Drug Overdose Deaths])/ SUM([Population]) * 100000**" then click "OK"

2 Build Map view of 2015 Death Rates

» Ensure that "18 – Motor Vehicle Incident Deaths" data source is selected

» Double click "State Name" to create map

» Hold down Control key to select two Death Rate fields, then drag them to map

» Drop fields onto middle of map

» On Marks card, drag and drop "Measure Values" pill from Size to Color

» Move "Measure Names" pill from Rows shelf to Columns shelf to position maps side by side

» Drag and drop "Date" onto Filters Shelf; choose discrete Years; and select only "2015"

» Select "17 – Drug Overdose Deaths" data source

» Click linking icon next to "Report Date" to reactivate link

» Rename worksheet title and tab "2015 Death Rates"

» Click "Map" on Menu bar, then select "Map Layers"

» In left "Map Layers" pane, under "Map Layers" section, deselect all but "Base" option

3 Create dashboard with Cross-Data Source Filter

» Open new Dashboard and rename tab "America's Drug Problem"

» Drag and drop "Deaths Timeline" to dashboard; position "2015 Death Rates" worksheet so that it occupies lower half of space

» Drag Text box to top of dashboard; add title "America's Drug Overdose Death Problem." Change font to 18-point bold

» Resize text box to appropriate title size

4 Create Cross-Data Source Filter for field Census Region

» Navigate to "Deaths Timeline" worksheet

» Ensure that primary data source "17 – Drug Overdose Deaths" is selected

» Drag and drop "Census Region" field onto Filters shelf

» Select all Census Regions, then click "OK"

» Navigate back to "America's Drug Problem" Dashboard

» Click "Deaths Timeline" worksheet to highlight it

» Click caret at top right, select "Filters," then "Census Region"

» Click "Census Region" filter in right column to highlight, then click caret near top right corner

» Click "Apply to Worksheets"; select "All Using Related Data Sources"

» Change filter display format to "Multiple Values (dropdown)"

» Move "Census Region" filter to top of dashboard next to title

5 Format dashboard

» Click Measure Names color legend in top right corner to highlight, then click "X" to remove it

» Click Measure Values color legend to highlight it, then click caret

» Select "Floating"

» Move color legend to float between two Death Rates maps

» Click color legend caret and uncheck "Show Title"

CHAPTER 29

Tips and Tricks

This chapter includes a collection of techniques and nuanced development considerations to improve your understanding of Tableau and assist you in navigating, customizing, and optimizing your Dashboards and Reports.

Navigation and Organization

Below are some quick features to help navigate and annotate a Tableau Workbook.

- **Field finder**. It's not uncommon to have a large number of field names display in the Data pane, which can make a particular field hard to find. To quickly locate a desired field, perform one of two options to open a Field Search box: (1) enter Control-F, or (2) click the Magnifying Glass icon to the right of the Dimensions header in the Data pane.

- **View data**. Underlying data can be viewed either in its entirety or down to the aggregation level of a mark.

    - To view an underlying dataset, click the Spreadsheet icon to the right of the Dimensions header in the Data pane.

    - To view aggregated data for a specific mark, right-click the mark and select "View Data" from the menu that appears.

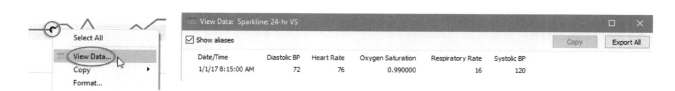

- **Commenting calculated field names**. Hovering the cursor over a calculated field name displays a tooltip. The default display is the field name; however, this can be edited to display the field calculation instead (saving time when trying to locate a field with the desired calculation). To copy the formula, right-click the calculated field, then select "Edit" to open the calculated field dialog box. To access the calculated field tooltip and paste the formula, right-click the calculated field name again, and select "Default Properties," then "Comments."

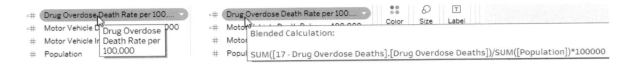

Report/Dashboard Performance Improvement

While no single trick is guaranteed to improve performance, these may help:

- **Performance Recording tool**. Tableau can record workbook performance details (extracts, queries, data blending) to analyze and identify any factors contributing to low speed and poor efficiency. Under "Help" on the Menu bar, choose "Settings and Performance," then "Start Performance Recording." Open a workbook and perform a few sample interactions on the dashboard—click a filter, modify a parameter. When finished, click "Stop Performance Recording." Tableau then generates a Performance Summary identifying any areas contributing to lags or delays.

- **Extract vs. Live connection**. When experiencing poor workbook performance with large file-based data sources, use extracts to take advantage of Tableau's fast data engine. Live connections to databases can hamper performance due to slower connections and processing speeds. Server-based databases may also benefit from using extracts, however results will depend on the processing power of the database and the size of the extract to be generated.

- **Dataset size reduction**. The number of rows and columns affects speed and responsiveness. Consider the following to reduce the size of the dataset:

  - Use Data Source and Extract Filtering. Render data connections more manageable by applying Data Source Filters. Extract data sources have an added benefit as these can be reduced in size via Extract filters.

  - Aggregate the dataset to the level necessary for the report to reduce the number of rows.

- **Workbook size**. Simplify workbook elements. Limit the number of worksheets, dashboards, and quick filters. While there is no imposed limit, each additional element can affect performance. To counteract this, consider splitting a workbook into several smaller ones. Reduce the number of quick filters. Quick filters set to show "Only Relevant Values" are particularly performance-intensive.

Calculation Optimization

The following tips can help improve the performance of calculations:

- **Strings vs. Integers**. Strings are slow; use integers instead.

- With Functions: `COUNTD([Int])` will be faster than `COUNTD([text])`.

- With Logical Statements: `IF [Field #] = Integer` will be faster than `IF [Field #] = "text"`.

- **Performance implications of functions**. `SUM()` will be faster than `COUNTD()`. COUNTD tallies the number of unique items in a dataset, comparing every single record against every other record. Consider this formula, for example:

```
COUNTD(IF [Age]>60 THEN [Patient_ID] ELSE NULL END)
```

For every patient over age 60, the Patient ID will be listed. COUNTD will then count the number of unique records of Patient ID. Assuming one row per patient in the data source, a faster way to do this is:

```
SUM(IF [Age]>60 THEN 1 ELSE 0 END)
```

This formula will interpret every patient over age 60 as an integer of 1. SUM will then rapidly add up all the integers.

- **CASE / WHEN statements are faster than IF / THEN statements**. When structuring logical calculations, put the most common cases first, so that they are evaluated before less common ones.

- **Leverage speedy mathematical functions**. Imagine a situation where the goal is to create three categories in order to organize Measures in groups for positive, zero, or negative values. One way to illustrate this situation would be:

```
IF [Field]>0 THEN "Positive"
ELSEIF [Field]=0 THEN "Zero"
ELSE "Negative"
END
```

However, this formula (while accurate) uses strings and requires logic checks, adversely affecting performance. A faster calculation would look like this:

```
SIGN ([Field])
```

This calculation will group the field into 1's, 0's, and -1's very quickly. If needed, rename these values with more descriptive aliases (1="Positive," 0="Neutral," -1="Negative," for example).

- **Boolean calculations**. Instead of writing an IF / THEN statement to create two Dimension buckets, use a Boolean calculation, then create aliases. For example:

```
IF [Total Patient Falls Rate] < 1.5 THEN "Good"
ELSE "Poor"
END
```

This formula uses strings and logic checks. Instead, use a Boolean calculation:

```
[Total Patient Falls Rate] < 1.5
```

The values can then be renamed with descriptive aliases (TRUE = "Good" and FALSE = "Poor").

Order of Operations ▶

Tableau performs operations in a specified order. Understanding this order ensures that analytics perform as intended, and can help troubleshoot any unexpected results. The diagram to the right conveys the order in which Tableau performs its operations (filters are in blue text; calculations and functions in black). A full understanding of the upstream effects of the steps preceding an operation is crucial to its success. For example, if a FIXED Level of Detail calculation is not returning the desired result, it is likely being affected by an Extract, a Data Source, and/or Context Filters, so check those first.

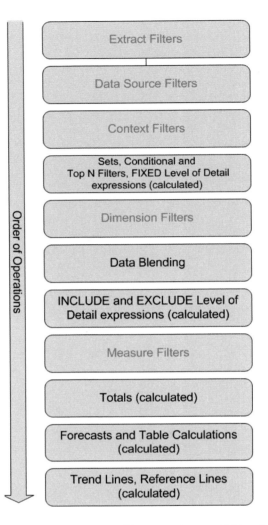

Diagram taken from Tableau Online Help Manual at: www.tableau.com > Support > Tableau Desktop (Resources) > Manuals & Guides > Main Tableau Help > Get Started > Tableau Concepts > Tableau's Order of Operations

Alternative Data Connection Methods

- Open Excel or CSV file in Tableau. Before opening Tableau, locate the desired Excel or .csv file. Drag it to the desktop and drop it onto the Tableau icon there. This action simultaneously launches Tableau and opens the file.

- Copy/paste Excel. Copy a selection of cells from an Excel spreadsheet and paste them into Tableau, generating a new data source. After copying the Excel selection, open Tableau, select "Data" from the Menu bar, and click "Paste."

- Web Data Connectors. Are open source and offer a great short cut to new data connections.

Custom Colors & Shapes

- **Custom shapes** can be added to the Tableau Shapes menu. Navigate to the local Tableau Repository and add the image file(s) to the Shapes folder there. To find the Tableau Repository, click "File" on the Menu bar, then "Repository Location..."

- **Custom color palette**. Categorical, sequential, and/or diverging custom color palettes can be added to Tableau by editing the Preferences.tps file in the Tableau Repository. The palettes then appear on the Select Color menu. Tableau's Knowledgebase Articles provide clear, detailed instructions for creating these palettes.

Other Visual Techniques

- **Move discrete column header to the top of a chart**. Click "Analysis" on the Menu bar, then select "Table Layout," and "Advanced." In the Table Options dialog box, uncheck the option "Show innermost level at bottom of view when there is a vertical axis."

- **Replace field reference**. If the name of a field in a chart is modified for any reason, Tableau is unable to find the correct destination for updated data. It flags this mismatch with a red exclamation point. To correct this error, right-click the invalid field in the Data pane and select "Replace References." In the dialog box that appears, select the replacement field name.

- **Sort nested dimensions**. To sort by more than one Dimension, use one of two options:

Option 1 - Combined Field
Create a combined field by pressing Control and clicking each field to highlight. Right-click the highlighted fields, then select "Create" and "Combined Field." Place the resulting Field between the Dimensions, then sort on it. (To hide the combined field, right-click its pill and uncheck "Show Header.")

413

Option 2 – Rank function

Copy the Measure pill of interest, apply a Quick Table Calculation selecting Rank, then set "Compute Using" to "Pane (down)." Change the pill to discrete and place it between the two Dimension pills on the rows shelf. (To hide the Rank pill, right-click it and uncheck "Show Header.")

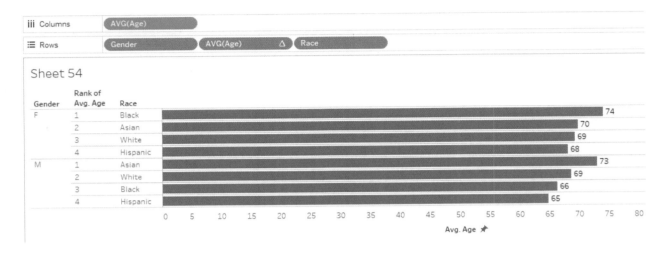

Distribution

CHAPTER 30

Report & Dashboard Distribution

S o far, this book has presented information on how to create data visualizations using Tableau Desktop. This chapter guides the reader to the best product offerings for sharing reports and dashboards based on the most common types of audience and distribution situations.

Consider the questions that follow to select the appropriate tool to develop and distribute your visualizations. A comparison chart and in-depth analysis of each product come later in the chapter, further clarifying features and design.

- **Connectivity:** What data sources do you need to access?
- **Distribution:** How do you intend to share your dashboards and reports, and control who can see them?
- **Automation:** Do your reports need to be automatically refreshed?
- **Security:** Does your data need to be HIPAA-compliant? Do you require on-site-level security, or can your work be saved to the cloud?

Report Development Products: Tableau Desktop Variants

- **Tableau Desktop: Tableau Public Edition** – connects to Microsoft Excel, Microsoft Access, multiple text-file formats, statistical files, Google Sheets, and Web Data Connectors. Files may be saved only by taking extracts of the data source(s) and publishing them to Tableau Public. (This process makes an internet connection mandatory.)

- **Tableau Desktop: Personal Edition** – connects to file-based data sources (examples: Excel, CSV, Access, .tde, and statistical files); connects to Web-based data sources (examples: OData, Google Sheets, Web Data Connectors). Saves work as .twb or .twbx files. Not compatible with Tableau Server or Tableau Online, but can be used with Tableau Public and Tableau Reader.

- **Tableau Desktop: Professional Edition** – connects to almost any data source via 75+ connectors. Compatible with Tableau Public, Tableau Server, and Tableau Online.

Tableau Option	Cost	Data Sources	Comments
Reader	Free	Data extracts and local data files	• No built-in security • No ability to refresh data automatically • Workbooks can be viewed and interacted with, but not altered or developed
Public	Free	Data extracts and live Google Sheets	• Storage space is limited to 10 gigabytes per named user • Data source maximum size is 15,000,000 rows of data per workbook • Workbooks can be viewed by anyone. However, the option to download workbooks and their underlying data sources, while on by default, can be turned off.
Server	Paid	Any supported data source	• Enhanced security • Requires data-center space, server purchase, and IT support
Online	Paid | Hosted version of Server	Data extracts and live connections to some sources	• Secure (not publicly viewable), with limited security features • Live connections to some data sources, both hosted in the Cloud and on site via the Tableau Bridge client. While this syncing product offers some security for the transition, it may cause slight transfer delays. • 100 GB storage

Tableau Reader

As the name implies, Tableau Reader is a read-only application, available at no charge from the Tableau website. Once installed, Tableau Reader enables a user to open visualizations and interact with them by filtering, sorting, and examining data. However, Tableau Reader does not permit analysis or the creation of visualizations.

Tableau Reader can open only Tableau Packaged Workbooks (.twbx files). As explained in Chapter 2, these files contain visuals as well as underlying file-based data sources.

Tableau Reader has two significant weaknesses: security and automation. Anyone with a .twbx file can un-package it and access the underlying data; there is no built-in security for the distribution of a packaged workbook. Additionally, any such workbooks opened in Tableau Reader cannot make real-time connections to databases.

Tableau Public

Tableau Public is a free, hosted service that lets anyone publish Tableau Packaged Workbooks to the Web. Any version of Tableau Desktop can be used to publish Tableau Packaged Workbook files to Tableau Public. If a user has not purchased Tableau Desktop, a free desktop product (Tableau Desktop Public Edition) can be downloaded and used to create workbooks based on Tableau Data Extracts and to publish them on the Web. The limitation to using the Tableau Desktop Public Edition is that all work developed with this free software can be saved only to the Tableau Public cloud.

Tableau Public is an open sharing platform. It is possible to toggle on and off the ability for others to download a published workbook, but all data and worksheets posted are fully viewable and accessible by the public, making this an unsuitable choice for proprietary business data or PHI. There are also limitations on the amount of data that may be included in each workbook, and a total storage cap per user. It is worth repeating: Tableau Desktop Public Edition saves work to Tableau Public Web servers, not locally on the user's computer. To save workbooks to Tableau Public, choose Server > Tableau Public > Save to Web. Bloggers, non-profit organizations, and periodicals are typical users of Tableau Public. However any organization looking to enhance its website with interactive data visualization using public data could also find it useful.

Tableau Server

Tableau Server provides a central repository for all Tableau workbooks accessible by an organization's business users via a Web browser. Server also offers two significant advantages: a data-refresh feature, and the ability to keep data and workbooks onsite to satisfy robust security protocols. New products have emerged to deploy Tableau Server hosted on a cloud platform (Amazon Elastic Compute Cloud | EC2, Azure Virtual Machines, and Google Compute Engine, among others).

This enterprise-class business analytics platform can scale up to vast numbers of users. The server can connect live to databases or automatically refresh data extracts published to Tableau Server by scheduling updates from their original source. Tableau Server provides enhanced security, and permits users to customize access to reports with specifications defined by the server administrator. Tableau Server is ideal for large companies that need to share live content with a high degree of security.

Tableau Online

Tableau Online is similar to Tableau Server, but is hosted via a third-party Tableau partner. This product retains the advantages of cloud distribution and automatic refreshes, but is hosted offsite. This arrangement can lead to security challenges in some cases.

Tableau Online provides ease of use, speed, and security without the need to manage the physical infrastructure of a server network. It is well suited to small companies that lack an IT department (or larger companies with overloaded IT departments).

Tableau Online's big difference is security. Access to content is controlled by the user's set-up in the Tableau Online interface. Tableau Online is unable to publish workbooks with a live connection to data behind an organization's firewall; instead, the data can be "pushed" (manually or on an automated schedule) or connected to certain cloud-hosted data environments like Amazon Redshift and Google BigQuery. (The exceptions to this limitation include data sources that are already cloud-based.) Tableau Online requires additional per-user licensing, even if those users already have access to Tableau Desktop.

Tableau and HIPAA

HIPAA, the Health Insurance Portability and Accountability Act, sets the standard for protecting patient data. Any company that deals with protected health information (PHI) must ensure that all required physical, network, and process security measures are in place and active. Note particularly, however, that Tableau is not a Business Associate, and Tableau Online is not HIPAA-compliant. Tableau Server is the *only* option for a distribution system of PHI that can be made HIPAA-compliant.

Publishing Reports to Tableau Server or Tableau Online

While Tableau Reader and Tableau Public have limited security capabilities, Tableau Server and Tableau Online allow distribution of reports and dashboards with a large degree of control over what is visible. Below are the general steps to publishing a workbook once Tableau Server has been deployed at a company. This walk-through assumes that users, groups, and projects have already been configured.

> » Finalize reports and dashboards and ensure that all reports to be published have descriptive tab names. These names will be visible to users.

> » Select Server > Publish Workbook and type in server name and credentials.

> » Type information into all required fields in the publishing menu.

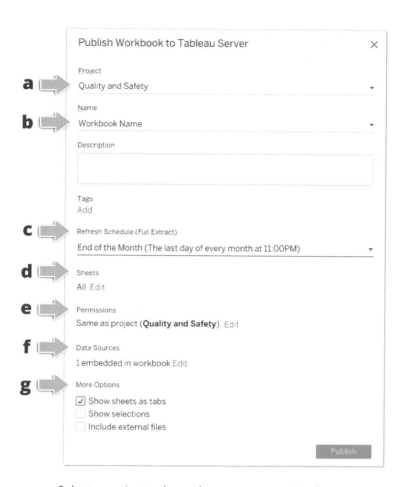

a. Select a project to keep the reports organized.

b. Give the project workbook a descriptive name.

c. Schedule an Extract Refresh (for packaged workbooks only).

d. Select the dashboards and worksheets to publish by checking or unchecking the appropriate tabs.

e. Assign and add permissions for users or groups. Select viewer, interactor, and editor for predefined permissions settings, or customize permissions for greater precision. See image below for permissions details.

f. Decide on an authentication method for the data sources: embedding the database connection credentials or having the report prompt the user.

g. Select additional options to display tabs across the top for easy navigation.

Best Practice

Be very careful when specifying who can see more than just the displayed data. Certain permission options (Web Edit and Download Full Data, for example) allow end-users to see all data underlying a report.

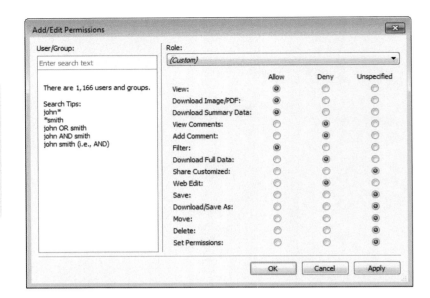

CHAPTER 31

Gallery of HealthDataViz Dashboards

A software application alone cannot enable even the most technically savvy person to create reports and dashboards that bring out the story in the data, and thereby both urge and empower users to take action. For this to occur, designers and developers require an entire toolbox of skills, including subject-matter expertise, database savvy, awareness of design and data visualization best practices, and intense curiosity that pushes them to find and bring to light what is most crucial to grasp.

We offer here four examples of dashboards and reports designed by HealthDataViz that build on these skills along with many of the Tableau techniques and best practices discussed throughout this book. Each example is prefaced by an explanation of the healthcare requirement and design approach used, and illustrated by call-outs of specific Tableau techniques used to develop the view.

Hospital CEO Dashboard

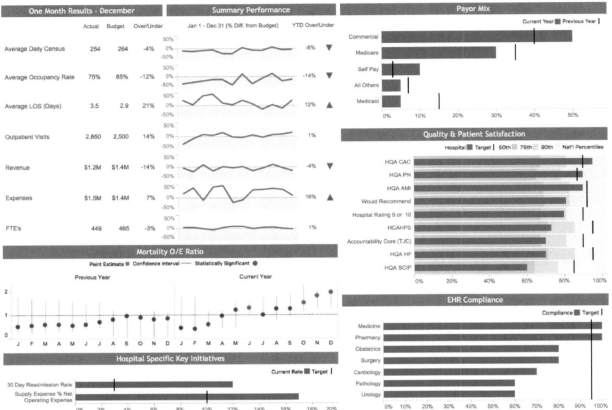

This prototype dashboard was designed for a hospital Chief Executive Officer (CEO) and included in the revised edition of data visualization expert Steve Few's book *Information Dashboard Design*.

The dashboard takes into account the current environment in which hospital CEO's navigate—one shaped by Value-Based Purchasing (VBP) and public reporting, and where financial, clinical, information technology, and patient satisfaction metrics are inextricably linked. Driving VBP and indeed all the information that these leaders require is the conviction that healthcare buyers (payors, patients) should hold healthcare providers (hospitals, doctors) accountable for both the cost and the quality of the care they deliver. This dashboard displays:

- Industry-standard metrics on the hospital's occupancy rate and average daily census along with high-level financial results (revenue and expenses) compared with budget. Up- and down-arrow icons alert the CEO to areas that may require further inquiry, and to deviation graphs that show the difference between budget and performance for the preceding 12 months.

- Bar charts indicating any changes to payor mix from the previous to the current year.

- The hospital's quality and patient-satisfaction results for mandated performance measures are displayed in the form of a black vertical line for each measure. (This line also encodes a target or goal.)

- EHR compliance by subspecialty ranked on a horizontal bar graph that includes a target compliance rate.

- Special initiatives in the bottom left corner with a simple horizontal bar graph to encode year-to-date performance compared to target or goal.

- The hospital's mortality observed-to-expected (O/E) ratio, with confidence intervals (in the middle-left panel).

Tableau Techniques Used

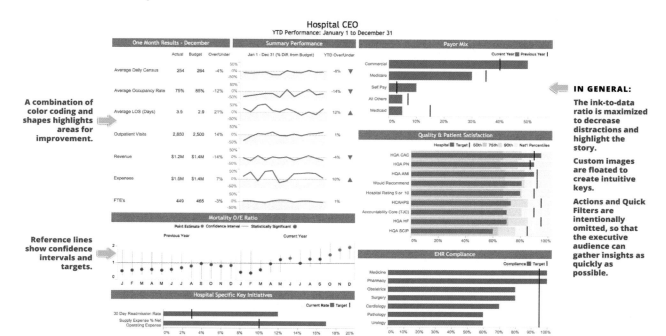

Public Health - Self-Reported Health Survey

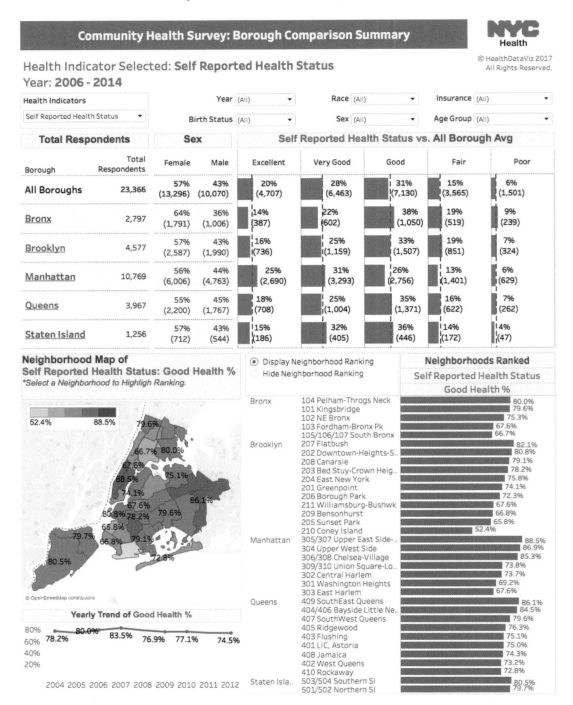

According to the American Public Health Association (APHA), public health's chief objective is to promote and protect the health of people and the communities where they live, learn, work, and play.

While clinicians deliver care to people who are sick, professionals working in public health try to prevent illness and injury in the first place by promoting wellness and healthy behaviors. Much of this work begins with understanding the health of communities and the factors that may affect it—in both negative and positive ways. With this in mind, we created an Overview Dashboard using publicly available Self Reported Health Status Survey data from the New York City Department of Health and Mental Hygiene (NYC Health) website. In this display, we arranged the data so that the viewer can easily and directly see results by each NYC borough's count of survey respondents, the proportion who are male or female, and how each group reported its health status: Excellent, Very Good, Good, Fair, or Poor. The arrangement allows for comparison between boroughs and for each unique borough. We also added additional context by overlaying a vertical line to indicate the average response rate in each category.

The second half of this dashboard uses an interactive Choropleth Map to display a composite score called "Good Health %." Dark blue map areas signal neighborhoods with a higher rate of people reporting good health; lighter colors mean lower rates. Directly to the right of the map is the same information displayed in ranked bar charts organized by Borough. Clicking different areas of the map highlights the related bar chart for ease of viewing.

At the top of the dashboard are several filters that allow a viewer to refine the target group of people under study. This dashboard is paired with a second, Borough-specific view (not pictured) with a greater level of contextual information, to help users consider some of the factors that may be affecting residents' self-reported health.

Tableau Techniques Used

Dynamic title based on Health Indicators filter selection

Action Filters adjust the Neighborhood Map below

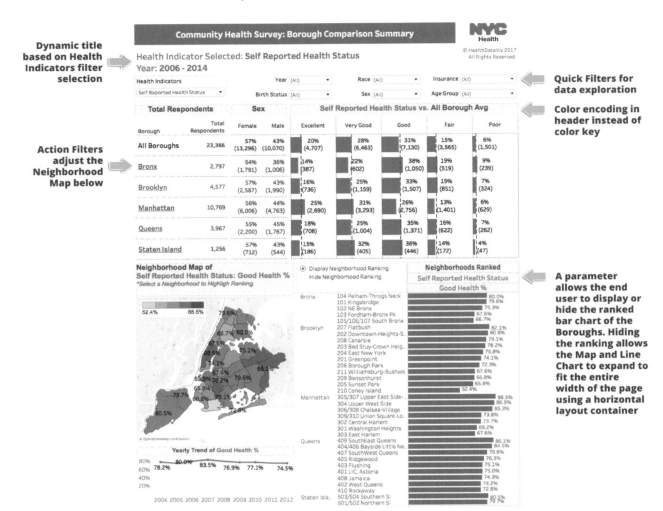

Quick Filters for data exploration

Color encoding in header instead of color key

A parameter allows the end user to display or hide the ranked bar chart of the Boroughs. Hiding the ranking allows the Map and Line Chart to expand to fit the entire width of the page using a horizontal layout container

Operating Room (OR) Utilization

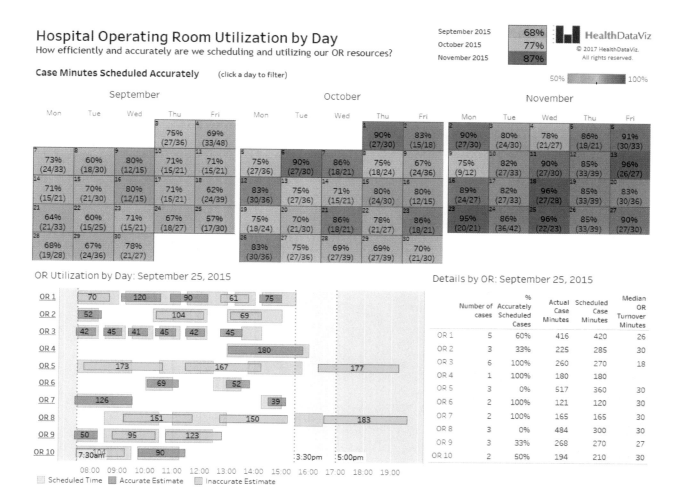

Extensive research by HealthDataViz on surgical outcomes makes it clear that high-quality, cost-effective surgical care stems in large part from efficient and productive use of operating rooms. The Hospital Operating Room dashboard above, created by HealthDataViz and show-cased in *The Big Book of Dashboards: Visualizing Your Data Using Real-World Business Scenarios* (Steve Wexler, et al., 236-245), makes it easy to see how effectively procedures are scheduled and OR resources used.

This dashboard displays surgical case and OR scheduling information to help OR managers, other staff, surgeons, and anesthesiologists identify potential opportunities to improve. They can then build strategies for more efficient deployment of facilities and resources. Note the following particularly useful features of this database's design:

- The calendar view displays the percentage of cases that were scheduled accurately for each day. Blue signals higher accuracy; orange, lower.

- A click on any one day makes associated data on the Gantt chart and text table change to display that day's information, providing even greater levels of detail.

429

- The combination of summary data in the calendar heat maps and detailed data in the Gantt chart and text table makes it possible to identify any scheduling or use patterns. Contextual details help foreground opportunities to improve.

Tableau Techniques Used

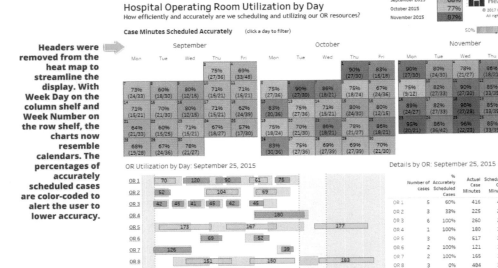

Headers were removed from the heat map to streamline the display. With Week Day on the column shelf and Week Number on the row shelf, the charts now resemble calendars. The percentages of accurately scheduled cases are color-coded to alert the user to lower accuracy.

Selecting a day on the calendar activates an action filter that displays (in the chart below the calendars) all cases occurring on that day across the page.

Hospital Patient Care Revenue versus Expense Margins by Payor

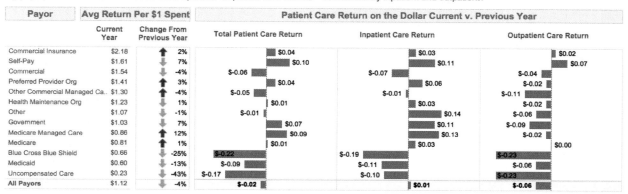

© 2017 HealthDataViz. All rights reserved.

The importance of Payor Mix ("who's paying the bills?") for any provider delivering health-care services cannot be overstated: the slightest change in it can deliver boom or bust to the bottom line. Healthcare-service purchasers pay at different levels, and patients require different types and amounts of services. An increase in private insurance versus Medicare, for example, or compared to Medicaid or uncompensated care, can make the difference between profit and loss.

How each payor contributes to (or compromises!) a provider's financial health can be powerfully displayed in a well-designed report like the one above. Note the design elements that contribute to clarity, flow, and impact:

- The top half displays the example hospital's payor mix, and how it has changed from the previous fiscal year.

- The arrow icons are gray (rather than a more "emotional" color such as red or green): the change is noted, but not judged, and the icons are visible to all, including the 10% of males who are red-green colorblind.

- Three deviation graphs display revenue after expenses both in total, and broken out for inpatient and outpatient care.

431

Tableau Techniques Used

Trend indicated by both shape of up/down arrow and hue.

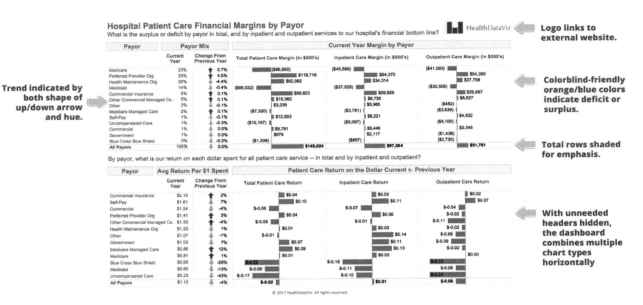

Logo links to external website.

Colorblind-friendly orange/blue colors indicate deficit or surplus.

Total rows shaded for emphasis.

With unneeded headers hidden, the dashboard combines multiple chart types horizontally

© 2017 HealthDataViz. All rights reserved.

Here's the bottom line: the key to creating an effective dashboard is to understand the people who will use it, and the decisions they need to make. Once you know this, you can build dashboards that deliver both big-picture and detailed versions of current performance and desired goals, giving users the vision and the tools to see problems and solve them fast and well.

References

Books

Few, Stephen. *Information Dashboard Design: Displaying Data for At-a-Glance Monitoring.* Analytics Press, 2nd edition, 2013.

Few, Stephen. *Show Me the Numbers: Designing Tables and Graphs to Enlighten.* Analytics Press, 2nd edition, 2012.

Lidwell, W, Holden, K, Butler, J. *Universal Principles of Design, Revised and Updated: 125 Ways to Enhance Usability, Influence Perception, Increase Appeal, Make Better Design Decisions, and Teach through Design.* Rockport Publishers, 2nd edition, 2010.

Tufte, Edward R. *Envisioning Information.* Graphics Press, 1990.

Ware, Colin. *Visual Thinking: for Design.* Morgan Kaufmann, 1st edition, 2008.

Online Help

Tableau Help: https://onlinehelp.tableau.com/current/pro/desktop/en-us/help.html#default.html

Articles

Goodman, DC, Fisher, ES, Chang, CH, Morden, NE, Jacobson, JO, Murray, K, Miesfeldt, S. *Quality of End-of-Life Cancer for Medicare Beneficiaries, Regional and Hospital-Specific Analyses.* A Report of the Dartmouth Atlas Project. The Dartmouth Institute for Health Policy & Clinical Practice. 16 Nov 2010. http://www.dartmouthatlas.org/downloads/reports/Cancer_report_11_16_10.pdf

Rehmeyer, J. Florence Nightingale: The passionate statistician. *Science News: Magazine of the Society for Science & the Public.* 26 Nov 2008. https://www.sciencenews.org/article/florence-nightingale-passionate-statistician

Data Sources

Reshaping Data Files: Using Data Interpreter, Pivot, and Column-Splitting

World Health Organization. (2012). Health Statistics and Information Systems. Projections of mortality and causes of death, 2015 and 2030 > Mortality 2015 and 2030 – Baseline Scenario > WHO regions. Retrieved from: http://www.who.int/healthinfo/global_burden_disease/projections/en/

Table Lens chart

World Health Organization. (2015). Global Health Observatory data repository. Mortality and Global Health Estimates > Life Expectancy, Data by country. Retrieved from: http://www.who.int/gho/en/

World Health Organization. (2015). Global Health Observatory data repository. Mortality and Global Health Estimates > Child Mortality > Child Mortality Levels > Probability of dying per 1,000 live births, Data by country. Retrieved from: http://www.who.int/gho/en/

World Health Organization. (2014). Global Health Observatory data repository. Health Financing > Health expenditure per capita by country. Retrieved from: http://www.who.int/gho/en/

Line chart, Highlight Table/Heat Map chart

Centers for Disease Control, Flu Portal dashboard. Influenza positive tests reported to CDC for flu seasons 2013 to 2016. Retrieved from: http://gis.cdc.gov/grasp/fluview/fluportaldashboard.html

Small Multiples chart

Trust for America's Health. The State of Obesity: Better Policies for a Healthier America, Sep 2016. Issue Report. Retrieved from: http://stateofobesity.org/files/stateofobesity2016.pdf

Area chart

Centers for Medicare & Medicaid Services, National Health Expenditures by Type of Service and Source of Funds: CY1980 to 2015. Retrieved from: https://www.cms.gov/Research-Statistics-Data-and-Systems/Statistics-Trends-and-Reports/NationalHealthExpendData/NationalHealthAccountsHistorical.html

Maps, Top N Parameter

Centers for Disease Control and Prevention, United States Cancer Statistics. 2013. Retrieved from: https://www.cdc.gov/cancer/npcr/uscs/download_data.htm

Table Calculation, Running Total

Centers for Disease Control and Prevention, National Center for Health Statistics. Multiple Cause of Death 1999-2015 on CDC WONDER Online Database. UCD-ICD-10 113 Cause List > Accidents > Motor vehicle accidents. Retrieved from: wonder.cdc.gov/mcd.html

Story

Centers for Disease Control and Prevention, National Center for Health Statistics. Multiple Cause of Death 1999-2015 on CDC WONDER Online Database. UCD-ICD-10 (T40.1 & T40.4). Retrieved from: wonder.cdc.gov/mcd.html

Data Blending

Centers for Disease Control and Prevention, National Center for Health Statistics. Multiple Cause of Death 1999-2015 on CDC WONDER Online Database. UCD-ICD-10 113 Cause List > Accidents > Motor vehicle accidents. Retrieved from: wonder.cdc.gov/mcd.html

Centers for Disease Control and Prevention, National Center for Health Statistics. Multiple Cause of Death 1999-2015 on CDC WONDER Online Database. UCD-ICD-10 (X40-X43). Retrieved from: wonder.cdc.gov/mcd.html

About the Authors

Daniel Benevento, AB

Dan Benevento is a data-visualization consultant and trainer passionate about using health and healthcare data to save the world. He collaborates with business stakeholders and IT professionals nationwide to design and develop hundreds of timesaving, high-impact reports and dashboards in healthcare and other fields. When not working to create better healthcare visualizations, he spends his time climbing cliffs, paddling rivers, strumming guitars, savoring fancy cheeses, and calling his mother every Sunday.

Katherine S. Rowell, MS, MHA

Kathy Rowell is co-founder and principal of Katherine S. Rowell & Associates and of HealthDataViz, a Boston firm that specializes in helping healthcare organizations design and present data displays that effectively inform decisions and bring decisive action. She advises providers, payers, policymakers and regulatory agencies on aligning systems, designing reports, and developing staff to make clear to all concerned what needs to be done—soon—and why. Kathy and her colleague Ann Cutrell wrote the award-winning first volume in The Best Boring Book Ever™ series Select Healthcare Classification Systems and Databases, available from Amazon.

Janet Steeger, MEd, RN

Janet Steeger is a clinical and educational consultant with over 20 years of experience in curriculum design and implementation in healthcare quality improvement, electronic medical records, and Tableau software. When she steps away from computer and classroom, two of her four Belgian Malinois become her students in training and coaching for competition in a variety of dog sports. Making it clear how thoroughly she understands the way learning works, Janet would probably say that they teach her at least as much as she teaches them.

Ann Cutrell, MS, RPh

Ann Cutrell is a research consultant intent on and delighted by finding the healthcare story buried in the masses of data the industry generates. Ann combines pharmacy experience with medical informatics training to help organizations apply data to support optimum clinical outcomes and manage costs. As for managing her Type A personality? She participates in Ironman triathlons. For fun.

Marnie Morales, PhD

Marnie Morales is a neuroscientist who turned technical consultant after immersing herself in the culture of Tableau data visualization. Marnie develops HDV's striking and effective data visualizations, and is also an expert Tableau software trainer. She enjoys local food (and beer) culture, time in the community garden nearby, and relaxing with friends. When she can, Marnie visits her extended family in Ambato, Ecuador.

About HealthDataViz

ealthDataViz specializes in helping design, organize, and present data displays that inform decisions and drive action. Extensive knowledge of and experience with healthcare, and skilled data visualization guide every client engagement, transforming data into compelling stories and people into compelling storytellers.

Design and Communication

HealthDataViz harnesses the best practices of data visualization to craft reports and dashboards that display healthcare data accurately, clearly, and compellingly. Our solutions solve complex problems, improve care and its delivery, and reduce errors and loss.

Do the statements here drain your resources and prevent your teams from making informed decisions? We can help!

- Report specs don't get through to the IT team.
- Reports make no sense.
- Good decisions are compromised by bad|missing information.
- Viewers can't find the opportunities in the data.
- Information systems don't communicate with reporting requirements.
- Dashboards look like ransom notes: fragmented, confusing, scary.

Data Literacy Training

Staff competence in the use, interpretation, and reporting of healthcare data varies widely. HDV adapts customized training programs for each organization's individual levels and situations, to improve knowledge, understanding, and capabilities, and enable the production of extraordinary reports. Its meticulously tailored curricula meet the needs and reporting requirements of each particular client with courses on:

- Fundamentals of Data Analysis and Statistics
- Data Visualization Workshops
    - » Communicating Healthcare Data with Tables and Graphs
    - » Dashboard Design for Communicating Healthcare Data
- Tableau for Healthcare Workshops
    - » Beginner|Intermediate
    - » Intermediate|Advanced

Public Workshops

Best practices of data visualization guide the creation of these hands-on, interactive sessions—including the tremendously popular and well-attended "Tableau for Healthcare" two-day course, the genesis of this book. Visit www.HealthDataViz.com for full details and a calendar of upcoming workshops.

Write us at *info@healthdataviz.com*!

Index

437

439